"Choice architecture provides a context for orienting ('nudging') citizens toward choices aimed at their well-being. *The Practitioner's Guide to Ericksonian Choice Architecture* by Dan Short offers a further way of privileging the role of context: the psychotherapeutic dimension of ECA (Ericksonian Choice Architecture). As in the ecological rationality approach of Gerd Gigerenzer's school, and inspired by the pragmatism of William James, Short's interesting book shows how what are commonly considered biases, errors, and distortions can become strengths and sources of personal growth when they are placed within a frame and a decision environment that reinterpret and enhance them. ECA represents a new challenge to traditional normative psychotherapy."

Riccardo Viale, *Professor of Cognitive Economics, University of Milano-Bicocca and LUISS, Italy; author of* Nudging

"Dr Short's views on Milton H. Erickson's communication skills offers new insight into mysterious successes that have lingered beyond logical understanding. While previous scholars explored Erickson's techniques and hypnotherapeutic ideas, Short examines case materials from an unexplored direction. This remarkable contribution illustrates integrated permissive decision-making used rationally to promote independent autonomy. Finally, we can appreciate how Erickson's confusing creative directives elicited generative responses. This work on Ericksonian Choice Architecture brings new understanding even to those of us who have studied Erickson for decades."

Roxanna Erickson-Klein, *Board of Directors—The Milton H. Erickson Foundation*

"The intuitive therapist will recognize many of the approaches subsumed under the framework of Ericksonian Choice Architecture (ECA) to nudge the unconscious towards problem solving and foster self-awareness and insight. Covering a broad swath of ideas Short provides a comprehensive and meticulous integration of psychological, philosophical, and economic literature and theory, highlighting numerous techniques to increase agency and confidence; to honor autonomy; and to utilize client resources. The cases, his own and Erickson's, are carefully analyzed to illustrate the applied suggestions built on the ECA foundation. Unpackaged and carefully explained he names the processes and then guides us through their usage, an architecture of both choice and change. A compendium that deserves to be on each psychotherapist's bookshelf of resources."

Julie H. Linden, *Editor-in-Chief,* The Routledge International Handbook of Clinical Hypnosis

"If you want to know ways you can help clients to embrace healthy choices that are consistent with their values and personal autonomy, rather than seeing them as resistant or noncompliant, this book is for you. Kudos to Dan Short—highly recommended!"

Michael F. Hoyt, *author of* Brief Therapy and Beyond: Stories, Language, Love, Hope, and Time *and* Single Session Therapy: A Clinical Introduction to Principles and Practices

"This new book by Dan Short offers clinicians and counselors new ways to utilize Milton Erickson's contributions. He invites readers to exercise flexibility in reframing and restructuring taken-for-granted thoughts and attitudes. The author urges a deeper understanding of cognitive biases to help understand threats and opportunities, and to identify a new language for managing complexity with collaborative relationships that instill security and foster commitment, self-determination, and discernment. A particularly interesting aspect of the architecture of choice, according to the Ericksonian pragmatics proposed by Dan Short, concerns the scrupulous attention to the autonomy, dignity, and identity of the individual with whom this new approach is applied."

Consuelo Casula, *author of* Metaphors for Personal & Professional Evolution

The Practitioner's Guide to Ericksonian Choice Architecture

The Practitioner's Guide to Ericksonian Choice Architecture bridges the gap between behavioral economics and the helping professions and provides a model for guiding without controlling. This empowers clinicians to develop collaborative relationships with their clients, leading to positive and sustainable outcomes.

This book establishes Ericksonian Choice Architecture (ECA) as a legitimate extension of behavioral economics, applied to the clinician–client dyad. It offers a coherent, ethically grounded framework for choice-centric care, in which the enduring outcome is not engineered change but an increased capacity for authored choice that respects client autonomy and values. By treating decisions as both psychological acts and designable events, the author demonstrates how communication can shape choices rather than correct them. Explaining how clinicians can work with biases and mental heuristics rather than against them, this book supplies evidence-based strategies to design "optimal choice environments" that make progress feel self-directed rather than imposed.

Full of rich case material and thought experiments, this book is essential for Ericksonian practitioners, hypnotherapists, psychotherapists, and licensed counselors, as well as graduate students and trainees in these fields. It will also interest healthcare clinicians, leaders, and behavioral economists.

Dan Short is a practicing clinical psychologist who also serves as director for the Milton H. Erickson Institute of Phoenix, Arizona, adjunct faculty for the Milton H. Erickson Foundation's hypnosis training program, and the originator of ECA. Short served for five years as Editor-in-Chief for the Milton H. Erickson Foundation Newsletter and two years as Assistant Director at the Foundation. During that time, he oversaw the preservation of nearly 1,500 hours of audio recording from Milton Erickson. Short has taught medical hypnosis at Sonoran University of Health Sciences for more than a decade. Short has published five books, served as guest editor for the *American Journal of Hypnosis* (AJCH), and authored dozens of scholarly articles and book chapters. Short's research interests have focused on Ericksonian hypnosis, resulting in a research-based treatment manual for Ericksonian therapy (ET), which is used by training institutes around the world.

The Practitioner's Guide to Ericksonian Choice Architecture

Integrating Clinical Wisdom and the Science of Choice

Dan Short

Routledge
Taylor & Francis Group
NEW YORK AND LONDON

Designed cover image: sarayut © Getty Images

First published 2027
by Routledge
605 Third Avenue, New York, NY 10158

and by Routledge
4 Park Square, Milton Park, Abingdon, Oxon, OX14 4RN

Routledge is an imprint of the Taylor & Francis Group, an informa business

ISBN: 978-1-041-35465-9 (hbk)
ISBN: 978-1-041-35178-8 (pbk)
ISBN: 978-1-003-79787-6 (ebk)

DOI: 10.4324/9781003797876

Typeset in Sabon
by codeMantra

Access the Support Material: www.routledge.com/9781041351788

I wish to express my sincere gratitude to the many people who played a role in the creation of this body of work.

This project would not have begun without the support of Jeff Zeig, who "nudged" me toward developing a communication model that more fully addressed Erickson's evocative communication posture. Roxanna Erickson and Consuelo Casula offered essential feedback on the earliest drafts, helping to refine both its structure and its intent. I also deeply appreciate the insightful foreword by John Beahrs, which situates this work within a broader intellectual and clinical landscape. My daughter, Elise Short, brought extraordinary attention to detail and a genuine gift for language, greatly enhancing both the clarity of the ideas and the ease of reading throughout.

I am also grateful to Routledge and to Hannah Rich for her editorial guidance in nurturing this project and helping bring it to those who care deeply about their influence on others.

Contents

Acknowledgment

During the preparation of this book, generative artificial intelligence (AI) tools (OpenAI; GPT-5.2 model) were used for limited purposes including stylistic refinement, sentence-level editing, and phrasing alternatives. AI tools did not generate nor determine the book's core arguments, theoretical positions, or conclusions. All conceptual content, claims, interpretations, and scholarly judgments are the authors' own. The author critically reviewed, edited, and verified all AI-assisted text for accuracy, coherence, originality, and fidelity to the published scholarship.

Foreword

Who is responsible for what, to whom, and at what levels? Such questions weigh heavily on mental health practitioners charged with helping their clientele "get better." But what does this mean? To cure illness? Resolve repressed conflict? Counter-condition maladaptive habits? Offer counter-suggestions? Or something else? Clinicians must assess what is wrong and what can be done about it, all under the Hippocratic exhortation to "first do no harm."

From the 1930s until his death in 1980, Milton H. Erickson, M.D., built a psychiatry practice while becoming widely known for achieving seemingly magical outcomes with formidably difficult patients. Using indirect communication heavily weighted toward patients' "unconscious," he pioneered a flexible "utilization" approach: taking patients as they are and reframing their self-defining parameters in order to nudge them toward healthier well-being (Beahrs, 1971; Erickson, 1959). Many "strategic" and "problem-focused" therapists followed in his footsteps, seeking to identify and reverse problem-maintaining behaviors in pursuit of well-planned, operationalized, and measurable outcomes (Haley, 1963; Watzlawick et al., 1974).

In this important new book, Dr. Dan Short takes all of this complexity to yet another level: Ericksonian choice architecture (ECA). Rather than pursuing specific change goals that can be operationalized and then measured, he seeks to enhance clients' ability to act as change agents themselves. "Agency" is simply the ability to "make things happen," with "accountability for their consequences." Here, change agency itself is granted priority over designing, seeking, and measuring any specific changes. How can this happen? If "the power is in the patient" (Goulding & Goulding, 1979), what is left for us therapists? Essentially, we are being asked to influence our clientele to do what only they can do for themselves. How can this happen? Tough questions. No easy answers. Heavily debated by healers and philosophers throughout the ages, these questions remain unanswered. This is the book's topic.

Symbolic language is of the essence. Language virtually defines human experience—our unprecedented power over much of nature (Darwin, 1876; Deacon, 1997; Pinker, 2003), as well as the formidable complications that include psychopathology and mass wrongdoing. Milton Erickson's genius resided in an uncanny, both intuitive and learned, appreciation of language's multidirectionality and its resulting capacity to reframe meanings in ways that modify people's personal experience. Word combinations not only have traditional "meanings," but also potentially infinite others. These symbols profoundly affect how we think and feel about things, how we define ourselves and our social identities, and how we try to understand and solve our problems. Their multidirectionality confers both a fundamental "psychic uncertainty" and a corresponding capacity for adaptive reframing when circumstances become problematic (Beahrs, 1986). With ECA, Dan Short offers a heuristic framework for meaningful change that can be simultaneously direct and indirect.

Most people want to change and to stay the same. Yes, both at once. Usually, the optimal course of action is to find a satisfactory balance. But many patients focus on one pole to the exclusion of the other, creating stubborn biases that push against healthy balance and then resist change as if it were a matter of survival. Short elaborates on eight of these biases, each paired with its polar opposite. Two are exemplary: "Status Quo Bias" (Chapter 3) and "Change Bias" (Chapter 4).

The first can be viewed as a rigidification of the life-preservation instinct. Here, ECA seeks to "make change feel like a natural extension of the individual's existing state." Instead of adding something new, which might unintentionally threaten one's identity, a "subtractive" approach that limits options may paradoxically open new ones by respecting and building on a person's pre-existing foundation. In his earlier introduction to this book, Dr. Short had already set the stage by itemizing five reasons he eschews explicitly seeking specific changes: implicit authoritarianism can (1) invite reactance, (2) imply negative judgment, (3) undermine self-trust, (4) lead to overcontrol, and (5) usurp clients' own agendas. It works better to emphasize continuity over change and to accept authorship of one's status quo, with creative variations.

Now look the other way. "Change Bias" is the popular progressive idea that change is desirable in itself, wherever it leads. This finds support by analogy to growth, maturation, exploration, science, and technology. But left unsaid are the many ways change can "go bad": regressive dissolution, destabilization, and behavioral catastrophes. History shows how often utopian social schemes become unspeakable tyrannies, and experienced clinicians note how trying to "rescue" distressed clients can sometimes foster regressive destabilization. What might we do instead? As he does with other heuristics, Short usually endorses clients' change bias overtly while adding limiting patterns that anchor it in more constructive directions. "Temporal self-comparison" is exemplary. Taking repeated measures of a relevant variable over extended time is apt to redefine what might otherwise seem like an ungrounded disruption into a well-formed empirical reality—or, as Dr. Short puts it, "finding progress that holds."

Like Milton Erickson, Short also grants relative primacy to "unconscious" processing over conscious control—that is, "trust your unconscious" to intuitively "sense" and "let things happen." But we all know this is fraught, and that people sometimes do harmful things while claiming no control. Conscious intervention is needed here. What, how, and when? How does one assess what works and what does not? Most therapists go by intuitive "feel" and others' feedback. How can we assess and improve our skills more reliably? In a small uncontrolled pilot study of two quite different treatment protocols, therapeutic results correlated most consistently with patients' self-therapeutic effort (Beahrs, 2006), heightening my concurrence with Short's emphasis on clients' change agency itself as a principal treatment goal.

This book underscores the importance of ethical guidance, accountability, and transparency. Building on Erickson's extraordinary understanding of how language and symbolic meaning shape human experience, Short offers a framework for redesigning those meanings when they become limiting or maladaptive. Readers will find in these pages a thoughtful extension of Erickson's legacy, one that translates clinical wisdom into a practical guide for fostering agency, discernment, and adaptive choice.

John O. Beahrs, M.D., Portland, OR, March 23, 2026

References

Beahrs, J. O. (1971). The Hypnotic Psychotherapy of Milton H. Erickson. *American Journal of Clinical Hypnosis*, *14*(2), 73–90. https://doi.org/10.1080/00029157.1971.10402155

Beahrs, J. O. (1986). *Limits of Scientific Psychiatry: The Role of Uncertainty in Mental Health*. Psychology Press.

Beahrs, J. O. (2006). Assessing attributive causation in psychiatry: Psychotherapeutic results correlate with self-therapeutic activity. *Clinical Neuropsychiatry*, *3*, 154–161.

Darwin, C. (1876). *The Descent of Man, and Selection in Relation to Sex*. D. Appleton and Company.

Deacon, T. W. (1997). *The Symbolic Species: The Co-evolution of Language and the Brain*. W.W. Norton.

Erickson, M. H. (1959). Further Clinical Techniques of Hypnosis: Utilization Techniques. In E. L. Rossi, R. Erickson-Klein, & K. Rossi (Eds.), *Collected Works of Milton H. Erickson: The Nature of Therapeutic Hypnosis* (Vol. 1, pp. 271–306). Milton H. Erickson Foundation Press.

Goulding, M. M., & Goulding, R. L. (1979). *Changing Lives Through Redecision Therapy*. Brunner/Mazel.

Haley, J. (1963). *Strategies of Psychotherapy* (pp. x, 204). Grune & Stratton. https://doi.org/10.1037/14324-000

Pinker, S. (2003). *The Language Instinct: How the Mind Creates Language*. Penguin Books Limited.

Watzlawick, P., Weakland, J. H., & Fisch, R. (1974). *Change; Principles of Problem Formation and Problem Resolution*. Norton.

Preface

Stories convey forms of meaning that cannot be captured by abstract classifications alone. They carry emotional resonance, preserve context, and provide the kinds of memory cues through which knowledge becomes resonant and usable. For this reason, this book is built around stories.

While factual, all case material has been carefully anonymized to protect personal privacy. The narratives themselves are drawn primarily from the clinical work of Milton H. Erickson. I compiled the teaching tales from multiple sources, including Erickson's journal articles; books written by those who interviewed him; more than 1,000 hours of archival recordings that I listened to and analyzed; interviews I conducted with several of Erickson's former clients; and conversations with members of the Erickson family. For readers who wish to trace these accounts to their published origins, each case is numbered to correspond with a case index located at the back of this book.

Good stories do more than illustrate methodology. They reveal who we are and who we might become. They illuminate what truly matters by placing ideas within the lived complexity of human experience. My hope is that, as you read this book, your personal story will be subtly expanded, clarified, enriched, and brought into closer alignment with your deepest values.

Dan Short
January 23, 2026

Introduction

Choice and the Core Principles of Ericksonian Choice Architecture

Choice and the Core Principles of Ericksonian Choice Architecture

In September 2016, I met with an established client who was kind, devoted to his wife, and in a terrible state of panic. He was struggling with fatigue and had doctors at Mayo Clinic inform him that there were problems with his red blood cell count. It was dropping rapidly and they did not know why. In my office, he expressed his overwhelming fear that he will become horribly fragile or die soon. Because he had anxious, pessimistic tendencies, I helped him discover some optimistic possibilities. He returned a couple weeks later, freshly overwhelmed with anxiety. His greatest fear was that he had a deadly disease. Once again, I helped him envision some hopeful outcomes, explaining that until we know for certain that his life will soon end, he might as well counter-balance the negative possibilities by envisioning a desirable outcome.

By mid-November, it was determined that he had myelodysplastic syndrome (MDS). His physician told him that he would probably die from MDS but not in the immediate future. Wanting to learn more about his dysfunctional bone marrow, my client researched information on bone marrow expansion and how this can lead to intolerable pain deep within one's bones. Now, he was not only terrified that he might die of MDS but more so that it could be a slow, unbearably painful form of death. He stated that his doctor had told him that he may have the option of a bone marrow transplant, which might cure the MDS. However, he disclosed that he did not want to get hopeful about that, until it was certain that he was eligible.

Then in early-January 2017, he called my office from his hospital bed. He was even more distraught than before. The oncologist at Mayo had given him an additional diagnosis of prolymphocytic leukemia (PLL), a rare and aggressive form of leukemia. He was being kept at Mayo waiting to see whether he could become strong enough for a bone marrow

DOI: 10.4324/9781003797876-1

transplant. If not, the cancer was certain to kill him within a matter of months.

He asked if there was anything I could do to help him, as he was concerned he would go mad with fear and anxiety. I replied that we all must face death at some point—but only the most fortunate get to choose the type of death they experience. I reminded him of the earlier statements he had made about dying slowly from MDS, or even rapidly but in excruciating pain. I asked, "Do you think leukemia will be a less painful way to die?" He answered in the affirmative. So, I asked, "If you were given a choice of dying from leukemia now or MDS later, which would you choose?" Using a calmer tone of voice, he replied that leukemia did seem to be the better option. This cleared his mind enough that we were able to discuss how he wanted to spend his final days. We then discussed plans for what he could do to make this loss less painful for his wife.

What makes one option preferable to another is not an objective fact but the result of an individual's subjective interpretation. Choices are guided by personal priorities, emotional responses, and contextual meaning, all of which are deeply personal and vary from one individual to another. These subjective realities can also change over time.

A month later, my client was given a bone marrow transplant, which caused both the MDS and the PLL to go into remission. At the time of this writing, he has been cancer-free for exactly eight years and is really enjoying the end of his life, however long these precious and uncertain days may last.[1]

How should my nudge, the question about which type of death he would choose, be classified? The introduction of this choice was not based on a psychological diagnosis or personality trait. There was no use of hypnotic suggestion or trance. We did not process emotions or explore childhood experiences. There was no coaching or counseling, because behavioral change was *not* the goal.

Instead, I was using a form of state-based psychology, which views innate behavioral patterns as fluid, context-dependent regulatory priorities that can reorganize within minutes. The approach described in this book is not a medical model offering diagnostic labels and treatment interventions but a *communication model* that provides an organized set of semantics recognizable to mental processes that operate largely outside conscious awareness, including implicit attitudes, cognition, emotion, perception, and recall. While there are other approaches that emphasize how adaptive growth emerges automatically from tacit learning processes evoked through a relational process, such as motivational interviewing (MI) (Miller & Rollnick, 2024) and Ericksonian therapy (Gilligan, 2013), the approach you are about to discover is unique in that it applies systematic choice-environment design and state-based principles to make adaptive actions feel easier, more accessible, and self-generated.

For instance, in the example above, an implicit attitude toward death was renegotiated rapidly and without conscious deliberation. My goal was not to fix a broken psyche (clinical model) but to design meaningful opportunities that could be recognized, given the present state of mind (communication model).

As you read through this book, you will learn how to create an *optimal choice environment*. This was achieved in this case by creating a contrast between the possibility of dying slowly (option 1), or painfully (option 2) from MDS versus dying rapidly from PLL (option 3). The specific tactic, of using two undesirable aspects of MDS to make leukemia seem good in comparison, is known as the decoy effect (Huber et al., 2014). That occurs when an inferior option makes another more attractive. This "nudge" is a feature of what has recently come to be called choice architecture.

What Is Choice Architecture & Why Does It Matter?

Choice requires two attributes: intelligence and agency. It is the capacity to identify a problem or solution and to *move autonomously* in a direction that serves the organism's needs. Before his celebrated work in intelligence testing, Alfred Binet argued that even protozoa exhibit a rudimentary form of choice through approach versus avoidance behavior (Trewavas, 2015). From this perspective, the modern question is not whether choice can occur without conscious thought, but how the pre-cognitive presentation of options can be structured so that individuals experience choices that are clearer, more usable, and more aligned with their goals. This is the domain of choice architecture.

The term *choice architecture* was coined by Richard Thaler and Cass Sunstein in their 2009 book *Nudge: Improving Decisions about Health, Wealth, and Happiness*. Choice architecture is defined as the professional use of information framing and context effects to optimize the experience of choice, including choices for behaviors not subject to conscious intention. A choice architect is someone who strategically frames information and designs the presentation of choices to decision-makers. This is a research-based movement inspired by recent advances in behavioral economics (Milkman, 2021; Nease et al., 2013; Thaler & Sunstein, 2009).

As illustrated in the story of a man facing terminal illness, the very act of recognizing that a choice exists is subjective. Whether someone perceives themselves as having freedom and opportunity in each situation depends on their focus of attention and interpretation of circumstances. This internal experience of choice becomes especially crucial in moments of uncertainty, where the mind navigates between fear and hope, shaping one's sense of control over the unknown.

An important discovery by Inesi and colleagues (2011) is that choice and power are interchangeable in fulfilling the human need for a sense of control. Thus, when individuals feel powerless in one aspect of their lives, the ability to make choices elsewhere can restore their sense of agency and control. It is at this juncture that the work of a skillful choice architect can play a pivotal role. By strategically presenting meaningful options, the application of choice architecture can effectively enhance personal agency and engagement, even when a person's power is restricted. Nelson Mandela's life illustrates this principle. During twenty-seven years of imprisonment, he preserved a sense of agency through disciplined exercise, study, and reflection, drawing inspiration from *Invictus*: "I am the master of my fate; I am the captain of my soul."

What Is Ericksonian Choice Architecture?

Ericksonian Choice Architecture (ECA) draws on Milton Erickson's distinctive approach to indirect communication, particularly his pioneering use of information framing, symbolism, and context effects. Erickson transformed hypnosis into a practical form of problem-solving that supported individual autonomy and self-expression. His work also influenced later therapies. Motivational interviewing promotes change without coercion (Miller & Rollnick, 2024); solution-focused brief therapy structures useful options (de Shazer, 1988); and strategic self-therapy treats agency or free will as central to adaptive functioning (Beahrs et al., 1992). While sharing all these qualities, ECA moves beyond the *change-centric* paradigm these models use to identify success. Instead, it prioritizes the experience of choice over change. ECA can therefore be defined as the strategic design of options, cues, and environments that guide implicit choice in ways that support clients' emotional needs, unstated preferences, explicit values, and long-term goals. As discussed later, ECA functions as a contextualized-care framework.

ECA assumes that people self-organize moment-to-moment around shifting regulatory priorities (safety, control, belonging, energy conservation, etc.). These priorities show up on the surface as what behavioral science calls "cognitive biases." The ECA practitioner's job is not to correct the bias but rather to design opportunity. As will become clearer in the discussion of ECA's core principles, this communication model belongs to the same philosophical lineage as person-centered, competency-oriented, and motivational approaches, while placing distinct emphasis on the state-dependent, contextual design of choice environments rather than on conversational semantics alone.

Unlike traditional models of influence that emphasize compliance or behavior modification, ECA is used to create an *optimal choice environment*, allowing individuals to explore their autonomy within the parameters of structured guidance. For example, in the 2009 book, *Nudge*, Thaler and Sunstein describe a field study conducted at Amsterdam's Schiphol Airport, where small images of flies were etched into the urinals. The addition of these targets resulted in an 80% reduction in unsanitary spillage. Most men enjoy hitting targets. The ECA slogan, "meet people where they are," encapsulates the principle that effective guidance begins with accepting the individual's current inclinations, not as an obstacle to be overcome, but as an essential foundation for designing choice environments that naturally activate their inherent capacity for adaptive growth. However, mainstream choice architecture is often static, institutional, and aimed at population level (macro-level choice architecture), rather than being moment-to-moment, collaborative, and responsive to the fluid relational dynamics shaping an individual's experience of choice (micro-level choice architecture).

Grounded in principles of psychology, cognitive science, and neurobiology, the ECA branch of choice architecture designs choices that adapt to a person's changing motivations and circumstances. The goal is for guidance to feel collaborative, self-directed, and naturally connected to the person's process of adaptation. It involves engaging unconscious processes to expand and optimize choice-realization, even beyond conscious awareness. Applying Inesi and colleagues' (2011) *substitution principle* (the finding that power and choice can psychologically substitute for one another), choice-centric care offers an alternative when people feel a lack of control over life outcomes. In essence, both power and choice fulfill the basic human need for autonomy and agency, so when one is restricted, the other becomes more desirable or compensatory.

ECA leverages indirect communication, permissive exploration, and unconscious processing to guide individuals toward outcomes that align with their own goals. This approach reflects behavioral economics research, which shows that structuring environments subtly (altering default options or providing choice cues) can significantly impact decision-making without restricting autonomy (Johnson et al., 2012). The use of environmental cues in decision-making has been extensively studied in consumer behavior, demonstrating how subtle modifications to choice architecture can encourage beneficial choices (Dolan et al., 2012).

Unlike change-centric care, which tends to increase the practitioner's reliance on applying outside pressure to achieve predetermined outcomes ("healthy" behavior), choice-centric care prioritizes providing options that activate *intrinsic motivations* and adaptive tendencies. By doing so, it offers a sense of control that is experienced as authentic and self-directed, effectively enhancing initiative and engagement without imposing an artificial demand for change.

The assumption that *positive* change (growth) is a natural byproduct of the experience of free choice is axiomatic to ECA. Milton Erickson (1964) made essentially the same point when explaining the fundamental importance of shifting the burden of responsibility for therapeutic results onto patients, ensuring they repeatedly affirm their own desires, needs, and intentions both consciously and unconsciously. This makes the therapeutic goals truly their choice, rather than something imposed by the therapist. Recent research in psychology and behavioral economics has revealed that many choices are shaped by an interplay of unconscious processes, which include heuristics, biases, and social cues. After exploring historical trends and the recent innovations of behavioral economics and choice architecture, this chapter will clarify ECA's conceptual foundations, and then expand upon ECA's six foundational principles: *ethical guidance*, *choice-centric objectives*, *contextualized care*, *state-dependent functioning*, *dual processing*, and *autonomous problem-solving*.

Historical Trends and Theoretical Goals

Starting with Freud's introduction of psychotherapy in the late 19th century, the core value and defining identity of the mental health profession has been to act as agents of change. Freud conceptualized mental health care as a process of uncovering unconscious conflicts, bringing them into conscious awareness, and resolving them through insight. His focus on catharsis, personal growth, and transformation emphasized internal psychological change as the pathway to improved mental health.

Because the mission of psychotherapy was to change people on the inside, Freud's approach was less focused on symptom reduction and more on exploring the deeper meanings behind symptoms. This esoteric endeavor sometimes failed to produce meaningful results, and on some occasions, patients further deteriorated because of therapy (Kächele & Schachter, 2014).

The rise of behaviorism introduced a more pragmatic and measurable conception of change. Behaviorists sought to reframe mental health care as a problem-solving endeavor focused on altering observable behaviors through behavioral learning principles, such as operant conditioning. This mid-20th-century approach aligned with the emerging scientific emphasis on empiricism and verifiable outcomes. To justify its effectiveness as a field, mental health care began to prioritize demonstrable treatment outcomes. In this context, "change" became defined as measurable improvements in behavior or symptom reduction, often at the expense of more abstract or subjective concepts like self-actualization or self-determination.

Post-War Era and the Need for Justification

After World War II (WW-II), the demand for psychological services increased dramatically, particularly with the rise of veterans returning with psychological distress. At the same time, funding and credibility for mental health professions became contingent on producing measurable results. Empiricism, driven by the apparent successes of applied behavioral analysis, as well as the rise of cognitive-behavioral therapy (CBT) in the 1960s and 70s, cemented the focus on outcome-based change as central to mental health care. Therapy was increasingly seen as a way to produce specific, observable improvements in functioning, often defined by symptom reduction, productivity, and societal reintegration.

This cultural zeitgeist, which was marked by the industrialization of care and a focus on rapid results, established the perfect conditions for the development of brief therapy, an approach to behavioral change that was pragmatic, future-oriented, and pioneered by Milton Erickson.

The Permissive Approach to Naturalistic Change

For Erickson, the mission of change remained central to his teaching but, along with Carl Rogers, Abraham Maslow, and Viktor Frankl, Erickson expanded the definition of change to include subjective experiences, such as meaning-making, emotional resilience, and personal insight, alongside measurable behavioral and symptom-based outcomes. More uniquely, Erickson's therapeutic approach represented a groundbreaking integration of psychodynamic principles and early 20th-century behaviorism. His work uniquely focused on the unconscious mind, emphasizing its role in choice-realization, goal-setting, and planning, while simultaneously employing behavioral techniques to achieve symptom reduction. Erickson's perspective on human change set him apart: He viewed transformation not as something to be imposed but as a spontaneous byproduct of free choice, emerging naturally when individuals felt empowered to exercise autonomy. Erickson (1958) called this the naturalistic approach to change.

Though Erickson did not explicitly prioritize the experience of choice over the pursuit of change, his methods demonstrated a profound respect for individual autonomy. Most significantly, Erickson introduced permissive suggestion, a therapeutic method that emphasizes facilitating choice rather than exerting control. Erickson also introduced the applied practice of indirect suggestion, a hypnotic technique that resembles the practice of offering *affordances*, a concept later formalized in macro-level choice architecture by behavioral economics scholars (Norman, 2013; Viale, 2022). Erickson's use of indirect suggestion was designed to guide individuals toward productive outcomes while preserving their sense of self-determination, a key aspect of effective choice architecture.

Moreover, Erickson understood the principles of unconscious choice decades before modern behavioral economists and psychologists began to formalize these ideas. Long before Richard Thaler's work on nudges or Daniel Kahneman's insights into heuristics and biases, Erickson demonstrated a nuanced understanding of how unconscious regulatory priorities shape behavior. His therapeutic strategies aligned with these unconscious, context-dependent processes, subtly guiding individuals toward adaptive changes while honoring their autonomy.

In many ways, Erickson's work prefigured the fields of behavioral economics and choice architecture by recognizing that meaningful adaptation arises not from force or direct instruction, but from skillfully working with unconscious processes. His approach highlighted the importance of creating an environment where individuals feel empowered to make choices that align with their values and motivations. By doing so, Erickson not only revolutionized the field of psychotherapy but also laid the groundwork for concepts that would later transform our understanding of decision-making and human behavior.

Principe 1: Ethical Guidance

In his definitive work, *Nicomachean Ethics*, the renowned philosopher Aristotle addresses the question, "What does it mean to live a good life as a human being?" He argues that we live a flourishing life by cultivating virtues, which are guided by reason and aimed at our highest human potential. Similarly, there are certain fundamental virtues that are associated with ECA (accountability, transparency, and preservation of autonomy), which are guided by the logic of Aristotle's doctrine of the mean (finding the mean between excess and deficiency) and aimed at cultivating the highest human potential for those who seek out practitioners of ECA.

Accountability

The first concern many individuals voice about Erickson's casework or about modern choice architecture is that it sounds manipulative. However, contrary to that suspicion, a fundamental ethical principle of ECA is that it does not seek to manipulate individuals into compliance. Most of us have learned to respond negatively to the use of manipulation because, by definition, it involves deceptive intent, exploitation of vulnerabilities, and psychological pressure. Manipulation also denotes a lack of reciprocity or accountability. Thus, the interaction is one-sided, where the manipulator benefits at the expense of those manipulated and experiences no consequences for their actions. In contrast, ECA practitioners build accountability into client relationships (e.g., the use of outcome measures) and by pursuing oversight (e.g., affiliation with professional organizations or oversight through consultation).

More broadly, ECA functions similarly to good social etiquette, respecting autonomy while gently influencing behavior in a manner that is kind, respectful, and honest. For example, when you smile and shake someone else's hand you are both priming the individual to have certain unconscious expectations for the interaction as well as securing a commitment from them to follow a heuristic of social reciprocity. Thus, choice architecture and social etiquette both influence behavior in indirect, context-sensitive ways that respect individual autonomy while encouraging outcomes beneficial to the individual and society.

Unlike good social etiquette, some ECA tactics are emotionally provocative or paradoxically confront a defended value, and are therefore high risk (you will soon see an example of this involving a young paratrooper). These tactics are used only when contextually justified, such as in crises when harm is imminent or when conservative action would lead to slow but certain destruction. *Any* interaction between practitioner and client that falls outside the boundaries of respectful behavior is considered a *restricted-use tactic*. These maneuvers require: (1) a compelling safety objective, (2) an existing alliance or duty-of-care, and (3) rapid repair afterward to restore dignity and autonomy.

Transparency

ECA operates with transparency, shared purpose, and informed consent, ensuring that individuals remain aware of their equality and are motivated to exercise their autonomy throughout the decision-making process. As Erickson (1966) explained during a lecture:

> And what are those [motivational] forces? Well, you're a person, your patient is a person. It's an interpersonal relationship. You've got one goal in common. A patient wants dental or medical care, and you're prepared to give the desired care. So there are two people joined together, working for a common end, the welfare of the patient. And the welfare of the patient is your welfare.

This principle of *collaborative autonomy* is aligned with contemporary research on ethical nudging, where choice environments are designed to facilitate better decision-making without coercion (Thaler & Sunstein, 2009). This principle has been demonstrated in counseling arena by MI, which is an empirically grounded collaborative autonomy model (Miller, 2023). Accordingly, the ethical task is not to minimize influence but to ensure that influence never undermines personal authorship or informed ownership of the path taken.

Just as we do not stop to enumerate what we are trying to achieve each time we smile at someone, tell a joke, or shake their hand, choice architects are not compelled by ethics to explain their every move. However, they are taught to be forthright in explaining their intentions and accurately representing their skill sets. This transparency ensures that individuals retain ownership of their decisions, a concept supported by studies in moral psychology that emphasize the role of self-determination in ethical decision-making (Greene et al., 2001).

Preservation of Autonomy

In his work on ethics, Aristotle positioned self-sufficiency (αυτάρκεια) as a central ideal. He argued that the flourishing person lives in such a way that their well-being depends primarily on their own character and choices, not on external conditions. In contemporary thought, *libertarian paternalism* is a philosophy of decision-making that recognizes the responsibility of those in a position of leadership to guide vulnerable individuals toward beneficial choices while preserving their freedom to choose. Explicated by Thaler and Sunstein (2009), this process operates through "nudges," which are subtle changes in choice architecture that encourage better outcomes without restricting options. In keeping with this philosophy, a core virtue of ECA is to nurture and protect self-sufficiency in others (what we now call the right to autonomy) while working through a variety of communication channels (both conscious and unconscious).

When we apply Aristotle's logic to libertarian paternalism, we see that it represents a balanced approach between two extremes: strict behaviorism, which undermines autonomy, and analytic neutrality, which neglects necessary guidance. John B. Watson, in his book *Behaviorism* (1924), boldly shares his belief in the power of environmental conditioning saying:

> Give me a dozen healthy infants, well-formed, and my own specified world to bring them up in, and I'll guarantee to take any one at random and train him to become any type of specialist I might select—doctor, lawyer, artist, merchant-chief, and yes, even beggar-man and thief, regardless of his talents, penchants, tendencies, abilities, vocations, and race of his ancestors.

This reflects the deterministic nature of classical behaviorism, where individuals are seen as entirely moldable by external conditions. However, this contradicts research on human thriving, which highlights the importance of self-agency, *intrinsic motivation*, and personal meaning in decision-making (autonomy).

On the opposite end of the spectrum, the stance of not directing, not gratifying, and not influencing the client toward any particular insight, choice, or emotional direction (analytic neutrality) rests on the assumption that lost individuals can independently discover the path forward. While it is difficult to argue with Carl Rogers' (1951) logic that "It is the client who knows what hurts, what directions to go, what problems are crucial, what experiences have been deeply buried" (p. 11), it is important not to overlook the foundational role of distributed cognition and social modeling for human growth and adaptation (Mehr et al., 2020). Modern research has shown that thinking and problem-solving are enhanced through structured interactions with others, verbal tools, and information-rich environments (leadership). When we pursue *a middle way* (balancing structure and freedom), we see the value of offering gentle guidance through the mechanisms of choice architecture while preserving individual autonomy and avoiding coercion.

Principle 2: Choice-Centric Objectives

While most modern psychotherapeutic approaches rightly emphasize the central importance of choice in promoting human well-being, their underlying frameworks often prioritize change as the primary objective. This emphasis, though rooted in well-established clinical traditions, can inadvertently marginalize individuals who are not amenable to change. This is a stance we will later examine through the lens of reactance or status quo bias. As a result, those who express a preference for continuity may be prematurely labeled as resistant, and if their position remains unchanged, they may ultimately be deemed beyond the reach of "therapeutic benefit."

ECA, in contrast, is *choice-centric*: it prioritizes the experience of exercising choice, with functional adaptation occurring as a natural byproduct. Aptly described by the ancient philosopher Heraclitus, "No man ever steps in the same river twice," meaning everything in life is in a constant state of flux or change. This includes the societies we live in, the physical space around us, our bodies, our actions, and even our memories are in a constant state of reconstruction (Hupbach et al., 2007). In *The Self Illusion* (2012), Hood even argues that the "self" is a construct, shaped by social and cognitive processes that lack any true consistency. Thus, it is not change that needs to be conjured but rather the quality of choice governing the flux of human existence. Change is constant, and without choice, it holds no special value.

Choice-centric care is established on the principle that individuals are most likely to thrive when they feel a genuine sense of ownership and active engagement in determining the course of their lives. Traditional approaches to well-being assume that people have a fixed, unchanging self and must be transformed into a different, supposedly better, static version. In contrast, choice-centric care views adaptation as an ever-evolving process. While choice-centric care emphasizes personal ownership and engagement, it does not assume that individuals have no need for guidance, leadership, or external support. The aim is to ensure that such influences are structured in a way that respects autonomy and fosters adaptive, self-directed growth rather than imposing a fixed idea of appropriate change. To achieve this, ECA emphasizes four key concepts: *leading from behind*, *autonomous stability*, *choice agnosticism*, and *data-biased decision-making*. Each of these ensures that individuals navigate positive change (growth) on their own terms while benefiting from rigorously tested psychological frameworks that support human thriving.

Leading from Behind

While explaining the starting point for collaborative relationships, Erickson and Rossi (1979) wrote,

> The senior author's first task was to recognize and accept their hostility and doubt and, if possible, actually to utilize it in some manner. He had to accept their negative frame of reference and yet introduce his own belief in the potential value of hypnotherapy.
>
> (p. 117)

The practice of accepting of the client's immediate frame of reference, while introducing conditions that support self-directed initiative, has been described by others as leading from one step behind (Cantwell & Holmes, 1994).

Beahrs (2006) captures this stance in two thematic communications: (1) "My job is not to change you, but to assist you in becoming more of who you already are." (2) "Who are you? What do you stand for? Where are you heading? What are your short-term and long-term goals?" (p. 159). For clients who seem ego-defensive, I will sometimes say, "After taking the time to understand you, I have become confident that we do not need to change who you are. Instead, let's figure out how you can show up, consistently, as the best version of yourself." Similar to Bearhs' second strategic communication, I lead from behind by asking, "What are your most important values? What should I be aiming for as I work with you?" Inquiring about a person's value system presupposes goodness and human decency and can elicit more constructive responses to critical feedback (Critcher et al., 2010).

Psychotherapy's roots in the medical model, where the goal is to diagnose and cure, have led to a primary focus on alleviating symptoms rather than cultivating a relationship grounded in strategic acceptance of the client's current state of mind. As a result, practitioners trained in this tradition are rarely taught to lead with acceptance, which can unintentionally foster power struggles, both between therapist and client and within the client's own internal experience.

More specifically, a therapist who is trained in *proceduralized care* is likely to insist that a client comply with the theory-based intervention for which the practitioner has some authority and expertise. For example, a therapist trained (and certified) in emotional process work would need to overcome any client resistance to uncovering suppressed emotions. But this type of pressure has been shown to result in higher rates of client deterioration (Mohr, 1995). Even if the client is not harmed, this unnecessary struggle not only slows progress but can also damage trust and rapport.

Another disadvantage of *change-centric care* is that the emphasis on symptom reduction and behavioral modification subtly implies rejection. Who the client is right now is not good enough. The therapist can state explicitly, "You are perfectly acceptable just as you are," but when their fundamental mission is to create change, the preceding message is seriously compromised. Because the identity-disaffirming message is merely implied, clients may struggle to articulate why they feel uneasy or self-conflicted, making it harder to challenge therapy's unstated suggestion, "You must change who you are." As a result, collaborative engagement suffers. The focus on correction overrides the client's need for self-trust and autonomy. In contrast, *choice-centric care*, as in ECA, *leads from behind* by prioritizing autonomy and cooperative engagement rather than reinforcing unconscious self-judgment.

Perhaps the greatest risk of *change-centric care* is that it can encourage controlling behavior. Research on Social Dominance Orientation (SDO) suggests that individuals who favor hierarchical social arrangements (e.g., doctor versus patient) are more likely to support or enact such dynamics, especially when change is framed as a top-down intervention (Pratto et al., 1994). Moreover, social dominance theory (SDT) posits that not only do dominant individuals maintain hierarchies, but so do subordinates by complying with controlling tactics. This was supported in a longitudinal study of students in hierarchical academic settings, where higher SDO at baseline predicted later compliance with harsh power tactics by authority figures, independent of prior compliance levels (Tesi et al., 2019).

These findings underscore a troubling dynamic: People in unequal relationships may come to accept and perpetuate the very power structures that limit their agency. In care settings, hierarchy-enhancing myths, such as the belief that clinical authority should be met with obedience, or that compliance is a sign of progress, can rationalize subtle forms of interpersonal dominance. If unchecked, helpers may unconsciously slip into behaviors that prioritize their own agenda over the client's, fostering a dynamic of control rather than collaboration. This dominance erodes the client's sense of agency and perpetuates *a spiral of inequalities*, where small initial imbalances in power are amplified over time through repeated patterns of deference, compliance, and control. This unconscious dynamic can occur in medicine, education, coaching, or any setting in which one person feels that they have the authority to change another individual.

As an anecdotal illustration, I have had clients tell me stories about being criticized by their medical doctor or by their previous therapist. These vulnerable individuals often felt humiliated when they did not respond to treatment with the anticipated changes. For example, one woman undertook gastric bypass surgery and lost 100 lbs. only to gain it all back a year later. In her follow-up visit, she was told by her surgeon, "You are in the failure group. There is a small percentage of people who cannot be helped." She said that after hearing this, she wanted to crawl under a rock and die (she literally struggled with suicidal ideation). Rather than seeking to change her, I helped her discover her most choice method of losing weight, which was Flow Yoga under the guidance of a kind female teacher. Over time, she developed a strong, lean body that reflected her core values of discipline and receptivity to nurturing guidance, qualities absent in her relationship with her mother. Admittedly, my knowledge of ECA did create an asymmetry of power. This is inevitable in helping relationships, just as when one person pulls another from a pit. The true ethical question is whether that power is used to serve the client's growth or the practitioner's self-interest.

Autonomous Stability

A second important marker of *choice-centric care* is *autonomous stability*, which means individuals have the right to remain as they are without pressure while also maintaining the freedom to experience growth on their own terms. In other words, true choice cannot exist without the freedom to stay the same. By affirming that staying the same is a valid choice, *choice-centric care* fosters psychological safety, reduces self-blame and reactance, while increasing the likelihood of self-agency. As Angela Duckworth explained in a recent dialogue with Katy Milkman (2025), personal empowerment begins when the question shifts from "What's wrong with me?" to "What is wrong with my situation?"

Research in positive psychology has consistently demonstrated that individuals who feel a greater sense of control over their choices experience lower levels of stress and higher overall life satisfaction (Seligman, 2011). This also aligns with research on self-determination theory (Deci & Ryan,

2008), which shows that *intrinsic motivation* is likely to increase when autonomy is respected. Moreover, when individuals experience low power or a diminished sense of control, the introduction of choices can effectively fulfill their need for control, restoring a sense of agency and stability (Inesi et al., 2011). Paradoxically, when people feel genuinely free not to change, they sometimes become more receptive to growth because the decision to reorganize the self is internally driven rather than externally imposed.

As an example, Erickson described the following interaction with a woman who came to his office and said she wanted him to do something about her weight:

Erickson: "I can help you, but you'll have to cooperate. You climb, Squaw Peak [mountain]."
Woman: "At sunrise?"
Erickson: "Yes."
Woman: "Well, I'd like some company."
Erickson: "You complain that your 16-year-old son is about 100 pounds overweight. Take him along for the company. Set a good example for him."

The next time Erickson saw her, she said, "You know, I don't believe I want to lose weight and I know my son doesn't. Do you mind if I stop trying to fool myself?" Erickson replied, "Not at all" (Rosen, 1982, pp. 126–127).

Choice Agnosticism

Choice agnosticism is a strategic stance in which the practitioner avoids endorsing a particular option. Instead, the focus is on protecting the client's sense of autonomy and control within a carefully designed set of alternatives. Rather than overtly directing individuals toward a specific choice, ECA designs psychological landscapes where multiple options are available. Although choice architecture is meant to influence decisions, and practitioners cannot eliminate their own biases, choice agnosticism requires that the client retain final authority over every choice.

As suggested by research on self-determination theory, when individuals perceive control over their decisions, they are more likely to experience *intrinsic motivation* and long-term behavioral alignment. Similarly, offering choices in negotiations leads to better outcomes and increased satisfaction, as counterparts feel others have their best interest in mind (Galinsky et al., 2017). Finally, studies on MI reinforce this principle, showing that autonomy-supportive counseling approaches yield better behavioral outcomes compared to directive strategies (Arkowitz et al., 2015).

Data-Biased Decision-Making

By aligning decision-making structures with principles of positive psychology and neurological functioning, ECA ensures that options are shaped by scientific insights (data biased) rather than subjective personal opinions or a single theoretical doctrine.

Mainstream choice architecture often treats the existence of a bias as problematic, yet this contradicts the presumed value of giving greater weight to empirical data during decision-making (being data-biased). ECA, by contrast, views bias not as a flaw but as an inherent aspect of cognition. The "bias effect" reflects what is easiest to notice and what a person prefers. Depending on the situation, it may improve judgment or lead to errors in perception. Research on heuristics and biases (Tversky & Kahneman, 1974) supports this perspective, showing that cognitive shortcuts, when understood and applied strategically, can enhance wise decision-making. Just as a left-handed dinner guest is better accommodated by strategic seating arrangements, ECA structures choice environments to work with, rather than against, natural cognitive tendencies.

Instead of imposing change, ECA incorporates six essential strategies: *utilization*, *framing*, *commitment*, *priming*, *redirection*, and *critical thinking*; to create environments where individuals recognize their own power to choose, making growth self-directed and sustainable. Each of these strategies draws on well-established findings in behavioral science showing that decision outcomes are shaped by heuristics, identity, emotional state, and relational context. While *change-centric care* highlights the power of the change agent, *choice-centric care* strategically shifts the focus to the choice agent, thereby fostering autonomy and *intrinsic motivation*. This is achieved by pursuing a strategy of *utilization* (discovering preexistent abilities, established resources, or hidden potentials). ECA also relies on a strategy known as *framing* to introduce the experience of choice, rather than seeking to cure immutable realities, such as the inevitability of suffering (at some time, in some form) or end of life. Instead of relying on external "interventions" to impose change, ECA focuses on fostering a personal sense of *commitment* prior to obtaining guidance from the choice architect. Also, ECA uses the strategy of *priming* to produce spontaneous mental shifts rather than using formal persuasion. Similarly, rather than using confrontation, ECA uses the strategy of *redirection*. And finally, rather than offering advice or formal counseling, ECA establishes the necessary conditions for clients to do their own *critical thinking*. Rather than performing "interventions," ECA practitioners design *affordances*, which are features of the environment that invite and enable adaptive choices without imposing them.

Principle 3: Contextualized Care

ECA acknowledges that human needs must be addressed at different levels of specificity, ranging from long-term societal needs to immediate personal concerns. For large-scale decisions, such as government health policies or hospital surgery protocols, we rely on quantitative statistics to determine how to best meet the needs of the greatest number of people (the ethics of utilitarianism). This approach identifies "populations" to be served based on diagnostic traits, such as major depressive disorder, or personality traits, such as introversion or high hypnotizability. Trait-grouping has enabled effective industrial-scale responses to complex social problems and has also led to the development of treatment protocols in various schools of therapy. This model, known as *proceduralized care*, is most effective for policy implementation and population-wide interventions. For example, a business that wishes to help its employees save money for retirement can set the retirement savings plan as a default option in employee contracts, with an opt-out option. This policy (standard procedure) preserves individual freedom while significantly increasing enrollment rates and long-term financial security.

In contrast to proceduralized care, we can focus our attention on the needs of any given individual. At this more personal level, care providers use individual history and past behavior as guides for tailoring the delivery of care to specific, individual needs. This approach, called *individualized care*, works best for helping someone whose needs or reactions do not conform to majority norms. Erickson sharply opposed strict procedural approaches to therapy, which he believed to be a violation of individual rights. While preparing a quote for what would have been one of his final speeches, Erickson wrote,

> Each person is a unique individual. Hence, psychotherapy should be formulated to meet the uniqueness of the individual's needs, rather than tailoring the person to fit the Procrustean bed of a hypothetical theory of human behavior.
>
> (Erickson, 2000, p. xvii)

Similarly, behavioral science researchers now criticize the "one-nudge-for-all" approach and advocate for more studies on nudging based on individual differences, which appear to be substantially more effective, and have a more robust and consistent evidence base (Mills, 2022).

ECA does not dispute the documented benefits of *proceduralized care* but instead recognizes its limitations. For example, while baby aspirin has been shown to reduce the risk of heart attack in most men (not women), there are some individuals who have severe allergic reactions to aspirin. Erickson described one such instance when a woman told her doctor that she did not respond well to aspirin. The physician insisted that she would be fine and prescribed it to her. As a result, the woman died. Erickson used this anecdote to make the point that the needs of the individual do not always correlate with the needs of the group. For that reason, Erickson advocated strongly for the practice of tailoring psychological care to the needs of the individual.

Moving to an even more granular level of analysis, ECA introduces the possibility of *contextualized care*, as displayed in Figure 0.1. This perspective enables its practitioners to discern the needs of the moment. I learned the importance of this level of specificity early in my career. I had been asked to evaluate a teenage boy for emotional disturbances by a school district. I collected behavioral rating scales from each of his teachers, examined his grades, read his school file, and administered the Minnesota Multiphasic Personality Inventory-Adolescent, the Beck Depression Inventory, and the Rorschach Ink Blot test. On a Friday afternoon, I interviewed the boy and learned that he was optimistic about his chances at this new school and very eager to try out for the basketball team. Every piece of information that I collected came back positive, so I called his mother Monday morning to share the good news that she did not need to worry about her son having emotional difficulties. However, she cut me off, saying, "Perhaps I should tell you that my son has been committed to a psychiatric ward. Late Friday afternoon, while I was still at work, he attempted suicide."

I later discovered that after meeting with me, he had gone to the gym and been treated harshly and unfairly by the basketball coach. He had

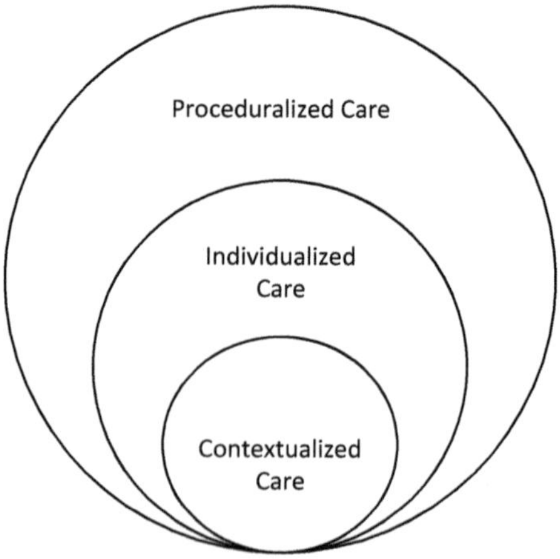

Figure 0.1 Three Levels of Specificity.

been told that his type was not welcome on the basketball team (because his single-parent mother was poor). He was shocked by the fact that he was not allowed to shoot a single basket. This brutal rejection sank any hope he had of fitting in at this school. While sitting at home alone, and in a state of acute crisis, he came to the conclusion that he was nothing but a financial burden. In other words, he had experienced a significant state shift since leaving my office.

Humans are complex, seemingly paradoxical creatures who can experience radical shifts in state of mind that may continue to evolve from one minute to the next. Studies in adaptive decision-making have shown that individuals exhibit different problem-solving strategies depending on environmental cues and stress levels. Under calm and controlled conditions, people tend to rely on deliberate, analytical reasoning, weighing options carefully before making a choice. However, when faced with high-pressure situations or rapidly changing environments, they often shift to heuristic-based, intuitive strategies that prioritize speed over precision. Research on dynamic decision-making models (Busemeyer & Townsend, 1993) highlights how choice structures must remain flexible to accommodate these shifts in cognitive load and emotional state. For instance, individuals experiencing heightened stress may default to habit-driven or emotionally charged responses rather than logical analysis. This variability underscores the importance of designing decision-making frameworks that can adapt in real time to changing conditions. By doing so, ECA fosters more effective and contextually relevant support.

While scholarship has been dominated by a trait perspective for the past century, the importance of state psychology is known to anyone experienced in hypnosis. Hypnotic phenomena (such as dissociation and age regression) are predicated on radical changes in state of consciousness. Also, equally surprising displays of state shifts can occur in ordinary psychotherapy, when a fully functioning adult suddenly regresses to childlike sobbing, their toes turned inward, and their thoughts dominated by childhood logic. More paradoxical examples, such as the powerful CEO who submits at home to domestic violence, highlight the fluid nature of human behavior, emphasizing that context and situational forces can override stable traits, leading individuals to act in ways that may seem entirely out of character. Though Erickson did not use the term *contextualized care*, he suggested this degree of precision and immediacy, stating, "the problem isn't trying to adapt therapy to that particular classification [proceduralized care], but: what potentialities does the patient disclose to you of their capacity to do this or to do that?" (Haley, 1985, p. 123). Thus, contextualized care is any model that can adapt to shifting mental states, which requires responding dynamically to evolving scenarios. It is the model of care that is most granular and most effective for meeting the needs of the moment.

In summary, *proceduralized care* is most effective for large-scale, population-wide interventions where standardized protocols based on statistical trends and trait-groupings can maximize benefits for the majority. *Individualized care* is best suited for addressing the unique, long-term needs of a specific person whose responses may not align with group norms. Contextualized care is most advantageous in immediate, state-dependent situations, requiring dynamic responsiveness to a person's shifting psychological state and present circumstances.

Principle 4: State-Dependent Functioning

The principle of contextualized care aligns with research on *state-dependent functioning*, which shows that cognitive processing is dynamic and shifts with changes in neurological arousal levels (Perry, 2006). These shifts impact not only cognition but also emotions, motivations, physiology, perception, and memory, emphasizing that these processes function as an integrated whole. ECA builds on this principle by recognizing distinct *states of mind* that encompass cognitive, emotional, motivational, perceptual, and somatic domains.

According to Perry (2006), when individuals experience heightened stress, fear, or emotional intensity, their ability to process information, regulate emotions, and make decisions is altered. In high-arousal states, functional control shifts from complex brain systems (cortical region) to reflexive systems (diencephalon and brainstem), resulting in greater reliance on instinctual or survival-oriented responses rather than rational analysis. Conversely, in low-arousal states, the same person may shift to reflective and abstract thinking. For traumatized or hyper-aroused individuals, Perry recommends a *sequence of engagement*: First, you must regulate (calming the body), then relate (forming social bonds), and then reason (engage in critical thinking).

The dynamic nature of adaptive functioning underscores the necessity of contextualized care in ECA, as affordances must be tailored to the person's current psychological and physiological state. Rather than assuming that it is always business as usual with a given individual, ECA recognizes that an individual's needs and capacities vary depending on their moment-to-moment experience, necessitating flexible and responsive strategies for meaningful engagement and support.

Reversal Theory

A second state theory that illuminates a key dimension of ECA is *reversal theory*. This theory, developed by Michael Apter (Apter, 1984; Apter et al.,

2014), has had a significant influence on the organization of ideas within ECA. Reversal theory revolves around the idea that people shift between different motivational states in response to situational cues, attitudes, emotions, and goals. Since survival depends on adaptation, and adaptation requires flexibility, the ability to shift motivational states dynamically is essential for responding effectively to changing circumstances. For example, at one moment a mother may need to gently nurture her infant and, at the sight of a predator, suddenly shift to a violent posture. When individuals become stuck in a single state, reversal theory presents the possibility of triggering state reversals to activate a type of motivation that is better suited to the situation.

Recognizing that human behavior is not primarily governed by reason or conscious awareness, the theory instead emphasizes emotions and implicit motivation as key forces in decision-making. It introduces the concept of meta-motivational states, which shape how people interpret and respond to choices. Crucially, reversal theory addresses the paradoxical nature of human behavior and non-linear decision-making. Often a series of choices, by the same individual, will appear contradictory. It also suggests that opposing motivational states can coexist within the same personality, shifting dynamically in response to internal and external cues.

As an example of how to trigger a state reversal, a leading contributor to brief therapy, Nicolas Cummings (2002) discussed with me the psychological tactic that inspired him to become a psychologist. The historical context was WW-II and for the first time in history, the army was using paratroopers. Cummings explained it this way:

> I was a paratrooper in World War II. Forty percent of the fatalities for paratroops was psychological. There was a superstition among the troops that the average life expectancy of a paratrooper was four jumps. If he was an officer, it was only two jumps. This belief helped alleviate anxiety and allowed the solider to jump into combat for their first, second, and third battle. But when it came time for the fourth jump the solider would freeze at the door. This is what we called "jump door fever." The jump sergeant would then use the boot-in-the-back technique to force them out the jump door. Invariably, under these circumstances, the trooper would go into a panic state and when he hit the ground, he would forget all his training and be dead within minutes.
>
> Dr. William Menneger (Carl Menneger's brother), the Chief Psychiatrist for the military during WW-II, conceived the idea that if the soldier could choose to jump, he would not go into a panic state. So, he brought several of us paratroop combat officers in for special training at a school in Long Island. My teacher was Frieta Fromm-Reichman. She taught us how to talk the paratrooper out the door in five seconds. The five second interval was critical because jumping sooner than that would cause

> the paratroopers to run into each other. If the jump was delayed the paratroopers would be spread too thin when they landed. After I took that course from Frieta Fromm-Reichman, I never lost another solider to jump-door-fever.

The actual tactic was not published because it sounded too controversial. But it was war and people's lives were on the line. When I asked Cummings to explain this tactic, he gave several examples, all of them involving the use of highly insulting language to transform fear into rage (state reversal). For example, one solider, who was of Italian descent, was told by Cummings, "It's just like a fucking wop to freeze up at the moment he's truly needed." This was a racial slur, an attack on his dignity and heritage. The man responded by saying, "Fuck you, sir!" and then proved him wrong by bravely jumping out the door.[2]

Reversal theory helps explain such shifts by providing a structured understanding of how and why people transition between motivational states. Importantly, these changes in motivation also bring shifts in perception, attention, memory recall, emotion, cognition, and physiology (as predicted by Perry's neurology-based state theory). Each of these contributes to how a person adapts to the demands of the moment. Together, these highly synchronized mental processes shape an individual's overall state of mind.

While Apter's theory uses unique terminology (e.g., "paratelic") to describe four sets of opposing states, ECA instead adopts established research on cognitive biases. This conceptual approach ensures that ECA's terminology is widely recognized and can categorize a broader range of opposing or contralateral states.

In ECA, a state is defined at the intersection of a regulatory priority (e.g., belonging), a target (i.e., a person or event), and the attitudinal valence or energy-orientation toward that target (state = priority × target × valence/energy). In the same way that a doctor checks the pulse to know what is happening with the cardiac systems, ECA practitioners focus on cognitive bias expressions as real-time surface evidence of that intersection. While there are many different conceivable states, this volume will focus on eight mutually exclusive states, as displayed in Figure 0.2.

These states of mind are especially relevant when navigating or designing collaborative relationships. As illustrated in the compass chart, each primary bias is best understood in contrast to its binary opposite. Although not shown in the chart, each bias can also be expanded into complementary subcategories. For instance, *social conformity bias* complements *authority bias*, just as *action bias* complements *change bias*.

The vertical axis is distinctive in that it represents an orthogonal dimension (Negativity vs. Positivity) which operates independently from, yet

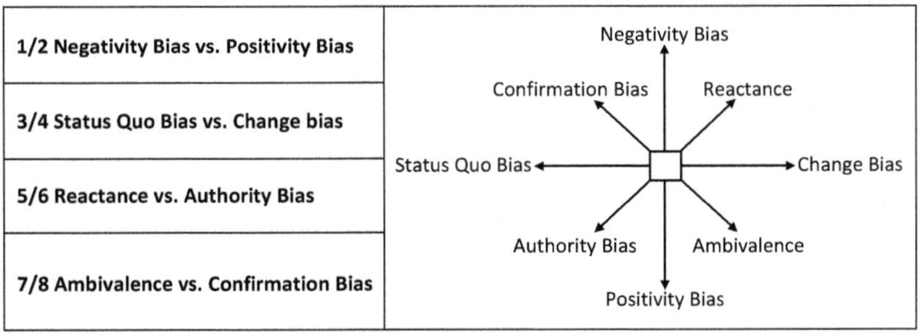

Figure 0.2 Diametrically Opposed States of Mind.

modulates, other psychological states involved in alliance formation. This was described earlier as the attitudinal valence or energy-orientation. For example, *reactance* reflects negativity toward authority, whereas *authority bias* reflects positivity toward authority. Similarly, *ambivalence* reflects negativity toward cognitive closure, while *confirmation bias* reflects positivity toward it.

As stated above, each state can be said to have a target. Ambivalence, for example, may target marriage (producing mixed feelings about that domain) without influencing attitudes toward work. This distinction underscores that ECA is not focused on trait psychology—we do not say someone "has an ambivalent personality." Rather, a state of ambivalence (or any other bias) represents a context-dependent regulatory function that targets specific variables. This conceptual framework (one that avoids pigeonholing individuals with maladaptive characteristics) is designed to enhance the precision of ECA while promoting choice through the construction of optimal choice environments.

Counter-Regulation

Like reversal theory, Rothermund's (2011) *counter-regulation theory* explains how people manage emotions without conscious effort by shifting between opposite emotional states. For example, after experiencing high anxiety during a stressful event, the natural tendency is to feel relief after encountering a signal that the event is over. Similarly, laughter is often used to counter-regulate fear, after escaping danger. The reversal helps restore emotional balance in a way that is spontaneous and automatic. It does not rely on cognitive resources.

According to this theory, people naturally seek emotional balance by shifting between opposing emotional states, a process known as *counter-regulation*. This shift helps reduce emotional saturation or fixation, allowing individuals to maintain emotional equilibrium without conscious effort. Research shows that counter-regulation also impacts attention and motivation. When people focus on achieving positive or negative goals, they become more easily distracted by stimuli with the opposite emotional tone (Rothermund et al., 2008). This automatic shift in attention helps individuals balance their emotions and adjust their actions without conscious thought. *It is a pre-conceptual choice that sets the stage for subsequent thoughts and actions.* Therefore, counter-regulation offers a nuanced understanding of how emotional and cognitive states shift in response to both internal and external cues, reinforcing the importance of ECA's flexible, contextually relevant affordances designed to guide implicit problem-solving processes.

Principle 5: Dual Processing

Aligned with widely accepted views in cognitive science, ECA recognizes that human decision-making operates through two distinct systems: System 1, which is fast, automatic, emotional, and heuristic-based (unconscious intelligence), and System 2, which is slow, deliberate, logical, and effortful or intentional (conscious intelligence). Thus, people can process information in both a conscious and unconscious mode.

While *intelligence* is defined as goal-directed adaptability, information processing, and problem-solving within real-life contexts (Kaufman, 2013), *heuristics* are rules derived from life experience that inform and shape the information processing that occurs outside of conscious awareness (System 1). These *heuristics* interact with biases in such a way as to reduce the amount of cognitive load on System 2 (conscious reason) resulting in the exercise of choice without conscious oversight. Most importantly, these hidden rules shape perception, decision-making, and behavior in predictable ways, as shown in Table 0.1.

While heuristics are adaptive strategies that facilitate quick decisions, they also introduce biases, such as an overconfidence or underconfidence bias, which affect the accuracy of those decisions. In ECA, cognitive biases are defined as *predictable mental processes that shape how we perceive, evaluate, and act on available options.* In some cases, the bias might be more so emotional, resulting in what researchers call *hot cognition.* In other instances, the bias might be highly rational, resulting in what is known as *cold cognition.*

In either case, contemporary cognitive psychology (not ECA) treats biases as a consequence of relying on heuristics to make fast decisions (Kahneman, 2011). The solution most favored by academics for addressing biased processing is to introduce critical thinking skills (cold cognition) to help mitigate the influence of cognitive biases. However, in addition to merely using new nomenclature to recycle Freud's prioritization of reason

Table 0.1 Predicting Implicit Information Processing

The Mental Process	*Behavioral Effects*	*The Heuristic*
Implicit attitudes	Rules determining good vs. bad, such as in-group favoritism	*Similarity Heuristic*
Implicit expectations	Rules guiding prediction and unconscious goal-setting, such as self-handicapping or procrastination	*Risk Aversion Heuristic*
Implicit attention	Rules determining what objects or ideas to monitor without conscious thought, such as automatically stopping at a red sign (red = danger)	*Representativeness Heuristic*

over instinct (insight), there are other serious conceptual problems with this logic.

The philosophy of *epistemological relativism* argues that our understanding of reality is *always* filtered through our subjective lens, making it impossible to achieve real objectivity. As an analogy, the reality of a river is one thing while viewing it from the top of a mountain, another thing while standing at its banks, and quite another while swimming across it. Until humans develop the ability to be omnipresent, perception, whether conscious or unconscious, will always be somehow biased. Erickson observed, "they are not just biases, they are part of the way we experience the world" (Erickson & Rossi, 1976, p. 180). Accepting this fact, ECA does not seek to eliminate heuristics and biases but rather seeks to optimize choice environments so that these mental operations lead to beneficial outcomes. As a brief example of optimizing a choice environment, an ECA practitioner might say to a person who is overwhelmed with hot cognition,

> You can take a few deep breathes and it will help you think more clearly. You can also close your eyes and know that you are not alone—you have someone else to help guide you through this problem. …And when you are ready, you can go forward in time. You can imagine yourself having successfully resolved this dilemma. And you can watch your progress through the eyes of an admiring friend, or someone who cares deeply for you. And, this will give you an entirely different perspective.

Those trained in hypnotherapy might call this a "trance" experience. Speaking more precisely, it is the use of physical relaxation, secure attachment, *choice previews*, and *perspective taking* to increase insight and cognitive flexibility. The result is a new mental landscape that favors the recognition of new possibilities. Erickson and Rossi (1979) explained essentially the same idea, saying,

> The development of a trance state is an intrapsychic phenomenon, dependent upon internal processes, and the activity of the hypnotist serves only to create a favorable situation. As an analogy, an incubator supplies a favorable environment for the hatching of eggs, but the actual hatching derives from the development of life processes within the egg. (p. 59)

ECA refers to this practice as "meeting people where they are." It involves recognizing a person's active biases and designing environments that guide them toward personally empowering and prosocial outcomes. This approach reflects research showing that communications aligned with existing motivational states produce less tension and greater collaborative engagement. For example, a common cognitive bias known as *loss aversion* can be effectively leveraged to strengthen commitment to positive choices by presenting positive habits as a way to avoid losses, such as declining health or missed opportunities (Ariely, 2009).

There seems to be no limit on what can be leveraged, including aggressive tendencies. As an example, Erickson[3] described the following interaction after a young woman walked into his office and glared at him. Her husband had arranged the appointment and warned Erickson to expect aggressive behavior:

Erickson: Your husband has told me that if I say a single wrong word here that you will slap my face and walk out. ...There is just one thing puzzling me...I don't know which way to duck. Are you right or left-handed?

Woman: Maybe you won't say the wrong thing.

Erickson: Maybe I won't. ...Well, you are my height. You are very nicely built. You weigh quite a bit less than I do and I'm not very heavy. You are as tall as I am. But none the less, you could really swing. So, are you right or left-handed?

Woman: Right-handed.

From that point forward, Erickson was able to gain further cooperation. Her initial mental state, known as *reactance*, might have come from the implicit attitude that vulnerability is bad and to be avoided at all costs. Erickson did not refute this rule but rather created an environment in which she felt safe and affirmed. This allowed her to choose a path of collaborative engagement. While academic scholars place greater emphasis on correcting the limitations of implicit cognition, ECA primarily seeks to utilize these unconscious processes to promote natural, self-directed decision-making.

Incubated Cognition

Incubated cognition refers to the mental processing that occurs outside of conscious awareness after a person has initially engaged with a problem but then steps away from it. Traditional models that prioritize System 2 critical thinking (e.g., CBT) risk undervaluing the subtle, emergent intelligence of System 1 (unconscious intelligence). Studies of incubated cognition show that true understanding and strategic choice can arise without direct reasoning or conscious effort (Short, 2022, p. 20).

While it is not obvious, the strategy of *critical thinking* is foundational to both mainstream choice architecture and ECA. What is unique to ECA is the assumption that critical thinking can occur without conscious oversight, if properly cued. As explained by Erickson in a 1960 lecture in Chicago:

> A patient may make an urgent appointment with you over the phone, only to come into the office and sit there very silently. You can confess your lack of understanding and tell them that no matter how silent they are, that their unconscious mind is beginning to think, beginning to understand, that they themselves do not need to know consciously what's going on in their unconscious mind.
>
> What are you saying to them? You are saying that their unconscious mind can now work, and you're making use of their silence, their conscious silence, and getting them to understand that they do not have to verbalize consciously at all. That their mere presence in your office allows their unconscious mind to work satisfactorily.
>
> I see no reason why one should resent a patient sitting quietly for a whole hour. I think it's a waste of time on your part if you don't use it for the patient. You don't need to say very much. All you need to do is tell a patient, let your unconscious mind work.

Incubated cognition reveals the mind's ability to generate insights through unconscious, associative processing, making it essential for any model of care (like ECA) that values dual processing, non-linear progress, and the role of time and context in psychological growth. As Erickson would often say to patients and his own family members, *you should learn to trust your unconscious mind.*

Bounded rationality, a term introduced by Herbert Simon (1955), suggests that while individuals strive to make rational decisions, their ability to do so is limited by factors such as information, time, and cognitive capacity. What Erickson argued was that unconscious thought (*incubated cognition*) addresses the problem of bounded rationality by introducing greater access to memories, emotions, and attitudes that operate outside the margins of conscious awareness.

The Advantages of Unconscious Processing

Understanding the power and precision of unconscious processing is central to ECA, which seeks to shape environments that engage both conscious deliberation and intuitive, emotion-informed responses. Unlike traditional care models that prioritize rational, effortful decision-making, ECA recognizes that much of human behavior (including adaptation, insight, and even critical thinking) can emerge from the mind's implicit systems. The following brief overview highlights the advantages and limitations of dual processing, with conscious processing requiring more time and energy and unconscious processes being more efficient and capable of producing rational, self-corrective, and goal-directed behavior (see Table 0.2).

Conscious thought (System 2) is capable of complex, logical, and structured inferential reasoning, such as deductive reasoning, hypothesis testing, and strategic planning. It is often used in tasks that require careful analysis and explicit rule application, such as engineering, math, and science. These conscious tasks often involve *extended cognitive frameworks* (Hutchins, 1995) to include social and material devices (*distributed cognition*). For example, complex math is not processed purely neurologically but also with pen and paper. Similarly, we talk through complex ideas with others and their input helps us understand ourselves better.

However, conscious awareness is not required to guide human behavior. Unconscious thought (System 1) excels in inferential tasks that involve pattern recognition, implicit learning, experiential knowledge, and muscle memory (embodied cognition). It integrates information from various sources to form inferences and judgments quickly and often accurately. While unconscious processing relies heavily on emotions and heuristics, these mechanisms still produce rational outcomes, and with greater speed and far less energy consumption (Kahneman, 2011). This is because implicit emotions provide important information. They shape our reasoning, guide our actions, and influence how we manage distress and experience spiritual fulfillment (Clore, 2011).

In keeping with Erickson's observations, modern cognitive researchers have rediscovered the mind's ability to make reasoned choices without conscious oversight (Dijksterhuis, 2004, 2009) and to engage in self-corrective behavior (Glaser & Banaji, 1999). Additionally, research suggests that unconscious processing has its own form of working memory,

Table 0.2 Six Qualities of Unconscious Choice

Unconscious Choice Is:	*Behavior That Is Complex, Adaptive, and Predictable Can Occur without Conscious Awareness*
Intelligent	Choices made outside of conscious awareness can access higher cognitive functions, such as planning, weighting of options, goal pursuit, and evaluation of outcomes (Bargh, 2004).
Arational	It is not motivated by reason or logical arguments (schematic representations) in the same way that conscious decisions are (Weinberger & Stoycheva, 2019). Rather, it uses parallel processing and non-sequential thought (e.g., dreaming, symbolism, metaphor, innuendo).
Context dependent	It relies upon context markers to execute sequenced chains of activity (O'Hanlon & Wilk, 1987), which can be any combination of habit (associational learning) and instinct (heuristics, biases, and emotional behavior).
Experience-bound	Decisions made unconsciously are heavily influenced by an individual's past experiences. Choices that involve risk are made based on potential outcomes relative to a reference point, which is often the status quo (Kahneman, 2011).
Divergent	It is less bound to fixed mental sets (Einstellung bias) and likely to ignore standards (rules, negation contingencies, and social norms), making these choices more creative and defiant (Dijksterhuis & Nordgren, 2006).
Complex	It has a much higher processing capacity than conscious thought (access to a larger pool of information), using a more far-reaching weighting of options, unconscious choices are sometimes not understood by conscious reason (Einstein, "I know the answer, but I don't yet know how to get there"). For complexity to occur, a time delay (incubated cognition) is needed (Dijksterhuis & van Olden, 2006). A delay of at least 10 minutes allows impulsivity and emotion to move through the brain.

with a greater capacity than conscious working memory, leading to superior evaluative abilities (Gambarota et al., 2022; Kihlstrom, 1987). As stated by the influential researcher John Bargh (2019), all of our higher cognitive functions, including *critical thinking*, can be conducted in a conscious or unconscious mode.

Principle 6: Autonomous Problem-Solving

The implications of ECA for behavioral health and social well-being are profound, as it reframes decision-making structures in ways that enhance autonomy, resilience, and adaptability. We begin this section on *autonomous problem-solving* with a list of the most important implications:

- **Enhancing Psychological Flexibility:** By leveraging cognitive biases and heuristics strategically, ECA fosters state reversals resulting in greater adaptability and allowing individuals to respond constructively to challenges rather than being rigidly attached to a single perspective or solution.
- **Reducing Psychological Reactance:** Traditional interventions can trigger automatic pushback when people feel their autonomy is threatened. ECA bypasses this by framing any choice as an opportunity for engagement in a collaborative process, ensuring that choices feel self-directed rather than imposed (affordances).
- **Optimizing Decision-Making for Mental Well-Being:** Rather than treating biases as flaws, ECA structures choices in a way that helps individuals make decisions aligned with their well-being, as described in the philosophy of libertarian paternalism but with a stronger emphasis on unconscious processes.
- **Encouraging Intrinsic Motivation and Ownership:** Through autonomous responsibility, individuals are given ownership of their personal progress (self-control), reinforcing sustained passion and perseverance for long-term goals (grit) (Duckworth & Gross, 2014). This effect parallels locus of control research demonstrating that perceived personal control increases persistence and long-term health benefits (Mozafari et al., 2024).
- **Leveraging Distributed Cognition for Social Well-Being:** ECA acknowledges that cognition is not confined to a single mind but is shared across people, environments, and communication tools. By designing choice environments that harness social and contextual intelligence, ECA fosters collective well-being and community resilience.
- **Mitigating the Negative Effects of Biases:** While biases like status quo bias, *change bias*, and reactance sometimes lead to maladaptive choices, ECA transforms these tendencies into pathways leading to adaptive self-organization (growth) without requiring an explicit overhaul of beliefs.

By reconfiguring the choice environment rather than trying to force change through direct persuasion, ECA offers a sophisticated, autonomy-supportive framework for improving mental and social well-being in a way that is both strategic and sustainable. This is particularly relevant in helping contexts, where client autonomy is directly correlated with long-term adherence to personal growth plans (Williams et al., 2009).

Human Flourishing

ECA aligns with principles of human flourishing, drawing from multiple independent lines of investigation. For example, from neurobiology we know that neuroplasticity, the brain's ability to adapt and reorganize itself, thrives on challenges and novel problem-solving. Research by Michael Merzenich (2013) and others has shown that the brain functions as a dynamic, problem-solving machine, continuously rewiring itself in response to new experiences. This adaptability is closely linked to neurogenesis, which is the process of generating new neurons. Most importantly, neurogenesis is activated when we engage in mentally demanding tasks under conditions of autonomous problem-solving.

Similarly, research into happiness and optimal experience suggests that autonomous problem-solving plays a crucial role in well-being. Flow psychology, pioneered by Mihaly Csikszentmihalyi (2014), highlights that humans thrive when engaged in tasks that are both challenging and intrinsically motivating. This state, colloquially referred to as "being in the zone," occurs when a person's skills are stretched just beyond their comfort level, creating deep focus and a sense of effortless control. When individuals are given both the necessity and the freedom to solve problems creatively (whether in work, learning, or play) they activate neural pathways that enhance cognitive flexibility, strengthen problem-solving abilities, and contribute to long-term mental resilience.

An internal locus of control, the implicit expectation that one's actions directly influence outcomes, has been shown to enhance persistence, stress management, and overall life satisfaction (Rotter, 1966). When individuals perceive themselves as active agents in shaping their circumstances rather than passive recipients of external forces, they are more likely to take responsibility for their decisions and efforts. This sense of ownership fosters resilience in the face of challenges, as people with a strong internal locus of control are more inclined to view setbacks as opportunities for growth rather than insurmountable obstacles, which aligns with more recent research on the growth mindset (Burnette et al., 2023). Those who feel in control of their lives experience lower stress levels, as they engage in proactive coping strategies rather than feeling helpless. Over time, a growth mindset contributes to greater well-being, motivation, and long-term success across various life domains.

This research supports ECA's emphasis on structured autonomy by showing that people thrive when they engage in meaningful, self-directed problem-solving. Influential concepts such as flow, internal locus of control, and growth mindset all highlight the benefits of environments that support active engagement, personal ownership, and adaptive responses, which are core principles in ECA's design of choice environments.

Defying the Resistance Label: Reframing Opposition as Engagement

The anecdote of the woman who threatened to slap Erickson brings us to another important feature of ECA. On a conceptual level, it *rejects the categorization of resistance as an obstacle* to overcome. Instead, ECA interprets non-compliance as a meaningful component of the choice landscape. Prioritizing understanding above influence, ECA practitioners strategically engage non-cooperative behavior, after asking themselves:

- What is this response revealing about the individual's choice framework?
- How can this preference be included as a functional part of the next step?
- What nearby options fit the choices they have already expressed?

By moving beyond the traditional concept of resistance, ECA avoids struggles for compliance and instead works with the person's existing motivations to create an optimal choice environment. The assumption is that individuals are always making meaningful choices, even when they appear to be resisting or self-handicapping (self-sabotage). This perspective, which is derived from functional psychology (Short, 2020), requires the adoption of three essential attitudes: *reframing opposition as engagement*; *designing for autonomy, not compliance*; and *engineering dynamic reversibility*.

When someone pushes back, hesitates, or says "no," it's not a sign of failure. It is a sign that something meaningful is happening (*reframing opposition as engagement*). Instead of trying to push through the opposition, we treat it as a clue. This response shows what the person values, fears, or is unsure about. By listening closely and working with their response, not against it, we can reshape the situation to include their concerns and create choices that feel more acceptable and aligned with implicit motivations.

Since ECA operates within the principle of *autonomous responsibility*, it does not seek to force or override decisions but rather to create structures that allow for spontaneous shifts in behavior (*dynamic reversibility*). Rather than trying to get someone to do what we want, choice architects design the environment so clients can choose what works best for them. That means offering attractive options rather than applying pressure. When people feel free to choose, they are more likely to engage, stay motivated, and take ownership of their actions.

Traditional influence models assume a linear path toward treatment goals, where resistance is seen as a problem to be corrected. In contrast, ECA embraces *dynamic reversibility*, the idea that any response, whether agreement, hesitation, or avoidance, can be redirected into a useful trajectory without coercion or persuasion. By designing flexible, non-binding choices, ECA reduces fear and defensiveness, making it easier for people to spontaneously explore new possibilities. As demonstrated in other highly successful communication frameworks, such as MI, when individuals know they can always change course, progress feels more like exploration and less like entrapment.

I can illustrate these principles with a brief story about a minor failure in my care delivery, followed by a counterfactual reflection on how I could have created space for dynamic reversibility, if only I had known about it then. On this occasion, I was leading a workshop for Ericksonian therapists and wanted to demonstrate the power of embodied emotion–cognition. It was my first experience teaching at a congress. I had given audience members a variety of symbolic objects to respond to (e.g., a spoon, a rose, a doll). After working in small groups, several volunteers came to the front so that I could demonstrate Ericksonian *utilization*. One woman had selected a knife. Pointing it toward my chest, she said, "For some reason, I feel like stabbing you." I was absolutely unprepared for this and tried to manage the moment by redirecting her into a discussion about her needs and aspirations. She looked embarrassed, and I knew I had failed her.

If, at the very start of my career, I had understood the concept of *dynamic reversibility*, I would have told her that she is free to stab me in the chest—*very slowly*. I might have said, "Take at least 60 seconds to complete the movement. This will allow you to experience a range of emotions and revisit different moments from your life as the knife moves slowly toward my heart." This would have created an opportunity for reversibility: She could have experientially explored one direction, then spontaneously chosen to reverse course based on her own timing and emerging needs. This mirrors findings that reversible or low-commitment choices create space for significant shifts in emotional and motivational states, leading to new experiential outcomes. Such a permissive stance fosters growth through engagement rather than through external persuasion or pressure.

In summary, by understanding an individual's underlying preferences and integrating them into the decision-making process, ECA transforms opposition into an opportunity for deeper engagement. This principle is supported by research in narrative psychology, which suggests that reframing negative responses as part of an evolving story can enhance motivation and resilience (McAdams, 2013).

Conclusion

ECA is more than a collection of isolated strategies and tactics. It is a psychological and philosophical framework that redefines behavioral guidance by integrating insights from social psychology, cognitive science, and behavioral economics. At its core, ECA departs from traditional models that rely on intervention protocols (i.e., externally engineered change).

Instead, it emphasizes structured autonomy, which is achieved by reshaping decision-making environments to support self-directed transformation. The result is an *optimal choice environment* in which the client can exercise autonomy and creative problem-solving. ECA's chief contribution is the concept of contextualized care, which prioritizes moment-to-moment responsiveness to shifting psychological states. This use of state psychology extends beyond trait-based or historically informed approaches by recognizing that meaningful progress often hinges on how choices are perceived and enacted in real time, making care more precise, adaptive, and human-centered.

This introductory chapter has explored the foundational theories and principles that underlie ECA, establishing a robust theoretical framework. That framework is essential not only for identifying effective behavioral tactics but also for knowing *when* and *why* to use them. While understanding *what* to do (the tactic) is necessary, it is insufficient without understanding the heuristics that are operative in each state of mind. This acts as a signal for the right moment (the when) and the deeper logic, or strategy, that justifies its use (the why). When practitioners grasp this full sequence (the what, when, and why) their ability to operate within ECA is elevated from technical proficiency to adaptive fluency.

As modern psychology continues to explore the intersection of unconscious processes and decision-making, ECA provides a critical bridge between research and practice. Whether applied in therapy, education, health care, business, or public policy, its principles empower individuals to problem solve in accord with their immediate needs and innate capabilities while benefiting from rigorously tested psychological frameworks. By strategically leveraging cognitive biases, leading from behind, and designing thoughtful choice landscapes, ECA offers a revolutionary yet grounded approach to fostering both personal and social well-being.

Notes

1 It is important to note that the case narratives used throughout this book are intended to clarify design principles rather than to establish causal claims. They illustrate how choice environments can be arranged so that options feel self-endorsed and internally consistent. The subsequent experimental studies cited throughout this chapter provide the empirical basis for the inferences that support ECA.

2 Nick Cummings also said that Frieda Fromm-Reichmann advised that although anger might produce quicker results in the short-run, love was much more powerful and enduring.

3 The sourcing for Erickson's casework draws on multiple sources: my interviews with his wife and children; review of more than 1,000 hours of archival recordings; interviews with several former clients; and the published record. Because Erickson sometimes recounted the same case with varying details,

these narratives cannot be reconstructed with absolute precision. The details I include reflect my best judgment about what he most likely said and did with a given individual. Each case's index number appears in the case index at the back of this book, which lists published versions of the report.

References

Apter, M. J. (1984). Reversal Theory, Cognitive Synergy and the Arts. In W. R. Crozier & A. J. Chapman (Eds.), *Advances in Psychology* (Vol. 19, pp. 411–426). North-Holland. https://doi.org/10.1016/S0166-4115(08)62361-4

Apter, M. J., Fontana, D., & Murgatroyd, S. (2014). *Reversal Theory: Applications and Development*. Psychology Press.

Ariely, D. (2009). *Predictably Irrational: The Hidden Forces that Shape Our Decisions*. Harper.

Arkowitz, H., Miller, W. R., & Rollnick, S. (2015). *Motivational Interviewing in the Treatment of Psychological Problems*. Guilford Publications.

Bargh, J. A. (2004). Bypassing the Will: Toward Demystifying the Nonconscious Control of Social Behavior. In R. R. Hassin, J. S. Uleman, & J. A. Bargh (Eds.), *The New Unconscious* (pp. 37–58). Oxford University Press.

Bargh, J. A. (2019). The modern unconscious. *World Psychiatry*, *18*(2), 225–226. https://doi.org/10.1002/wps.20625

Beahrs, J. O. (2006). Assessing attributive causation in psychiatry: Psychotherapeutic results correlate with self-therapeutic activity. *Clinical Neuropsychiatry*, *3*, 154–161.

Beahrs, J. O., Butler, J. L., Sturges, S. G., Drummond, D. J., & Beahrs, C. H. (1992). Strategic self-therapy for personality disorders. *Journal of Strategic and Systemic Therapies*, *11*(2), 33–52. https://doi.org/10.1521/jsst.1992.11.2.33

Burnette, J. L., Billingsley, J., Banks, G. C., Knouse, L. E., Hoyt, C. L., Pollack, J. M., & Simon, S. (2023). A systematic review and meta-analysis of growth mindset interventions: For whom, how, and why might such interventions work? *Psychological Bulletin*, *149*(3–4), 174–205. https://doi.org/10.1037/bul0000368

Busemeyer, J. R., & Townsend, J. T. (1993). Decision field theory: A dynamic-cognitive approach to decision making in an uncertain environment. *Psychological Review*, *100*(3), 432–459. https://doi.org/10.1037/0033-295X.100.3.432

Cantwell, P., & Holmes, S. (1994). Social Construction: A paradigm shift for systemic therapy and training. *Australian and New Zealand Journal of Family Therapy*, *15*(1), 17–26. https://doi.org/10.1002/j.1467-8438.1994.tb00978.x

Clore, G. L. (2011). Psychology and the rationality of emotion. *Modern Theology*, *27*(2), 325–338. https://doi.org/10.1111/j.1468-0025.2010.01679.x

Critcher, C. R., Dunning, D., & Armor, D. A. (2010). When self-affirmations reduce defensiveness: Timing is key. *Personality & Social Psychology Bulletin*, *36*(7), 947–959. https://doi.org/10.1177/0146167210369557

Csikszentmihalyi, M. (2014). Toward a Psychology of Optimal Experience. In M. Csikszentmihalyi (Ed.), *Flow and the Foundations of Positive Psychology: The Collected Works of Mihaly Csikszentmihalyi* (pp. 209–226). Springer Netherlands. https://doi.org/10.1007/978-94-017-9088-8_14

Cummings, N. A. (2002, October 25). *Nicholas Cummings, Ph.D., Sc.D.* (D. Short, Interviewer) [Newsletter]. Vol. 22, No. 3. https://static1.squarespace.com/static/617c39f42e5ed42978fb41e3/t/62166f0c7cf2aa6f27e13bbf/1645637390286/Vol-22-No-3.pdf

de Shazer, S. (1988). *Clues: Investigating Solutions in Brief Therapy* (pp. xxii, 202). W W Norton & Co.

Deci, E. L., & Ryan, R. M. (2008). Self-determination theory: A macrotheory of human motivation, development, and health. *Canadian Psychology / Psychologie Canadienne*, *49*(3), 182–185. https://doi.org/10.1037/a0012801

Dijksterhuis, A. (2004). Think Different: The merits of unconscious thought in preference development and decision making. *Journal of Personality and Social Psychology*, *87*(5), 586–598. https://doi.org/10.1037/0022-3514.87.5.586

Dijksterhuis, A. (2009). *The Beautiful Powers of Unconscious Thought*. Https://Www.Apa.Org. https://www.apa.org/science/about/psa/2009/10/sci-brief

Dijksterhuis, A., & Nordgren, L. F. (2006). A Theory of Unconscious Thought. In *Perspectives on Psychological Science*. Sage. https://journals.sagepub.com/doi/10.1111/j.1745-6916.2006.00007.x

Dijksterhuis, A., & van Olden, Z. (2006). On the benefits of thinking unconsciously: Unconscious thought can increase post-choice satisfaction. *Journal of Experimental Social Psychology*, *42*(5), 627–631. https://doi.org/10.1016/j.jesp.2005.10.008

Dolan, P., Hallsworth, M., Halpern, D., King, D., Metcalfe, R., & Vlaev, I. (2012). Influencing behaviour: The mindspace way. *Journal of Economic Psychology*, *33*(1), 264–277. https://doi.org/10.1016/j.joep.2011.10.009

Duckworth, A. L., & Gross, J. J. (2014). Self-control and grit: Related but separable determinants of success. *Current Directions in Psychological Science*, *23*(5), 319–325. https://doi.org/10.1177/0963721414541462

Erickson, M. H. (1958). Naturalistic Techniques of Hypnosis. In E. L. Rossi, R. Erickson-Klein, & K. Rossi (Eds.), *Collected Works of Milton H. Erickson: The Nature of Therapeutic Hypnosis* (Vol. 1, pp. 261–270). Milton H. Erickson Foundation Press.

Erickson, M. H. (1960). *A Lecture by Milton H. Erickson: Chicago, June 10, 1960. (Audio Recording No. CD/EMH.60.3.21)* [CD]. CD/EMH.60.3.21. The Milton H. Erickson Foundation Archives.

Erickson, M. H. (1964). The burden of responsibility in effective psychotherapy. *American Journal of Clinical Hypnosis*, *6*(3), 269–271. https://doi.org/10.1080/00029157.1964.10402352

Erickson, M. H. (1966). A lecture by Milton H. Erickson, Houston, February 18, 1966. (Audio Recording No. CD/EMH.66.2.18) [Audio recording]. The Milton H. Erickson Foundation Archives.

Erickson, M. H. (2000). *The Letters of Milton H. Erickson* (J. K. Zeig & B. B. Geary, Ph.D., Eds.). Zeig Tucker & Theisen Inc.

Erickson, M. H., & Rossi, E. L. (1976). Hypnotic Realities: The Induction of Clinical Hypnosis and Forms of Indirect Suggestion. In E. L. Rossi, R. Erickson-Klein, & K. Rossi (Eds.), *The Collected Works of Milton H. Erickson—Volume 10* (Vol. 10). Milton H. Erickson Foundation Press.

Erickson, M. H., & Rossi, E. L. (1979). Hypnotherapy: An Exploratory Casebook. In E. L. Rossi, R. Erickson-Klein, & K. Rossi (Eds.), *The Collected Works of Milton H. Erickson* (Vol. 11). The Milton Erickson Foundation Press.

Galinsky, A. D., Schaerer, M., & Magee, J. C. (2017). The four horsemen of power at the bargaining table. *Journal of Business & Industrial Marketing*, *32*(4), 606–611 (World). https://doi.org/10.1108/JBIM-10-2016-0251

Gambarota, F., Tsuchiya, N., Pastore, M., Di Polito, N., & Sessa, P. (2022). Unconscious visual working memory: A critical review and Bayesian meta-analysis. *Neuroscience & Biobehavioral Reviews*, *136*, 104618. https://doi.org/10.1016/j.neubiorev.2022.104618

Gilligan, S. G. (2013). *Therapeutic Trances: The Co-Operation Principle in Ericksonian Hypnotherapy*. Routledge.

Glaser, J., & Banaji, M. R. (1999). When fair is foul and foul is fair: Reverse priming in automatic evaluation. *Journal of Personality and Social Psychology*, *77*(4), 669–687. https://doi.org/10.1037/0022-3514.77.4.669

Greene, J. D., Sommerville, R. B., Nystrom, L. E., Darley, J. M., & Cohen, J. D. (2001). An fMRI investigation of emotional engagement in moral judgment. *Science (New York, N.Y.)*, *293*(5537), 2105–2108. https://doi.org/10.1126/science.1062872

Haley, J. (Ed.) (with Erickson, M. H.). (1985). *Conversations with Milton H. Erickson, M.D.*, Vol. I: *Changing Individuals* (1st ed.). Triangle Press.

Hood, B. (2012). *The Self Illusion: How the Social Brain Creates Identity*. Oxford University Press.

Huber, J., Payne, J. W., & Puto, C. P. (2014). Let's be honest about the attraction effect. *Journal of Marketing Research*, *51*(4), 520–525. https://doi.org/10.1509/jmr.14.0208

Hupbach, A., Gomez, R., Hardt, O., & Nadel, L. (2007). Reconsolidation of episodic memories: A subtle reminder triggers integration of new information. *Learning & Memory*, *14*(1–2), 47–53. https://doi.org/10.1101/lm.365707

Hutchins, E. (1995). *Cognition in the Wild*. MIT Press.

Inesi, M. E., Botti, S., Dubois, D., Rucker, D. D., & Galinsky, A. D. (2011). Power and choice: Their dynamic interplay in quenching the thirst for personal control. *Psychological Science*, *22*(8), 1042–1048. https://doi.org/10.1177/0956797611413936

Johnson, E. J., Shu, S. B., Dellaert, B. G. C., Fox, C., Goldstein, D. G., Häubl, G., Larrick, R. P., Payne, J. W., Peters, E., Schkade, D., Wansink, B., & Weber, E. U. (2012). Beyond nudges: Tools of a choice architecture. *Marketing Letters*, *23*(2), 487–504. https://doi.org/10.1007/s11002-012-9186-1

Kächele, H., & Schachter, J. (2014). On side effects, destructive processes, and negative outcomes in psychoanalytic therapies: Why is it difficult for psychoanalysts to acknowledge and address treatment failures? *Contemporary Psychoanalysis*, *50*(1–2), 233–258. https://doi.org/10.1080/00107530.2014.880321

Kahneman, D. (2011). *Thinking, Fast and Slow* (1st ed.). Farrar, Straus and Giroux.

Kaufman, S. (2013). *Ungifted: Intelligence Redefined*. Basic Books.

Kihlstrom, J. F. (1987). The cognitive unconscious. *Science*, *237*(4821), 1445–1452. https://doi.org/10.1126/science.3629249

McAdams, D. P. (2013). *The Redemptive Self: Stories Americans Live By - Revised and Expanded Edition.* Oxford University Press.

Mehr, K. S., Geiser, A. E., Milkman, K. L., & Duckworth, A. L. (2020). Copy-paste prompts: A new nudge to promote goal achievement. *Journal of the Association for Consumer Research*, *5*(3), 329–334. https://doi.org/10.1086/708880

Merzenich, M. (2013). *Soft-Wired: How the New Science of Brain Plasticity Can Change Your Life.* Parnassus Publishing.

Milkman, K. L. (2021). *How to Change: The Science of Getting from Where You Are to Where You Want to Be.* Penguin.

Milkman, K. L. (Host). (2025, October 19). *A Sit Down with Katy Milkman & Angela Duckworth—Choiceology with Katy Milkman | Podcast on Spotify* [Broadcast]. https://open.spotify.com/episode/2aSbDxRMMG5zJ7OZ6EPy1B

Miller, W. R. (2023). The evolution of motivational interviewing. *Behavioural and Cognitive Psychotherapy*, *51*(6), 616–632. https://doi.org/10.1017/S1352465822000431

Miller, W. R., & Rollnick, S. (2024). Why motivational interviewing is a person-centered approach. *SUCHT*, *70*(2), 97–101. https://doi.org/10.1024/0939-5911/a000862

Mills, S. (2022). Personalized nudging. *Behavioural Public Policy*, *6*(1), 150–159. https://doi.org/10.1017/bpp.2020.7

Mohr, D. C. (1995). Negative outcome in psychotherapy: A critical review. *Clinical Psychology: Science and Practice*, *2*(1), 1–27. https://doi.org/10.1111/j.1468-2850.1995.tb00022.x

Mozafari, S., Yang, A., & Talaei-Khoei, J. (2024). Health locus of control and medical behavioral interventions: Systematic review and recommendations. *Interactive Journal of Medical Research*, *13*, e52287. https://doi.org/10.2196/52287

Nease, R. F., Frazee, S. G., Zarin, L., & Miller, S. B. (2013). Choice architecture is a better strategy than engaging patients to spur behavior change. *Health Affairs*, *32*(2), 242–249. https://doi.org/10.1377/hlthaff.2012.1075

Norman, D. (2013). *The Design of Everyday Things: Revised and Expanded Edition.* Basic Books.

O'Hanlon, B., & Wilk, J. (1987). *Shifting Contexts: The Generation of Effective Psychotherapy* (pp. xii, 289). Guilford Press.

Perry, B. D. (2006). Applying Principles of Neurodevelopment to Clinical Work with Maltreated and Traumatized Children: The Neurosequential Model of Therapeutics. In N. B. Webb (Ed.), *Working with Traumatized Youth in Child Welfare* (1st ed., pp. 27–52). The Guilford Press.

Pratto, F., Sidanius, J., Stallworth, L. M., & Malle, B. F. (1994). Social dominance orientation: A personality variable predicting social and political attitudes. *Journal of Personality and Social Psychology*, *67*(4), 741–763. https://doi.org/10.1037/0022-3514.67.4.741

Rogers, C. R. (1951). *Client-Centered Therapy.* Houghton Mifflin.

Rosen, S. (1982). *My Voice Will Go with You: The Teaching Tales of Milton H. Erickson, M.D.* W. W. Norton & Company.

Rothermund, K. (2011). Counter-regulation and control-dependency: Affective processing biases in the service of action regulation. *Social Psychology*, *42*(1), 56–66. https://doi.org/10.1027/1864-9335/a000043

Rothermund, K., Voss, A., & Wentura, D. (2008). Counter-regulation in affective attentional biases: A basic mechanism that warrants flexibility in emotion and motivation. *Emotion*, *8*(1), 34–46. https://doi.org/10.1037/1528-3542.8.1.34

Rotter, J. B. (1966). Generalized expectancies for internal versus external control of reinforcement. *Psychological Monographs: General and Applied*, *80*(1), 1–28. https://doi.org/10.1037/h0092976

Seligman, M. (2011). *Flourish*. Nicholas Brealey Publishing.

Short, D. (2020). *From William James to Milton Erickson: The care of human consciousness*. Archway Publishing from Simon & Schuster. https://www.bokus.com/bok/9781480891623/from-william-james-to-milton-erickson/

Short, D. (2022). *Making Psychotherapy More Effective with Unconscious Process Work*. Routledge. https://doi.org/10.4324/9781003127208

Simon, H. A. (1955). A behavioral model of rational choice. *The Quarterly Journal of Economics*, *69*(1), 99–118. https://doi.org/10.2307/1884852

Tesi, A., Aiello, A., Morselli, D., Giannetti, E., Pierro, A., & Pratto, F. (2019). Which people are willing to maintain their subordinated position? Social dominance orientation as antecedent to compliance to harsh power tactics in a higher education setting. *Personality and Individual Differences*, *151*, 109390. https://doi.org/10.1016/j.paid.2019.04.045

Thaler, R. H., & Sunstein, C. R. (2009). *Nudge: Improving Decisions About Health, Wealth, and Happiness*. Penguin.

Trewavas, A. J. (2015). *Plant Behaviour and Intelligence*. Oxford University Press.

Tversky, A., & Kahneman, D. (1974). Judgment under Uncertainty: Heuristics and Biases. In L. C. MacLean & W. T. Ziemba (Eds.), *Handbook of the Fundamentals of Financial Decision Making, Part I* (pp. 261–268). World Scientific Publishing Co. Pte. Ltd. https://ideas.repec.org//h/wsi/wschap/9789814417358_0015.html

Viale, R. (2022). *Nudging*. MIT Press.

Watson, J. B. (1924). *Behaviorism*. Routledge.

Weinberger, J., & Stoycheva, V. (2019). *The Unconscious: Theory, Research, and Clinical Implications*. Guilford Publications.

Williams, G. C., Niemiec, C. P., Patrick, H., Ryan, R. M., & Deci, E. L. (2009). The importance of supporting autonomy and perceived competence in facilitating long-term tobacco abstinence. *Annals of Behavioral Medicine*, *37*(3), 315–324. https://doi.org/10.1007/s12160-009-9090-y

Chapter 1

When the Glass Is Always Half-Empty

Negativity Bias

When the Glass Is Always Half-Empty: *Negativity Bias*

An elderly gentleman sat next to his wife on my sofa. Dispensing with all pleasantries, he stated, "It was not my idea to see a therapist. I'm only here because my wife thinks it will help and the doctors at Mayo gave us your name." His wife quickly added, her voice filled with concern,

> I am worried about my husband. He is seriously depressed. He hardly eats and spends most of his time in a dark bedroom. I have never seen him like this. He has always been such a good father and caring husband, but now he has stopped talking to our adult children and doesn't spend any time with his grandchildren.

Turning to his wife, he snapped, "Do you want to tell him why I am depressed or should I?" I interjected stating that I thought it would be best if he told his own story.

The man leaned forward and spoke with bitterness.

> I've spent my whole life solving problems and being the leader for our family. If my wife or our children were in trouble, they'd come to me, and I'd find a solution. I've never needed anyone's help because I've always been healthy and strong. But after dealing with fatigue and pain, I went to Mayo Clinic, where the so-called best doctors in the world tell me I have advanced pancreatic cancer. They say I've got a few months left, at best. And then they suggest I talk to you so I won't be depressed. Now, you tell me this—what are you going to do for me that none of these other doctors can do? Are you able to cure cancer?

Here was a man used to being in charge and he was laying down a challenge. My task, as I understood it, was to present a challenge of my own.

My response was, "Looking at you, I can see you are a leader and a strong personality. You didn't need to tell me that." *I continued,*

DOI: 10.4324/9781003797876-2

> My guess is your children have never doubted whether their father would be there to help them face their challenges and make the most of the life they've been given. I imagine, in the eyes of your grandchildren, you are almost mythical. You are the person their mommy and daddy look to for advice.

After a brief pause, I continued,

> So, now I have a question for you. Would you rather focus your thoughts and energies on yourself and your impending death, or would you like to turn your attention back to your family and their needs? What do you think will be most meaningful to you, to focus on yourself or to focus on the greatest challenge your family has ever had to face?

He looked at me, his expression softening. "I've always been a servant leader, someone who took care of others rather than focusing on myself." His voice trembled slightly as he asked, "What can I do for my family… now that I have this disease? I've never felt so powerless."

Speaking bluntly, in a matter-of-fact tone, I replied, "You have no choice but to face death, eventually." I added,

> Of the three of us sitting in this room, you are most likely to encounter death first. But someday, I will die as well. And so will your beloved wife. Although we all hope it will be a long time from now, each of your children will also have to face death.

After pointing out that his wife and family are all going to die, I continued,

> It is something that can be done poorly, in a state of despair and panic, or it can be done nobly and with gratitude for all the goodness you've experienced during your time on earth. You see, you are leading your family into death. The lessons you teach now can potentially carry forward for generations. If you do this right, your great-grandchildren and great-great-grandchildren will benefit from the strength and leadership of a man that they learn about from stories told by their parents.

This is when I issued my challenge as a sort of dare, "Are you going to let depression stand in the way of this achievement? If not, then what do you need to do differently when you return home?"

He held my gaze with intense interest. After a long silence, he admitted,

> When I came here, I didn't think you were going to be able to tell me anything I didn't already know. But you've said some things I haven't thought about before. I'm going to need to think about this for a while.

I agreed and pointed out that his mind would likely be working on a meaningful response even if he focused on other things, like enjoying time with his wife and playing with his grandchildren. His wife asked me how she could best support him. I advised her to simply be the loving wife she had always been. He approved of this response, then reasserted his authority.

> I'll come back to your office because you clearly have some valuable things to say. But I want some time in between visits to work this out for myself. I think I'll be ready to see you again in three weeks.

I agreed, "That sounds like the right amount of time to let your thoughts incubate."

Three weeks later, the couple returned to my office holding hands. His wife beamed as she announced, "I'm so happy to have my old husband back. He's returned to interacting with family members in a loving, fun way."

He gave a sheepish smile and admitted, "I was caught off guard. I needed a little assistance getting over the depression." After some pleasant small talk, he thanked me for helping him see the big picture.

"I feel like I can handle my death moving forward," he said. "I don't think I need any more therapy."

I told him that he was the best judge of what he needed and assured him I would be here if the depression returned. He thanked me again and, as far as I know, he died with dignity, doing his life on his own terms.

In a different book (Short, 2022), I used this case to illustrate the tactic of *future contrasting*, where I subtly prompted him to envision two different ways of dying and primed him to make an implicit choice. This effect is consistent with research showing that vividly contrasting future outcomes can strengthen commitment to a new goal by making long-term consequences feel more important in the present moment. Another tactic we see illustrated in this example is *adaptive reuse*, which was achieved by turning the problem of dying into a unique opportunity.

This story highlights another intriguing principle. From the outset, it was clear that he would not be an easy patient to establish rapport with. So, I engaged him by issuing a challenge, reminding him that he was going to die soon, and pointing out that his wife would eventually die as well. I also noted that he could face death in a state of despair and panic. Although I didn't use the word "coward," the implication was there (making this a *restricted-use tactic*).

His response? He listened carefully, without interruption, and even complimented me by acknowledging that I had important things to say. Clearly, rapport was established. But how? Why did my seemingly negative approach resonate with him? This overarching question will be the focus of this chapter.

Recognizing *Negativity Bias* in Ericksonian Choice Architecture

Negativity bias is the psychological phenomenon where people tend to give more weight to negative experiences or information than to positive ones. In this state of mind, negative events have a greater impact on one's psychological state and processes than neutral or positive events of equal intensity. This results in a preconscious need to focus on threats and prioritize action aimed at reducing negative outcomes. This predisposes individuals to be more readily motivated by criticism than by praise or by negative forewarnings than by positive encouragement.

Evolutionarily, this bias likely served as a survival mechanism in threatening environments, prioritizing the detection and avoidance of danger over the pursuit of rewards. Paleolithic environments often presented asymmetrical risks, where losses (e.g., being injured, losing food) had more severe and immediate consequences than equivalent gains. Thus, a state of mind capable of heightened sensitivity to losses would have provided a survival advantage, promoting cautious and conservative behavior in certain contexts.

Negativity bias is evident across various psychological domains. In memory, negative events are more likely to be recalled than positive or neutral ones. In attention, people tend to focus more on negative stimuli, processing them more thoroughly. In emotion, negative experiences often evoke stronger reactions than positive ones. In decision-making, negativity bias can distort judgments by making negative outcomes seem more significant than they objectively are.

This bias is closely linked to emotions, such as anxiety and depression, which can arise from heightened sensitivity to negative stimuli and a persistent focus on adverse outcomes. Since attention can be directed inward or outward, this tendency toward negative evaluation may be internalized or externalized, reinforcing a negative outlook in both cases.

When negativity bias is internalized, it often leads to a deeply negative perception of one's abilities and self-worth. Individuals with this tendency may become hypervigilant about their perceived flaws, focusing excessively on mistakes and failures while overlooking their strengths and achievements. This mindset is reinforced by a pessimistic explanatory style, where setbacks are viewed as personal shortcomings rather than situational challenges. One clear example of this is the *worse-than-average effect*, which is the tendency to believe oneself to be less capable than others at difficult tasks.

This relentless focus on the negative aspects of the self can contribute to feelings of inadequacy and shame (low self-esteem), as well as an expectation that one's efforts are futile and unlikely to yield success (low self-efficacy). Left unaddressed, *internalized negativity* can severely impair self-compassion and problem-solving motivation, making personal growth and resilience increasingly difficult to achieve. Like visual perception, mental attention tends to focus in one direction or the other (either inwardly or outwardly), giving this bias different manifestations.

An alternate form is *externalized negativity*, which is characterized by a predominantly negative attitude toward others and the external world. Individuals manifesting this orientation may demonstrate a heightened sensitivity to potential threats or criticisms from others, often defaulting to suspicion, mistrust, or frustration when interpreting social interactions. This tendency can also involve magnifying negative traits in others while minimizing positive attributes, resulting in strained relationships and difficulty appreciating constructive feedback.

Research on violence in the schools by Kenneth Dodgeand Cynthia Frame (1982) sheds light on this phenomenon. In their studies, boys with more aggressive tendencies were found to misinterpret ambiguous social situations, perceiving benign actions as hostile. This misinterpretation reflects a broader pattern of externalized negativity, where individuals habitually assume negative intentions in others, even in neutral or unclear contexts. Furthermore, the *externalized negativity bias* may present as a habitual readiness to anticipate disappointment or failure in various situations, reinforcing a cycle of defensive or hostile responses. The overemphasis on external threats and negative perceptions can impede collaboration, social engagement, and the ability to recognize opportunities for positive connection and growth.

Operationally, negativity bias can be identified through patterns in memory recall, thematic focus, and behavioral tendencies. In terms of memory, individuals with a negativity bias tend to recall negative experiences more readily when prompted to retrieve memories. This bias also influences their expectations for the future. For example, if asked, "Do you think this is a problem that can be resolved?" in this state of mind individuals may respond entirely negatively, even after they have sought your help for a solution.

When asked to list personal problems and accomplishments, individuals experiencing a negativity bias often focus more on setbacks, risks, or self-criticism. Their attention is drawn to perceived failures or threats, while successes or strengths are frequently overlooked.

Emotional reactions can also reveal negativity bias. People in this state of mind may show discomfort when acknowledging positive remarks, such as compliments or achievements, often dismissing them with statements like, "I just got lucky" or "Yes, but..." Additional behavioral indicators include: rejecting or downplaying encouraging feedback, expressing reluctance to act due to fear of failure, and anticipating disappointment. These reactions are often reinforced by automatic behaviors that support negative expectations (self-fulfilling prophecies).

Research further highlights the complexity of negativity bias, with various studies identifying mediating and moderating factors. This means that negativity bias is not fixed; it is shaped by social, psychological, and contextual factors, as well as by how information is presented and processed. For instance, social connectedness and the use of cognitive reappraisal reduces negativity bias (Neta & Brock, 2021; Raio et al., 2021), while social anxiety and exposure to social judgment can increase negativity bias (Müller-Pinzler et al., 2019). Additionally, contextual factors, such as stress and fatigue, can exacerbate the bias, increasing susceptibility to negative information (Braund et al., 2019). Research by Rozin and Royzman (2001) shows that negative experiences often have a stronger effect than positive ones across many areas of life. They concluded that negativity also spreads more easily than positivity.

Erickson's Casework and the Application of Tactical Nudges

Recognizing negativity bias is only the first step. While this bias explains why individuals fixate on threats, shortcomings, and worst-case scenarios, the real challenge lies in reshaping their engagement with these thoughts in a way that fosters agency.

This is where Erickson's approach becomes particularly powerful. Instead of confronting negativity bias head-on or attempting to suppress it, he worked within its framework, applying tactics that subtly redirected attention and behavior toward constructive action. By structuring choice environments that aligned with his clients' natural inclinations, he created pathways for behavioral adaptation that felt both intuitive and achievable.

The following cases illustrate how Erickson used tactical nudges and state shifts to transform powerlessness into progress. Through strategic nudges such as *anchoring low*, *negatively calibrated prediction*, *the domino effect*, and *adaptive reuse*, he helped individuals regain control over their circumstances, not by trying to change their predisposition, but by repurposing their cognitive tendencies into tools for growth.

Case 1.1: Work without Pay[1]

A young man approached Erickson and said, "A Chicano has no chance of getting a job. I've only got a grade school education. I've looked for work, but nobody wants to hire a Chicano."

Erickson responded by instructing him to go to a particular restaurant and volunteer to mop the kitchen twice daily, for free. He cautioned, "Don't accept any pay. Don't accept any food. Eat only at home on food your mother supplies."

He then explained,

> They will ask you to peel potatoes and cut up vegetables. They won't offer you pay. But they will overwork you. And they will start to depend on you. In about a year's time, you will have a job. But you will have to work for it.

The young man followed Erickson's instructions. As time passed, the manager began assigning him additional tasks, and the chef came to value his assistance. More importantly, his feelings about himself started to improve.

One day, he confidently told Erickson, "A big convention is coming to town, and the restaurant will really need my help."

This was a good indication of increased self-esteem, so Erickson advised him, "You tell the manager that you think you can get a job for pay in Tucson, and you hope he doesn't mind if you apply for that job in Tucson."

When the young man relayed this to the manager, the manager responded by offering him a fair wage and making him a full-time employee.

From there, he continued to prove his usefulness and expand his skill set. About a year later, when another convention was approaching, he successfully negotiated a substantial raise using the same method Erickson had taught him.

Years later, he became one of the highest-paid chefs in Phoenix. Eventually, he opened his own restaurant, followed by a second.

Anchoring Low

Anchoring low is a behavioral tactic within Ericksonian Choice Architecture (ECA) that involves setting performance objectives intentionally below an individual's perceived capabilities. This approach reduces performance anxiety by directing the negativity bias toward the low-risk possibility of failing to meet a modest, easily achievable goal. Paradoxically, this can produce a sense of relief that would not occur for someone without this bias. For those whose anxiety stems from fear of failure, the reduced threat allows them to engage more freely and confidently with the task at hand.

Research on low anchors in social settings highlights their paradoxical effectiveness. For instance, Reynolds (2017) found that stating negative expectations (without controlling for cognitive bias) improved performance on non-cognitive tasks (e.g., physical tasks, routine activities) but hindered performance on cognitive tasks (e.g., analytical reasoning).

A similar counterintuitive pattern appears in auctions. Ku et al. (2006) challenged the traditional "start high, end high" negotiation strategy by showing that lower starting prices often lead to higher final prices. This effect operates through three key mechanisms: lower starting prices reduce barriers to entry and attract more participants; initial participation creates sunk costs, increasing commitment and persistence; and high bidder activity signals value to observers, reinforcing engagement. While the first two processes clearly apply to individuals and groups alike, the third requires more explanation.

A related effect occurs in conversations and debates, where "mental traffic" increases the salience of certain ideas. Erickson, for example, intentionally set an extremely low bar in discussions that neutralized negativity bias in clients. In response, they would argue that they could easily surpass the proposed standard. This verbal back-and-forth induces *counter-attitudinal advocacy*, which is a cognitive dissonance effect where arguing against one's initial stance leads to implicit attitude change (Kim et al., 2014).

Similarly, anchoring low in ECA leverages these dynamics to enhance accessibility to performance. By shifting the threat of failure (from performance failure to a failure of ambition), the tactic minimizes perceived risk, making engagement feel safer and more appealing. Once a low anchor is surpassed, the principle of successive approximation (incremental performance expansion) often triggers spontaneous motivation to outperform previous attempts, driven by the desire to consolidate small successes. This process resembles the escalation of commitment observed in auction studies where initial investment encourages continued effort.

Moreover, anchoring low is effective in disrupting rigid self-perceptions. Individuals who identify as "failures" or believe they are incapable of improvement are provided immediate, experiential evidence that their abilities are more adaptable than previously assumed. This mechanism aligns with research on mastery experiences and their impact on self-efficacy beliefs (Bandura, 2000).

Ultimately, anchoring low transforms perceived limitations into a foundation for growth, enhancing accessibility to higher performance through incremental, self-motivated progress.

Case Analysis

Erickson's nudge, anchoring low, ingeniously turned the young man's perceived powerlessness (internalized negativity) into a structured sequence of achievable actions that allowed his natural capacity for competence to gradually emerge. By assigning the task of working without pay and without any immediate reward, Erickson was essentially eliminating the risk of failure. In other words, you can't get fired from a job that you have not been hired to do. This reduction of perceived risk is consistent with findings that performance anxiety diminishes when potential losses are minimized.

Furthermore, the young man needed socialization and friendship outside of his mother's house. But this was not listed as a treatment goal. Therefore, again, there was no risk of failure. As time passed his initial persistence with unpaid work gradually earned him increased responsibilities and acknowledgment, providing tangible evidence of progress and reinforcing his sense of competence. His growing skill set and recognition within the restaurant cultivated resilience and agency, ultimately enabling him to achieve his goal through concrete actions.

If we dissect Erickson's use of anchoring low, we can see that it contained several key elements. One was *escalating commitment*, as the initial task of volunteering without accepting compensation prompted him to reflect on his own values and his willingness to pursue achievement without external reward. Another was *reverse positioning*, in which Erickson paradoxically argued against immediate rewards, thereby directing the young man's attention toward building long-term value and stability. A third element was social validation, as the progressive increase in his responsibilities served as visible proof of his skill development and the restaurant staff's reliance on him. Finally, Erickson encouraged a hardball negotiation strategy by guiding the young man to tell his boss that he was considering leaving for Tucson, thereby prompting the employer to consciously recognize his value.

Erickson's use of anchoring low served as a behavioral nudge that reframed the young man's initial sense of powerlessness not as a deficit, but as a starting point for low-stakes, high-value engagement. Through incremental gains and subtle reinforcement, Erickson's design of the choice environment enabled the client to rediscover agency, resilience, and belonging, not through coercion or correction, but by designing a set of choices that made growth the default option. This case reminds us that in *choice-centric care*, progress often begins not with a dramatic intervention, but with a reordering of possibilities (affordances) that makes progress feel both safe and self-directed.

General Application

Anchoring low involves setting performance objectives deliberately below an individual's perceived capabilities. This approach circumvents negativity bias by establishing modest, easily achievable goals. By shifting the threat of failure from performance to a failure of ambition, anchoring low reduces performance anxiety and allows individuals with strong negativity bias to engage more freely and confidently with the task at hand. While this technique has historical roots in Ericksonian methods, modern applications have evolved and been further refined through empirical research, practical advancements, and integration with technology.

Anchoring low can be applied across various domains to reduce anxiety, enhance motivation, and promote resilience. In therapy, setting minimal performance expectations alleviates pressure for clients with strong negativity bias, allowing them to build confidence gradually through small successes. For example, directing a socially anxious client to merely think of all the things they would like to say, during a high-value social exchange without verbalizing any of these thoughts. This task creates a failure-proof goal that fosters an increased desire to engage. In coaching, anchoring low can be used to create failure-proof scenarios, such as encouraging a client overwhelmed by the prospect of writing a book to write an outline (during session) that is no more complex than what a sixth-grader would write. This task is made failure-proof by adding that the outline is meant to be thrown in the trash. In career counseling, the technique can be applied by earnestly examining job roles that are below a job seeker's qualifications (and describing them as such), reducing perceived risk and cuing self-driven ambition. Just as illustrated in the case with Erickson, starting low does not mean that a person's career will end low. Even if our job seeker takes the lesser job, research has shown that early-career setbacks can lead to greater future success for those who persist (Wang et al., 2019).

Technological advancements have further enhanced the use of anchoring low by providing tools for monitoring incremental progress and adjusting low anchors to match client readiness. Digital platforms and gamified tactics frequently employ low anchors to facilitate engagement by framing simple tasks as low-effort activities. For instance, applications aimed at anxiety reduction may encourage users to complete basic breathing exercises or brief mindfulness practices, building confidence through consistent engagement and gradually increasing task complexity. Artificial intelligence (AI)–driven systems have also been employed to personalize low anchors based on individual performance metrics, providing tailored nudges that adapt as users progress. As research continues to illuminate the underlying mechanisms of anchoring low, its integration with technology is likely to produce increasingly sophisticated nudges designed to facilitate sustainable personal and professional growth.

Case 1.2: Fear of Sex

When asked to describe his approach to hard-to-reach clients, Erickson described the following scenario, which may or may not have been an actual case review.

If a woman were to come to Erickson (1985, p. 124) with deep-seated misgivings and inhibitions about sex, and if she was unable to discuss the topic directly, he would work with her using indirect communication. He argued that forcing her to talk about sex would be counter-productive.

Instead, he would ask her, "Do you think you might like to plant a flower garden?"

The first step was to get such a person working on a flowerbed in the backyard, which is more private. Once she knew she could enjoy that, Erickson would instruct her to plant another flowerbed in the front yard. This approach was designed to build a series of intrinsically rewarding accomplishments.

After she developed a sense of pride in her flowers, Erickson would shift her focus to the inside of the house. He would have her discuss her bedroom, asking whether she might enjoy adding new furniture or painting it a different color.

As Erickson explained, the goal is to foster a sense of accomplishment in the bedroom, allowing her to gradually associate positive feelings of ownership and pride with a space that was previously a source of discomfort.

Domino Effect

The *domino effect* in ECA bypasses negative expectations by establishing progress in a different area of life functioning that has symbolical parallels. This strategically chosen task is meant to spark a chain reaction, making it easier to adopt adaptive behaviors across various domains. This tactic draws from behavioral momentum (Ayllon & Azrin, 1968), the foot-in-the-door technique (Freedman & Fraser, 1966), and cross-domain substitution, where boosting self-esteem in one area can offset setbacks in another (Tesser, 2000). Most importantly, it includes spillover effects, where behaviors in one domain are linked, either consciously or unconsciously, by an underlying motive. Researchers have shown that when people decreased their amount of sedentary leisure time each day, they also reduced their daily fat intake, even with participants never being specifically told to eat less fat (Spring et al., 2012). This happens because there is often a deeper motive, such as a desire for self-improvement, control, or confidence, that connects these behaviors. Research shows that spillover effects are common across many fields (Dolan & Galizzi, 2015). Because it can be demoralizing to address a person's lack of progress directly, the domino effect works around self-imposed limitations by building momentum through small, seemingly unrelated successes that enhance self-efficacy and activate the needed motivation.

Those trained in Ericksonian therapy or solution-focused therapy may already be familiar with the snowball effect, also known as the goal-gradient effect or successive approximation. This approach resembles the domino effect but with a key distinction: While successive approximation involves breaking a larger task into smaller, manageable steps (baby steps), the domino effect redirects attention to a different task altogether. For instance, someone struggling to maintain a healthy diet might be encouraged to reduce their TV-watching time. This alternative task is symbolically related to the primary goal (greater self-discipline) yet outside the focal point of negative attention. Thus, the domino effect is well suited for those with a strong negativity bias.

The essential point is that the adaptive process begins with a small, subjectively achievable task that indirectly parallels the desired behavior. As an example, I recently had a client express immense shame (internalized negativity) over her failure to leave an abusive relationship. Her husband was both violent and unwilling to seek employment. Four years ago, she had found a divorce attorney who told her to leave the marriage. This attorney also said that her prenuptial agreement was worthless and that after a long, expensive battle in court, she would probably lose half of her assets to this man.

She was frightened because this volatile person had filled the house with guns and she did not know what he would do if she tried to divorce him. She was also deeply depressed because she did not want to give him half of her estate. Switching to a different domain, I asked how much she had been paying her attorney. She said it was a very large sum of money, with the attorney charging $500 each time she sent an email or left a voice message. I then asked if she wished to remarry. Without hesitation, she stated that she was unwilling to do a fifth marriage, stating, "I am not Elizabeth Taylor!"

Given those facts, I advised her to stop pursuing a divorce and fire her attorney.

She was only four months from retirement. So, I recommended she celebrate by going to visit her daughter in Scotland. I asked if her husband would try to follow her there. She said he never traveled with her when she went to see her children. I suggested that she could stay in Scotland for as long as she likes, and then go visit her son in Texas for several months, or years, all without pursuing a divorce. Her response was jubilant. She said no less than three times that the plan was brilliant.

Divorcing her husband was too overwhelming. But firing her attorney was a simple task that she accomplished that very same day. In other words, leaving the exploitative attorney was a symbolic parallel to leaving her exploitative husband. It showed her that she had the courage needed to move forward with her life. This mirrors research showing that successful action in one domain often increases confidence to act in psychologically related areas. This approach (domino effect) helps the person build confidence without the emotional pressure that comes from directly pursuing what seems to be an unreachable goal. Eventually, the individual's perception of what is possible shifts, making adaptive behavior feel increasingly natural and attainable.

Case Analysis

The domino effect in ECA refers to a behavioral tactic where a series of small, manageable actions is strategically designed to create a cascade of positive psychological shifts in one domain, ultimately influencing other domains of functioning. By initiating progress in a non-threatening area, this approach generates momentum that enhances self-efficacy and motivates the individual to tackle increasingly challenging tasks. This tactic draws on Bandura's concept of self-efficacy, where successful experiences build a sense of personal competence (Bandura, 2000), and aligns with behavioral activation principles, where engaging in rewarding activities promotes emotional resilience and protection from depression (Martell et al., 2010).

Returning to Erickson's example, we see that he did not confront the issue directly (fear of sex). Instead, Erickson asked, "Do you think you might like to plant a flower garden?" This innocuous task initiated a sequence of positive achievements, first with a flowerbed in the backyard, then expanding to the front yard. As the woman's pride in her gardening accomplishments grew, Erickson shifted her focus to her bedroom and encouraged her to enhance it by adding furniture or repainting, allowing her to gradually associate creativity and pride with that space.

If we dissect Erickson's illustration of the domino effect, we can see that it contained several key elements. He began by highlighting achievement, encouraging the woman to nurture her garden, and thus build confidence through tangible evidence of success. The visible growth of the garden served as concrete proof of her efforts, counteracting feelings of failure or stagnation. Finally, by ensuring that her progress was clearly the result of her own actions, Erickson reinforced her sense of agency and self-efficacy, empowering her to take further steps toward personal transformation.

This case illustrates how the domino effect within micro-level choice architecture can support natural momentum by organizing experiences in a way that feels safe, rewarding, and self-initiated. Erickson's approach was not about solving a problem outright. It was about creating a sequence of actions that made engagement feel increasingly worthwhile. Each step, from tending a garden to enhancing a living space, became an act of self-discovery that fostered a sense of pride, competence, and ownership. These cues were not corrective but affirming, making it easier for the woman to interact with parts of her life that had previously felt off-limits. This case reminds us that in *choice-centric care*, the goal isn't to push for resolution, but to build environments where adaptive action becomes the natural next step.

General Application

The domino effect in ECA leverages small, manageable tasks to create a chain reaction that promotes adaptive behaviors across different domains. Unlike successive approximation, which breaks down larger tasks, the domino effect redirects attention to unrelated yet symbolically equivalent tasks to enhance engagement and reduce emotional overload. This technique is especially useful for individuals in a state of mind characterized by a negativity bias, which makes them more prone to focusing on setbacks and anticipating failure. By starting with a simple, seemingly unrelated task, the individual avoids the psychological barriers associated with failure and builds confidence through a series of small, achievable steps.

Research on cross-domain self-efficacy shows that progress in one area can boost success in others, even if unrelated. For example, one study found that aerobic capacity and muscular endurance seem to positively affect academic achievement in middle school students, with students who participate in fitness programing three times more likely to meet or exceed reading and math test standards (Bass et al., 2013). Furthermore, Sheldon and Lyubomirsky's (2006) work on positive activity interventions suggests that engaging in small, enjoyable activities can elevate mood and enhance self-efficacy, thereby improving broader well-being and productivity. While the possible benefits of symbolic connections have yet to be elaborated in research, these findings underscore the interconnectedness of human motivation and the potential for strategic nudges to create powerful cross-domain improvements.

Case 1.3: Hysterical Arm Paralysis

Just one year away from retirement, a factory worker injured himself at work. Although the injury was minor, he lost the ability to move his right arm.

The company physician dismissed his condition as nonsense and threatened to terminate him without his pension if he did not return to work after one week in the hospital.

Erickson observed the man and confirmed the diagnosis of hysterical arm paralysis. However, he chose not to gather a detailed history because the man was continually moaning and complaining about overwhelming pain. This was a clear indication of a negativity bias.

To approach the issue strategically, Erickson arranged for two other doctors to join him in performing a thorough medical evaluation. Speaking in front of the man, they conversed in whispers with a tone of great pessimism, agreeing on a placebo diagnosis of "inertia syndrome" and describing the ominous stages of recovery.

They explained,

> The progression of the disease will result first in the relaxation of the shoulder joint, permitting arm movement within the next two days. Unfortunately, this will be accompanied by a warm, hard feeling in the right wrist. Then the elbow will lose its stiffness, but this will settle into the wrist.

At the next meeting, one of the physicians expressed excitement upon discovering muscle relaxation in the shoulder. Subsequent tests supposedly revealed, "changes in the first, fourth, and fifth nerves of the elbow."

After a debate, they all agreed, "He will recover full arm usage by the end of the week, but with permanent wrist fatigue."

The physicians checked on the man's progress daily, appearing gratified by their diagnostic precision. As predicted, by the end of the week, the man returned home with only a stiff wrist.

Negatively Calibrated Prediction

Negatively calibrated prediction is a behavioral tactic within ECA that involves presenting a pessimistic forecast in which negative information is deliberately given more weight, leaving some margin for success. This approach is indicated when there is a negativity bias, during which negative information is naturally prioritized over positive information in cognitive processing (Baumeister et al., 2001). By leveraging this bias, negatively calibrated prediction encourages individuals to engage in effortful action to confirm their negative expectations of slow or difficult progress.

A key feature of this tactic includes the deliberate avoidance of praise, because emphasizing negative information is more likely to engage cognitive effort and persistence. According to a concept known as *cue-diagnosticity*, negative information is often more diagnostic than positive information, meaning that people rely on it more heavily when making judgments and predictions (Unkelbach et al., 2020). For this reason, negatively calibrated prediction frames small improvements as minor disappointments. This reframe keeps those with a negativity bias focused and engaged.

Effort itself can also be framed in negative terms. When people expect a task to be difficult, progress is presumptively possible, and they may become motivated to test their negative prediction by taking meaningful action. Importantly, negatively calibrated prediction remains domain-specific; negativity is confined to a single area, such as health, relationships, or career opportunities, while positivity in other areas is met with genuine optimism and validation. This selective pessimism allows for a nuanced approach that acknowledges both challenges and strengths, and provides a powerful framework for fostering resilient engagement and growth.

Case Analysis

The preceding case involves a factory worker who developed hysterical arm paralysis following a minor injury at work. Faced with the threat of losing his pension if he did not return to work, the man's maladaptive behavior likely reflected both emotional distress and a psychological escape from perceived threats. Erickson did not focus on the psychological origin of the paralysis. Instead, he created a placebo diagnosis of "inertia syndrome" (a restricted-use tactic) providing the worker with a structured, predictable pathway to recovery that preserved his dignity.

This nudge worked by altering expectations for non-volitional behavior (Kirsch, 1990) and by gradually building progress through small successes, such as the relaxation of the shoulder joint and changes in nerve function, which were framed as concrete evidence of "disappointing" improvement. This reflects evidence that expectations themselves strongly shape behavioral outcomes and recovery trajectories. The doctors' calibrated predictions about his recovery subtly highlighted opportunities for progress, counteracting the worker's sense of helplessness and lack of choice. Their illumination of non-threatening options, such as "He will recover full arm usage by the end of the week, but with permanent wrist fatigue," respected the man's right to have a serious problem and yet make meaningful progress. Furthermore, the doctors' ongoing satisfaction with his recovery reinforced his motivation to continue improving.

If we dissect Erickson's use of negatively calibrated prediction, we can see that it contained several key elements. One was strategic reframing through diagnosis: Erickson's creation of "inertia syndrome" framed the man's struggle as a condition with a predictable progression, allowing him to invest in the narrative of gradual recovery without feeling judged or invalidated. Another was incremental progress, where breaking down recovery into stages transformed each step into an opportunity for success. This aligns with tactics known as goal granularity and successive approximation. Finally, the doctors normalized struggles as part of the growth process. The language they used presented difficulties as natural aspects of recovery, helping the man reinterpret his setbacks as signs of forward movement and fostering a growth mindset in the process (Dweck, 2016).

This case highlights how micro-level choice architecture can offer clients *structured autonomy* in the face of overwhelming constraints. Erickson did not interpret the worker's condition as avoidance or non-compliance. Instead, he treated it as a design cue to help him construct an optimal choice environment. Each stage of progress was framed not as a correction of error, but as a self-affirming choice within a safe, navigable structure. In doing so, Erickson modeled a core tenet of *choice-centric care*: Natural adaptation emerges not from confrontation or conscious insight, but from offering an array of viable, non-threatening options, each calibrated to reinforce agency, competence, and meaningful direction.

General Application

Negatively calibrated prediction involves forecasting negative outcomes or focusing on potential failures to elicit cognitive and emotional engagement in clients. While it initially appears counterintuitive, studies have shown that paradoxically acknowledging failure or disappointing progress can create opportunities for behavioral adaptation and new perspectives. For example, a study by Wang et al. (2019) found that early-career setbacks can serve as a catalyst for improvement. For this to occur, it is important for critical observations to be focused on process (e.g., this was the wrong choice) rather than aimed at the person as a whole (e.g., you have poor judgment) (Kamins & Dweck, 1999).

One key shift in the evolution of this tactic has been in how practitioners frame these predictions. The focus has moved from simply forecasting failure to providing opportunities for the client to experience failure in a way that is not only manageable but also potentially motivating. Carol Dweck (2017) coined the term "failure-as-feedback" to describe the idea that setbacks and mistakes are valuable learning opportunities that provide information for growth, rather than indicators of fixed ability or personal inadequacy. The *failure-as-feedback* concept is central when anticipated failure is positioned as a necessary stepping stone to progress, highlighting areas of potential success that may have previously been unrecognized.

With the rise of digital tools and AI-driven applications, negatively calibrated prediction has become more adaptable and precise. For instance, some platforms use sentiment analysis to assess the emotional tone of a conversation, automatically suggesting how to reframe a predicted failure in a way that aligns with the client's underlying emotional state. This real-time analysis allows choice architects to fine-tune their use of negatively calibrated prediction, offering predictions that are calibrated to the client's current psychological and emotional needs. The use of machine learning algorithms to track a client's progress can also adjust the predictions dynamically, offering increasingly personalized forecasts that reflect subtle shifts in mindset or behavior.

Case 1.4: Nauseated by the In-Laws

Erickson described a woman who couldn't stand her in-laws visiting three or four times a week. The stress led her to develop a stomach ulcer, causing severe pain that interfered with her work, family life, and social relationships.

Erickson remarked to her,

> You really can't stand your in-laws, but you can stand going to church. You can stand the card games with the neighbors. You like your work, but you really don't like your relatives. They're a pain in the belly. Why not have the pain in your belly every time they come? It ought to be usefully developed. They certainly can't expect you to mop up the floor if you vomit.

Taking Erickson's suggestion, the woman devised a plan. Whenever her in-laws came over, she would rush to the refrigerator as soon as she heard them drive into the yard and drink a glass of milk. When they entered the house, she would greet them, start talking, and then deliberately make herself sick to her stomach and vomit.[2]

After vomiting, she would leave the room, feebly and piteously asking her in-laws to clean up the mess. This happened every time they visited, and soon they grew tired of mopping the floor.

Eventually, the in-laws began calling ahead to ask if she felt well enough for a visit. She would often respond, "Not today, not today, not today."

The woman found satisfaction in having control over the situation. She learned to save all her stomach pain for their visits and used it to assert her own boundaries.

After a couple of months without their visits, she invited them over for an afternoon. They arrived warily, but she discovered she now had enough power to influence their behavior.

When she wanted them to leave, she simply displayed a distressed look and rubbed her abdomen. They quickly made their exit, not wanting to risk having to mop the floor again.

Adaptive Reuse

In ECA, the behavioral tactic known as *adaptive reuse* involves finding functional value in problematic habits, tendencies, or compulsions, and redirecting them to serve a positive or constructive purpose. This concept draws a parallel to adaptive reuse in architecture, where a defunct building is repurposed and renovated into something with a new functional application.

Because it is often counter-productive to oppose or suppress undesirable behaviors, adaptive reuse accepts and then channels their energy, focus, or intent into a context that aligns with beneficial goals. This tactic acknowledges the underlying purpose of the behavior, recognizing that even habits perceived as problematic may possess valuable traits when applied strategically. Research in behavioral psychology supports this approach, as it aligns with the principle of cognitive flexibility (Tversky & Kahneman, 1974), which emphasizes the potential for individuals to adapt and reshape their behaviors in purposeful ways.

The core components of adaptive reuse include the identification of maladaptive tendencies, reframing these behaviors as resources, and providing the conditions for redirecting their influence in a manner that facilitates goal achievement. In doing so, the tactic promotes an internal process of constructive adaptation.

Case Analysis

Erickson's nudge for a woman suffering from stomach ulcers (due to frequent, unwanted visits from her in-laws) exemplifies a *choice-centric* approach that transformed her experience of pain into a means of social influence. By suggesting that she "usefully develop" her pain, Erickson reframed her physical discomfort as a means of self-expression. This new frame stands in contrast to the construct of pain as an ailment to be eradicated. This approach addressed her resentment and added value to her physical distress by strategically using it to stop her in-laws' unwelcome visits (many small animals also use vomit to repel predators). Instead of passively enduring the pain, she learned to direct it toward achieving a desired outcome.

If we dissect Erickson's use of adaptive reuse, we can see that it contained several key elements. First, he highlighted her social competency by emphasizing her ability to enjoy other social activities, such as attending church and playing cards. This helped her reestablish her self-esteem. Second, he gave her a subjectively meaningful objective by assigning pragmatic value to the physical act of vomiting, transforming what had been purely distressing into something purpose-driven, keeping her in-laws away. Finally, Erickson framed her struggles as a form of growth, encouraging her to see her pain not as a burden but as a tool of empowerment and to view her body as a resource.

This case illustrates how *choice-centric care* can reorient a client's relationship to System 1 (unconscious) behavior by transforming distress into a resource. Instead of seeking to eliminate the woman's pain or reinterpret it through insight, Erickson invited her to experience it as a usable resource, an instrument for shaping social boundaries in a way that aligned with her unspoken preferences. This parallels findings that accepting and redirecting unwanted experiences often produces better outcomes than attempts to suppress them. This act of adaptive reuse did not require denial or suppression, but offered a new function for something already present. This is the strategy of *utilization*. By integrating her experience into a purposeful structure, Erickson created a low-friction pathway for reclaiming agency without introducing conflict or demanding explanation. The key takeaway is that, unlike change-centric approaches, choice architecture does not always require new behaviors. It can succeed by reassigning meaning to existing ones, allowing clients to interact with their world on terms that feel authentic, strategic, and affirming.

General Application

Within ECA, adaptive reuse is the practice of identifying functional value in problematic tendencies and redirecting them toward constructive purposes. Much like repurposing a defunct building for a new usage, this approach acknowledges that even seemingly maladaptive behaviors may contain useful elements when applied strategically.

For individuals experiencing *internalized negativity bias* (those who may fixate on personal shortcomings or engage in self-critical thought patterns) adaptive reuse offers a way to transform these tendencies into strengths. For example, in therapy a client who habitually ruminates on mistakes could be guided to fixate on which day his unconscious mind will surprise himself with a small breakthrough. Additionally, he can be encouraged to obsess over whether he will recognize this progress as it occurs or only see it in hindsight. In coaching, a perfectionist prone to excessive self-consciousness might be encouraged to pay special attention to the parts of themselves that deserve love, forgiveness, and encouragement, thereby increasing self-compassion. By shifting the focus of these ingrained patterns toward growth and self-acceptance, adaptive reuse not only nullifies a negativity bias but also leverages its intensity for behavioral adaptation. Rather than viewing maladaptive tendencies, such as self-criticism and rumination, as obstacles, individuals learn to repurpose them as tools for insight, resilience, and personal development. In this way, adaptive reuse transforms what once felt like a burden into a pathway to progress.

Designing an Optimal Choice Environment (OCE) for Negativity Bias

Designing an *optimal choice environment* for someone dominated by a negativity bias requires an understanding of the cognitive and emotional tendencies that underlie this bias. Individuals with a pronounced negativity bias tend to focus more on potential threats or negative outcomes than positive ones, which can lead to heightened feelings of anxiety, mistrust, and disengagement. To counter-balance these tendencies and help individuals with this bias access their full range of cognitive and motivational capabilities, it is essential to create an environment that facilitates reflective readiness. This involves establishing conditions that help dysregulated individuals re-engage higher cognitive functions (such as critical thinking) and flexible motivational states that enable adaptation. The optimal choice-environment design includes providing space for the person to process their feelings and thoughts in a non-judgmental environment, which reduces their internal struggle with new perspectives. Research on cognitive flexibility supports the notion that providing opportunities for people to shift their focus from negative outcomes to potential benefits can reduce the grip of negativity bias, fostering a more balanced perspective (Liu et al., 2017; Raio et al., 2021).

To manage the emotional state of individuals with a negativity bias, *creating a quiet mind* is useful. This entails introducing conditions that induce a sense of safety and relaxation, such as rhythmic stimulation, safe touch, gentle or slow tonality, and familiar anchors that signal security. These elements are effective in down-regulating fear and anxiety, which are often intensified by a negativity bias. Research in neuropsychology suggests that relaxation techniques, such as those used in mindfulness and trauma-informed practices, can help activate the parasympathetic nervous system, counteracting the fight-or-flight response that can be triggered by negative thinking (Perry, 2006).

Another important element for an optimal choice environment is *alliance building*. This plays a central role in fostering trust and collaboration. Cultivating feelings of respect, shared goals, in-group identity, and cooperative engagement creates an emotional foundation where individuals feel understood and supported. Trust-building strategies have been shown to enhance the effectiveness of behavioral tactics by down-regulating anger, which can arise when individuals feel their negative perceptions are ignored or invalidated (Metz et al., 2022).

Finally, *employing moral appeal* can help guide decision-making, encouraging individuals to transcend their personal desires through empathy, social obligation, or personal integrity. By appealing to value-based decision-making, it is possible to encourage individuals to focus on higher-order goals, reducing the grip of fear and redirecting focus away from short-term negative emotions. This approach was illustrated in the case review at the start of this chapter as I helped the elderly gentleman face his impending death. Together, these strategies help design an optimal choice environment that not only mitigates the effects of negativity bias but also encourages behavioral adaptation.

Thought Exercise

In this section, *you* (the reader) will have an opportunity to exercise your design skills using a thought experiment. Imagine what you would do to create an optimal choice environment for someone with a negativity bias. Remember that this environment can include mental landscapes, such as private conversations with one's self or it may involve the adaptive reconstruction of their physical surroundings. This includes adding anything that might serve as a source of motivation. The only requirement is that you respect their right to remain vigilant to any potential threats from their environment, especially the threat of failure.

For this thought exercise, imagine speaking with a man who brings his wife for help with recovery from a brain injury. The problem that is troubling her most is her decreased ability to speak or understand what others say. *You* (the reader) recognize that her current state of mind reflects a negativity bias. In this case, it is characterized by performance anxiety. Each time she fails to communicate, some deep part of her becomes increasingly frightened that she will never recover her linguistic abilities. Her husband tells you that his wife used to like to talk, but now it is becoming progressively worse. She will just sit there staring at him when he tries to engage her in conversation. Her husband clearly wants to help her, yet his intense desire for her to speak only increases the performance pressure.

Before reading further, consider how *you* would respond to this couple. What would *you* say or do to design an optimal choice environment that acknowledges her need for avoidance while implicitly creating opportunity for improved quality of life?

***

Erickson described a case (1.5 in the case index) involving a woman who suffered a cerebral hemorrhage and as a result developed aphasia. To start the therapy, Erickson told her husband, "I want you to buy a fish tank. Make it one of those 15-gallon ones. Set it up in the den, and stock it with tropical fish." Initially, the husband protested, "But my wife doesn't like tropical fish." Erickson replied, "I know. You can afford that tank, and you can afford the tropical fish." Erickson told him that if his wife complained about the fish tank, he was to tell her to talk it over with Dr. Erickson.

After his meeting with the husband, Erickson met with his wife. His statement to her was,

> Now your husband has purchased that fish tank, he's got it well stocked: you hate tropical fish. You hate aquariums. All right, now I want you every night at 7 o'clock to take your husband in there and you both sit there and silently watch those fish for half an hour. You don't know why. Your husband doesn't know why. Just spend half an hour there, and keep absolutely silent, and you tell him that he is to remain absolutely silent.

Erickson continued, "At the end of the half hour – you have a clock there that you can watch – you both leave the den, and then you can resume normal living. Anything you wish."

Erickson explained that his intent was to have the woman spend half an hour daily desperately wishing she could ask her husband, "What in the hell is going on here? Why? What is Dr. Erickson trying to accomplish?" Erickson believed that this situation would create a tremendous motivation for talking.

Erickson went on to explain that the fish tank was essentially a diversion. It was a reason for the two of them to sit there silently, wishing to speak. Erickson emphasized the importance of both of them being in the same motivational space (they were now both wishing they could speak). Erickson reports it took about a month for the woman to fully recover from the aphasia.

After their therapy experience concluded, the couple decided that they like tropical fish. Erickson learned that on Sundays, they would go visit aquariums and enjoy looking at fish. It was a recreational activity that they emotionally bonded over.

In this case, Erickson's approach exemplified anchoring low, making the task of relearning speech as simple as possible. They were merely asked to sit in silence for 30 minutes each day while wishing to speak. This removed all performance pressure. Additionally, there was no expectation to enjoy the process or adopt a positive attitude because Erickson understood that she didn't like fish—making it the ideal nudge for someone with a strong negativity bias.

When designing an optimal choice environment for individuals with a negativity bias, it is essential to prioritize self-protection over self-actualization. This reflects research demonstrating that perceived safety must be restored before individuals can effectively engage higher-order cognitive and motivational processes. The goal is to create an environment that feels non-threatening while gently expanding possibilities. By minimizing performance anxiety and creating opportunities for small, meaningful successes, the experience can encourage cognitive flexibility and adaptive self-perception. Erickson's approach demonstrates how subtle modifications to the choice environment (such as anchoring low, negatively calibrated prediction, domino effect, and adaptive reuse) can encourage progress without triggering psychological pushback. By working within the individual's existing framework, ECA facilitates natural, self-directed adaptation.

Conclusion

Throughout this chapter, we have explored how negativity bias shapes perception, decision-making, and emotional regulation, often leading individuals to fixate on threats, personal shortcomings, or anticipated failures. However, rather than viewing this bias as an obstacle to be eliminated, ECA demonstrates how it can be strategically redirected into constructive action.

By leveraging behavioral tactics such as anchoring low, negatively calibrated prediction, the domino effect, and adaptive reuse, ECA practitioners transform deeply ingrained negative tendencies into pathways for growth and resilience (Table 1.1). Whether guiding an individual to redefine their role in the face of mortality, nudging a young man toward self-efficacy through structured incremental progress, or channeling a woman's physical discomfort into boundary-setting, ECA tactics capitalize on existing psychological tendencies.

At its core, this approach acknowledges a fundamental truth: People are most likely to engage with strategies that align with their intrinsic ways of thinking. Instead of forcing optimism on those predisposed to anticipate difficulty, ECA *meets them where they are*, offering a way forward that feels both natural and achievable. By reframing negative attention patterns as tools for problem-solving, self-preservation, and adaptation, it becomes possible to convert perceived weaknesses into strengths, transforming what once seemed like a psychological trap into a catalyst for meaningful achievement.

Quick-Reference Tactic Map

Table 1.1 Tactics Suited for Negativity Bias and the Broader Architecture of Strategic Influence

If Client...	*Then Use...*	*Because*
Feels worthless, fears trying, or absolutely expects to fail	*Anchoring low:* Setting performance objectives below performance capabilities.	*Redirects* the threat of failure to the question of ambition.
Rejects compliments, fixates on difficulties, or cannot tolerate optimism	*Domino effect:* Creating an early win in a parallel domain so its momentum generalizes into increased confidence, agency, and follow-through.	*Primes* efficacy indirectly by making success feel real in a symbolically related domain, allowing confidence to generalize.
Asserts an inability to enact a skill	*Negatively calibrated prediction:* Any prediction in which negative information is given more weight, creating a pessimistic forecast that leaves some margin for success.	*Reverse primes* a feeling of efficacy through peripheral actions that symbolically generalize success.
Feels ashamed, hopeless, or demoralized by their behavior	*Adaptive reuse:* Finding functional value in problematic habits, tendencies, or compulsions and redirecting them to serve a positive or constructive purpose.	*Utilizes* available behavior to build self-confidence, pride, and social belonging.

Notes

1 The sourcing for Erickson's casework draws on multiple sources: my interviews with his wife and children; review of more than 1,000 hours of archival recordings; interviews with several former clients; and the published record. Because Erickson sometimes recounted the same case with varying details, these narratives cannot be reconstructed with absolute precision. The details I include reflect my best judgment about what he most likely said and did with a given individual. Each case's index number appears in the case index at the back of this book, which lists published versions of the report.

2 While the outcome demonstrates an increase in the patient's sense of control, the means by which it was achieved (self-induced nausea) were self-initiated and would not align with current standards of care. The clinical takeaway is the transformation of distress into leverage within a relational system, a process that can now be pursued through safer behavioral strategies.

References

Ayllon, T., & Azrin, N. H. (1968). Reinforcer sampling: A technique for increasing the behavior of mental patients. *Journal of Applied Behavior Analysis, 1*(1), 13–20. https://doi.org/10.1901/jaba.1968.1-13

Bandura, A. (2000). Exercise of human agency through collective efficacy. *Current Directions in Psychological Science, 9*(3), 75–78. https://doi.org/10.1111/1467-8721.00064

Bass, R. W., Brown, D. D., Laurson, K. R., & Coleman, M. M. (2013). Physical fitness and academic performance in middle school students. *Acta Paediatrica, 102*(8), 832–837. https://doi.org/10.1111/apa.12278

Baumeister, R. F., Bratslavsky, E., Finkenauer, C., & Vohs, K. D. (2001). Bad is stronger than good. *Review of General Psychology, 5*(4), 323–370. https://doi.org/10.1037/1089-2680.5.4.323

Braund, T. A., Palmer, D. M., Tillman, G., Hanna, H., & Gordon, E. (2019). Increased chronic stress predicts greater emotional negativity bias and poorer social skills but not cognitive functioning in healthy adults. *Anxiety, Stress, & Coping, 32*(4), 399–411. https://doi.org/10.1080/10615806.2019.1598555

Dodge, K. A., & Frame, C. L. (1982). Social cognitive biases and deficits in aggressive boys. *Child Development, 53*(3), 620–635. JSTOR. https://doi.org/10.2307/1129373

Dolan, P., & Galizzi, M. M. (2015). Like ripples on a pond: Behavioral spillovers and their implications for research and policy. *Journal of Economic Psychology, 47*, 1–16. https://doi.org/10.1016/j.joep.2014.12.003

Dweck, C. S. (2016). The remarkable reach of growth mind-sets. *Scientific American Mind, 27*(1), 36–41.

Dweck, C. S. (2017). *Mindset – Updated Edition: Changing the Way You think to Fulfil Your Potential.* Little, Brown Book Group.

Freedman, J. L., & Fraser, S. C. (1966). Compliance without pressure: The foot-in-the-door technique. *Journal of Personality and Social Psychology, 4*(2), 195–202. https://doi.org/10.1037/h0023552

Haley, J. (Ed.) (with Erickson, M. H.). (1985). *Conversations with Milton H. Erickson, M.D.*, Vol. I: *Changing Individuals* (1st ed.). Triangle Press.

Kamins, M. L., & Dweck, C. S. (1999). Person versus process praise and criticism: Implications for contingent self-worth and coping. *Developmental Psychology*, *35*(3), 835–847. https://doi.org/10.1037/0012-1649.35.3.835

Kim, S.-Y., Allen, M., Preiss, R. W., & Peterson, B. (2014). Meta-analysis of counterattitudinal advocacy data: Evidence for an additive cues model. *Communication Quarterly* (World). https://www.tandfonline.com/doi/abs/10.1080/01463373.2014.949385

Kirsch, I. (1990). *Changing Expectations: A Key to Effective Psychotherapy* (pp. xviii, 231). Thomson Brooks/Cole Publishing Co.

Ku, G., Galinsky, A. D., & Murnighan, J. K. (2006). Starting low but ending high: A reversal of the anchoring effect in auctions. *Journal of Personality and Social Psychology*, *90*(6), 975–986. https://doi.org/10.1037/0022-3514.90.6.975

Liu, H., Li, X., Han, B., & Liu, X. (2017). Effects of cognitive bias modification on social anxiety: A meta-analysis. *PLoS One*, *12*(4), e0175107. https://doi.org/10.1371/journal.pone.0175107

Martell, C. R., Dimidjian, S., & Herman-Dunn, R. (2010). *Behavioral Activation for Depression: A Clinician's Guide*. Guilford Publications.

Metz, A., Jensen, T., Farley, A., Boaz, A., Bartley, L., & Villodas, M. (2022). Building trusting relationships to support implementation: A proposed theoretical model. *Frontiers in Health Services, 2*, 894599. https://doi.org/10.3389/frhs.2022.894599

Müller-Pinzler, L., Czekalla, N., Mayer, A. V., Stolz, D. S., Gazzola, V., Keysers, C., Paulus, F. M., & Krach, S. (2019). Negativity-bias in forming beliefs about own abilities. *Scientific Reports*, *9*(1), 14416. https://doi.org/10.1038/s41598-019-50821-w

Neta, M., & Brock, R. L. (2021). Social connectedness and negative affect uniquely explain individual differences in response to emotional ambiguity. *Scientific Reports*, *11*(1), 3870. https://doi.org/10.1038/s41598-020-80471-2

Perry, B. D. (2006). Applying Principles of Neurodevelopment to Clinical Work with Maltreated and Traumatized Children: The Neurosequential Model of Therapeutics. In N. B. Webb (Ed.), *Working with Traumatized Youth in Child Welfare* (1st edition, pp. 27–52). The Guilford Press.

Raio, C. M., Harp, N. R., Brown, C. C., & Neta, M. (2021). Reappraisal—but not suppression—tendencies determine negativity bias after laboratory and real-world stress exposure. *Affective Science*, *2*(4), 455–467. https://doi.org/10.1007/s42761-021-00059-5

Reynolds, D. (2017). Restraining golem and harnessing pygmalion in the classroom: A laboratory study of managerial expectations and task design. *Academy of Management Learning & Education*, *6*(4), 475–483. https://doi.org/10.5465/amle.2007.27694947

Rozin, P., & Royzman, E. B. (2001). Negativity bias, negativity dominance, and contagion. *Personality and Social Psychology Review*, *5*(4), 296–320. https://doi.org/10.1207/S15327957PSPR0504_2

Sheldon, K. M., & Lyubomirsky, S. (2006). Achieving sustainable gains in happiness: Change your actions, not your circumstances*. *Journal of Happiness Studies*, *7*(1), 55–86. https://doi.org/10.1007/s10902-005-0868-8

Short, D. (2022). *Making Psychotherapy More Effective with Unconscious Process Work*. Routledge. https://doi.org/10.4324/9781003127208

Spring, B., Schneider, K., McFadden, H. G., Vaughn, J., Kozak, A. T., Smith, M., Moller, A. C., Epstein, L. H., DeMott, A., Hedeker, D., Siddique, J., & Lloyd-Jones, D. M. (2012). Multiple behavior changes in diet and activity: A randomized controlled trial using mobile technology. *Archives of Internal Medicine*, *172*(10), 789–796. https://doi.org/10.1001/archinternmed.2012.1044

Tesser, A. (2000). On the confluence of self-esteem maintenance mechanisms. *Personality and Social Psychology Review*, *4*(4), 290–299. https://doi.org/10.1207/S15327957PSPR0404_1

Tversky, A., & Kahneman, D. (1974). Judgment under Uncertainty: Heuristics and Biases. In L. C. MacLean & W. T. Ziemba (Eds.), *Handbook of the Fundamentals of Financial Decision Making, Part I* (pp. 261–268). World Scientific Publishing Co. Pte. Ltd. https://ideas.repec.org//h/wsi/wschap/9789814417358_0015.html

Unkelbach, C., Alves, H., & Koch, A. (2020). Chapter Three – Negativity Bias, Positivity Bias, and Valence Asymmetries: Explaining the Differential Processing of Positive and Negative Information. In B. Gawronski (Ed.), *Advances in Experimental Social Psychology* (Vol. 62, pp. 115–187). Academic Press. https://doi.org/10.1016/bs.aesp.2020.04.005

Wang, Y., Jones, B. F., & Wang, D. (2019). Early-career setback and future career impact. *Nature Communications*, *10*(1), 4331. https://doi.org/10.1038/s41467-019-12189-3

Chapter 2

The Bright Side Blind Spot

Positivity Bias

The Bright Side Blind Spot: *Positivity Bias*

My client had filed for divorce and spent the past six months thriving on her own. Yet, envisioning her ex-husband with someone new unsettled her. It was not just that he had moved on, it was how he kept pulling her into his dating life. He leaned on her for emotional support, treating her like a dating coach as he navigated his new relationship. There were also late-night confessions, his insistence that he would rather be with her than his new partner, and his claims that he could never love anyone else the way he loved her.

She had a term for it, love bombing. Then she added, "It is sort of endearing, hearing him worry about which shirt to wear or what to say. It's like he is a little boy in need of a mother."

The first half of our session was spent with me listening. She had a tangled web of emotions that needed to be talked through in the presence of an empathetic listener. She needed to somehow make sense of this post-divorce dynamic. Eventually she got to the heart of it, asking me, "Why does losing him feel so unbearable and what should I do about it? Are there some boundaries that I should set?"

I told her plainly, she owed him nothing beyond the essentials of co-parenting. No emotional support, no financial advice, and no mothering. If he needed those things, he could turn to a therapist, a financial planner, or his own mother. I emphasized that, as ex-spouses, their communication should focus solely on their two children and nothing more. She nodded in agreement, but her body language suggested that her longing for his positive attention might override any conscious effort to make wise decisions.

When the session was about three-quarters over, I recognized that a state shift was needed before she could engage in critical thought. Triggering a state reversal can be as simple as asking a single poignant question. With intense curiosity, I asked, "Do you remember why you divorced him?" Her head tilted sideways but she did not say anything. So, I continued,

DOI: 10.4324/9781003797876-3

> Do you remember him threatening to kill you—coming down the stairs with that gun held behind his back. Do you remember looking at the children and thinking that he would shoot them after killing you and then end his own life?

Her face turned pale. I continued, "Do you remember him forcing sex on you, and him wanting you to take LSD before sex so that you would be in a completely helpless position?" "Do you remember how hard it was to get this divorce? Do you remember telling me that he has people working for him that could simply make you disappear and that your body would never be found?" "Do you remember how hard we worked to get you safely out of the house with the children?"

As I spoke, the amnesic barrier lifted. The horrific memories had been covered by a vail of *euphoric recall*, a cognitive distortion in which past experiences are remembered more positively than they actually were. She had been so caught up in the illusion of their new friendship that she had blocked out the reality of their past. In a tone of disbelief she asked, "How does a person forget something like this? Until you reminded me, I had no memory of any of this."

While some psychotherapists might interpret this as repression, a more straightforward explanation is the influence of positivity bias, which often leads to *rosy retrospection*. This is the tendency to selectively recall positive aspects of past experiences while overlooking the negative ones. This phenomenon is particularly common after the loss of a significant other: For example, a person who endured an abusive marriage may, after their spouse's death, remember only their good qualities while ignoring the suffering they endured. In this case, her bias had shielded her from painful truths, allowing her to engage with her ex-husband as if the past had never happened, until the moment it all came rushing back.

Following this state reversal, I asked her how she felt about being divorced. This time, there was no trace of ambivalence. "I feel grateful that I got out alive! I have absolutely no interest in his mind-fucking manipulations."

It is important to note that her personality had not changed, rather, she had experienced a shift in state of mind. Previously, she had interpreted his words through the lens of *truth bias*, which is the optimistic inclination to believe that others are being honest, even when there is evidence to the contrary. The irony was that this bias persisted even as he openly *confessed* to deceiving the younger woman he was ostensibly dating. Until this moment, she had unwittingly extended the same misplaced trust to him, failing to fully recognize the pervasiveness of his manipulations.

She continued, "I feel sorry for the young woman who is dating him now. I think he's sociopathic. But there's nothing I can do about that, except stay as far away as possible."

As she spoke, I nodded, "I am in full agreement with YOUR decision," I told her. With the session having ended, we both agreed there was no need to schedule another appointment.

Two years later, I stumbled across an interview about her on the internet. She described herself as happy and thriving. The comments from her followers made it clear, she was deeply admired and seen as a strong female role model.

In this case, the word *insight* is a distraction. It doesn't encapsulate the contextual dynamics or the nudge I provided. My overarching strategy was to stimulate *critical thinking*, both consciously and at the deeper, gut level of feeling (unconscious intelligence). To achieve this, I employed a behavioral tactic known as a *history audit* (also called *cautionary reminders*). My goal was for her to draw her own conclusions from the context of her life story, ensuring that her future decisions were driven by the right motivational forces.

In organizations, audits are typically a status-driven process, an evaluation in which a subordinate is assessed by someone with greater power. But in Ericksonian Choice Architecture (ECA), the client is the executive, the decision-maker, and the sole beneficiary of the audit. A history audit helps increase executive functions (higher-order thinking) and can lead to reversals, or shifts in state of mind. This type of structured assessment has been shown to curb overconfidence (Moore & Healy, 2008) and is particularly valuable when optimism is incongruent with serious environmental threats. In such cases, reflecting on hard-learned lessons is almost always beneficial.

Recognizing *Positivity Bias* in Ericksonian Choice Architecture

Positivity bias is the cognitive tendency to interpret experiences, memories, and future possibilities in an overly favorable light, often minimizing risks and challenges. In the case above, this showed up as euphoric recall: Her ex-husband's "endearing" love bombing and pseudo-co-parenting closeness temporarily eclipsed the history of coercion and lethal threat until a brief history audit ("Do you remember why you divorced him?") reinstated the missing risk context and produced a rapid state reversal. The downside of positivity bias is that in this state of mind individuals tend to be overly optimistic, greatly underestimating the probability of undesirable outcomes and overestimating favorable and pleasing outcomes (also known as *optimism bias* or *positive outcome bias*).

This state is characterized by *approach motivation*, which can manifest as a pursuit of closer relationships, achievement goals, or personal growth challenges. Individuals high in positivity bias exhibit optimistic thinking: favoring confidence and enthusiasm while showing little interest in hesitation or regret. In this state, attention automatically focuses on positive contextual, social, and individual variables that can be used to disrupt negative outcomes, resulting in greater resiliency. This bias can be beneficial in promoting ambition and persistence, but may also lead to overestimation of control, resource misallocation, and susceptibility to deception.

Operationally, positivity bias can be measured by assessing individuals' tendencies to rate uncertain situations as more favorable than neutral observers do, persist in goal-oriented tasks despite obstacles, and overcommit resources, such as time or money. Research shows that optimism drives persistence and success in fields requiring resilience (Carver & Scheier, 2001) but also increases risk-taking in entrepreneurship (Hmieleski & Baron, 2009) and decision-making (Armor & Taylor, 2002). Additionally, individuals high in this bias may dismiss warning signs in relationships, making them more susceptible to scams or manipulative tactics (Korn et al., 2014).

The *illusion of control* further compounds these risks (Langer, 1975). This cognitive distortion occurs when individuals overestimate their ability to control or influence events and outcomes, even in situations where they have little or no actual control. It reflects a strong sense of personal agency, often more than is realistic. As a result, people may take unnecessary risks, thinking their skills, effort, or character gives them more control over the outcome than they actually have. For example, individuals in manic states exhibit extreme forms of this bias. More commonly, entrepreneurs may invest excessive capital in a failing venture, convinced that persistence alone will guarantee success. Similarly, individuals in toxic relationships may assume that their actions can "fix" or change an abusive partner, despite evidence to the contrary. In financial decision-making, the illusion of control can lead investors to take high-risk bets based on overconfidence in their predictive abilities, increasing their exposure to market volatility. By fostering an unrealistic sense of agency, the illusion of control amplifies the negative consequences of positivity bias, making individuals more prone to miscalculations, overcommitment, and disappointment when reality does not align with their expectations.

Another psychological phenomenon that fits under the umbrella of positivity bias is the *Dunning–Kruger effect*, which occurs when individuals with low knowledge or skill in a particular area overestimate their own competence (Kruger & Dunning, 1999). This effect arises because those who lack expertise also lack the ability to recognize their own limitations. As a result, they remain highly optimistic, not because they have a well-founded sense of confidence, but because they are unaware of what they do not know. As Confucius reportedly stated, "To know what you know and what you do not know, that is true knowledge." When the Dunning–Kruger effect is at play, this crucial self-awareness is missing.

For example, an inexperienced investor may confidently make high-stakes financial decisions without understanding market risks, or an untrained leader may push forward with an ill-conceived plan, oblivious to its flaws. This misplaced confidence reinforces the illusion of control, creating a dangerous feedback loop in which individuals persist in misguided actions, unaware of the gaps in their understanding.

Understanding the nuances of positivity bias is essential for leveraging its benefits while avoiding its pitfalls. When properly regulated, it fosters motivation and resilience. However, unchecked, it can lead to miscalculations and vulnerability to manipulation. Recognizing the conditions that amplify or mitigate its effects is key to making informed, balanced decisions.

Erickson's Casework and the Application of Tactical Nudges

Having recognized the effects of positivity bias (how individuals may unknowingly dismiss risks or overestimate their control) the next step is understanding how to guide them toward more adaptive choices. Rather than relying on persuasion or debate, which often triggers defensiveness, a more effective approach is the use of a gentle nudge.

Erickson masterfully employed this method to guide individuals who might be operating under overly ambitious goals or with insufficient planning. By structuring situations in ways that preserved autonomy while steering behavior toward promising outcomes, he demonstrated how the strategic design of choices can help evolve individual's adaptive capacity. The following examples illustrate how Erickson used *implementation intentions*, *anchoring high*, *permissive destabilization*, and *perspective taking* to create an environment where behavioral adaptation became the obvious, self-chosen path.

Case 2.1: Breaking the World Record

Donald was 6′6″ tall and 260 pounds, a powerhouse of an athlete with no excess fat on his frame. Recognizing his potential, his high school coach had trained him in shot put every night for an entire year, free of charge. However, with just two weeks left before the high school championship, Donald faced a frustrating barrier: He could only throw 58 feet, far short of the record.

His father was interested in hypnosis and brought him to Erickson who then taught Donald to expect automatic behaviors. For example, Erickson instructed him to "levitate his hand" and develop a deep awareness of his muscles. Then, he told Donald to return for the next session, enter a trance, and listen carefully.

When Donald returned, Erickson asked, "Did you know that a mile used to be four minutes long until Roger Bannister broke the record—after it had stood for many, many years?" Donald listened as Erickson continued:

> Bannister, who was well-acquainted with sports, realized that races are won by mere fractions of a second. He understood that a four-minute mile was 240 seconds. If he could run it in 239.5 seconds, he would break the record.

Then, Erickson shifted the focus to Donald's own challenge, saying, "You've already thrown the shot 58 feet. Tell me honestly—do you think you can tell the difference between 58 feet and 58 feet and 1/16th of an inch?"

Donald: "No, of course not."
Erickson: "How about 58 feet and 1/8th of an inch?"
Donald: "No."

Slowly, Erickson worked his way up, inch by inch, from 58 feet to 59 feet, each time reinforcing that Donald could not perceive the difference. Over two more sessions, he expanded Donald's belief in what was possible. Two weeks later, Donald set a national high school record.

That summer, Donald returned to Erickson with a new goal, stating, "I'm going to the Olympics. I want some advice." Erickson responded,

> The Olympic record for shot put is just under 62 feet. You're just an 18-year-old kid. It would be all right if you bring home the bronze medal. But don't bring home the silver or the gold—because then you'll be competing against yourself.

Donald returned home with the bronze medal.

Four years later, before the Mexico City Olympics, Donald came back. "I'm going to Mexico City," he told Erickson.

Erickson smiled, and said, "You're four years older now, Donald. It would be all right if you take the gold medal."

And Donald returned home with the gold.

Anchoring High

Anchoring high is a behavioral tactic in ECA that involves setting a benchmark slightly above an individual's current level of achievement, creating a psychological pull toward greater growth. This tactic draws on research demonstrating that initial performance benchmarks strongly influence later expectations and effort allocation. Unlike overly ambitious goal-setting, which can lead to frustration or disengagement, anchoring high strategically positions the next level of success as challenging yet attainable, reinforcing motivation and confidence.

However, this tactic must also account for the *hard–easy effect*, in which individuals tend to overestimate their ability to accomplish difficult tasks while underestimating their capacity for easier ones. For example, an overly confident mother might declare, "I'm going to make my teenage daughter respect me." But when asked to explain exactly how she plans to do that, she struggles to offer a clear or realistic approach. The practitioner then suggests a simple approach, "Would you be willing to dedicate some time to having a few enjoyable conversations with her?" Surprisingly, this easier task feels more daunting. The mother responds, "I don't know how to talk to her anymore," revealing an ironic reversal. While the mother has no direct control over her daughter's implicit attitudes (respect) she should know how to speak with her daughter about enjoyable topics.

When applied effectively, anchoring high can counteract these distortions by calibrating goals within an optimal difficulty range, a point challenging enough to inspire growth but not so overwhelming that they lead to discouragement. Using the same example with mother and daughter, the practitioner could introduce some structure and a modest goal, saying,

> Once a day, perhaps during dinner, ask your daughter her low point for the day and her high point. When she is unhappy about something (low point), sympathize, even if you disagree with her interpretation of things. When she describes the best part of her day (high point), smile and help her celebrate life's small daily pleasures.

Initially, the mother was overly confident she could prevail in the power struggle between her and her daughter. She did not account for the fact that many teenagers are willing to destroy themselves to win these types of power struggles.

This approach aligns with Vygotsky's (1978) *zone of proximal development*, which states that learning is maximized when tasks are slightly beyond current ability but still achievable with effort or guidance. It also leverages the *Pygmalion effect* (Rosenthal & Jacobson, 1968), where individuals tend to perform in ways that align with the expectations set for them. Without careful calibration, the hard–easy effect can disrupt this process. If an individual is anchored too high, they may fall into the trap of overestimating their readiness and become discouraged when they fail. Conversely, underestimating their ability may prevent them from even attempting tasks well within their capacity.

Research on *mastery-based learning* (Dweck, 2006) as well as research on grit and deliberate practice (Duckworth et al., 2011) support the gradual expansion of ability by prioritizing practice and steady progress over immediate results. By considering both the motivational benefits of anchoring high and the cognitive distortions introduced by the hard–easy effect, ECA practitioners can guide individuals toward ambitious yet achievable growth, balancing confidence with realistic self-assessment. This goal-setting process is of course a negotiation. For those with a strong positivity bias, the discussion should begin with a focus on high but realistic goals.

The core components of anchoring high in ECA include the *zone of proximal development*, *subjective proximity*, *positive expectancy effect*, and a *mastery agenda*. The *zone of proximal development* ensures that the next goal is slightly beyond current capability but still achievable with effort. *Subjective proximity* maintains that the goal must "feel" within reach to prevent disengagement caused by unrealistic expectations. The *positive expectancy effect* involves using implicit or explicit messages to convey confidence in the individual's ability to reach a higher benchmark. A *mastery agenda* removes pressure to perform by emphasizing gradual improvement over external comparisons. By applying these principles, individuals are encouraged to expand their self-imposed limits, fostering both immediate performance gains and long-term resilience.

CASE ANALYSIS

Donald was a highly trained athlete with exceptional physical ability, yet he was psychologically limited by his perception of what was possible. With only two weeks before the high school championship, he fixated on his current best throw of 58 feet, seeing it as a hard boundary instead of an expandable trajectory. Erickson recognized that Donald's challenge wasn't just physical training, it was mental framing. By introducing the concept of incremental improvement (granular goals), Erickson helped Donald shift his perspective. Instead of making success feel like an overwhelming leap, he *anchored high* by reframing the difference between 58 feet and 59 feet as imperceptible increments of progress, making the next level of achievement seem not only possible but also inevitable.

This tactic is supported by research on goal-setting and performance enhancement. Studies on anchoring effects (Tversky & Kahneman, 1974) suggest that people's judgments and expectations are influenced by an initial reference point, or "anchor." By slowly expanding Donald's mental anchor, showing him that he couldn't perceive small increments of progress, Erickson made a new, higher performance standard feel within reach. Additionally, research on self-efficacy (Bandura, 2000) emphasizes that belief in one's ability is a key driver of achievement. By systematically adjusting his frame of reference, Erickson bridged the gap between belief and performance, leading Donald to break a national record.

The central choice opportunity in this case was expansion versus limitation. Donald had to decide whether to continue viewing his personal best as a hard ceiling or to accept the possibility that he could push beyond it. By subtly guiding him to realize that he couldn't detect small increments of improvement, Erickson dismantled the psychological barrier of perceived impossibility. This set the stage for Donald not only to break the high school record but also to later pursue Olympic success. This was done first by anchoring high at a bronze medal, ensuring he did not limit himself to merely competing in the Olympics, and then four years later by anchoring even higher, allowing him to claim the gold.

If we dissect Erickson's use of anchoring high, we can see that it contained four key elements. First, there was *incremental reframing*, as Erickson slowly adjusted Donald's mental reference point, expanding his belief in what was possible by working from 58 feet to 59 feet in imperceptible increments. Second, he used *temporal self-comparison*, encouraging Donald to measure himself not against an impossible goal but against his own recent progress, making improvement feel gradual and attainable. Third, Erickson employed *expectation management* by strategically introducing achievement anchors, initially allowing Donald to aim for bronze in his first Olympics to prevent self-competition in future events, and later setting gold as the next logical step. Finally, he boosted Donald's self-efficacy by guiding him to *recognize his own potential*, ensuring that motivation came from within and reinforcing a deep sense of personal mastery.

This case demonstrates how design elements can shift an individual from performance maintenance to performance innovation. Erickson did not urge Donald to "try harder." Instead, he focused the young athlete's attention on moments when the boundary between current ability and potential felt fluid or invisible. Donald's success emerged through a reframed interaction with possibility itself. This illustrates a core lesson in *choice-centric care*: High achievement is often unlocked not by invoking ambition, but by making the next step feel so close, so naturally aligned, that movement becomes almost reflexive. The architecture of choice here wasn't motivational. It was perceptual, removing the friction between belief and action until the two moved as one.

GENERAL APPLICATION

Anchoring high is a behavioral tactic that sets achievement benchmarks above an individual's current abilities, encouraging growth by subtly shifting their perception of what is possible. For individuals with a positivity bias, who may overestimate progress or set overly optimistic goals without clear structure, anchoring high ensures that aspirations remain challenging yet realistic, preventing complacency or premature satisfaction. Effective anchoring works best when goals feel attainable, reinforcing *intrinsic motivation* without triggering discouragement.

In therapy, a client who believes they are already improving despite a lack of action might be encouraged to *anchor high* by committing to measurable progress, such as journaling emotional shifts over weeks. In coaching, an entrepreneur with inflated confidence might be guided to *anchor high* by setting revenue goals that require structured milestones. In counseling, a student with natural talent but little effort might be encouraged to reach beyond their comfort zone, reinforcing a mastery mindset rather than relying solely on innate ability. By applying anchoring high, practitioners help individuals with positivity bias stay goal-directed, resilient, and accountable to concrete progress.

Case 2.2: There Can Be Only One Jesus Christ

While working at the psychiatric hospital in Worcester, Massachusetts, Erickson encountered two patients who both believed they were Jesus Christ. To address their delusions, Erickson introduced them to each other, seating them together on a bench and allowing them to converse. One of the men, whom Erickson identified as Alfredo, loudly insisted that he was Jesus Christ. Following this debate, the other man, John, confided in Erickson, saying, "Listen to that crazy guy—he says he's Jesus Christ, but I am. You know it, and I know it."

Erickson then approached Alfredo, who made the same claim about John, "He says he's Jesus Christ—that man's crazy. I'm Jesus Christ." Playing along, Erickson would respond sympathetically, "Yes, that man is crazy; he claims to be Jesus Christ." He then returned to John and said, "Alfredo claims he's Jesus Christ, and you know damn well he's crazy. But Alfredo thinks the same about you—he believes you're crazy because you claim to be Jesus Christ." This pattern continued for days, with Erickson prompting John to reflect, "Now John, you say you're not crazy, yet I hear you saying the exact same things as Alfredo."

Eventually, John had a realization.

> You know, I've been thinking it over. He claims to be Jesus Christ, and I know he's crazy. But he doesn't know he's crazy—that's why he keeps saying it. I say the same thing, and he thinks about me the way I think about him. It looks like we're both crazy.

Erickson validated this insight, saying,

> That's how I feel about it, and that's how every nurse on the ward feels. You know, Jesus Christ wouldn't need to shout about being Jesus Christ. But John, you've yelled, screamed, and insisted on it—that doesn't seem very Christ-like. It just seems like crazy behavior.

John then proposed an experiment, "Take me to the library. I want to look at a book." In the library, he scanned the pages and said, "There's a capital T, an H, an O, an R, and an N: T-H-O-R-N. And there's a T and an O, and an N—that's my name, Thornton. And there's my name again. This book is written about me." Erickson modeled the same behavior, flipping through the pages and replying, "Well, let's see. There's an E, an R, an I... yes, a C-K, and S-O-N. E-r-i-c-k-s-o-n. John, I think this book is written about me."

John paused, then concluded, "Somebody's crazy. And it isn't you. Let me think it over."

Soon after, John abandoned his delusions entirely. He became the hospital librarian, then secured a job outside the hospital. Four years later, he was still gainfully employed and free of delusions. Occasionally, he would visit the hospital, checking in on Alfredo to see how he was doing.

Perspective Taking

Within ECA *perspective taking* is defined as the act of perceiving a situation, or understanding a concept, from an alternative point of view. This can include adopting the vantage point of another individual (third-person perspective) or taking an embodied perspective through the eyes of another person, or through those of a different version of oneself (first-person perspective). Research shows that psychological distancing reduces emotional reactivity, enabling more balanced reasoning and decision-making. This enables individuals to analyze their choices from an external viewpoint. This shift in perspective enhances *metacognition*, which is the ability to think about one's own thinking. It also reduces emotional biases that might cloud judgment or self-awareness. By distancing themselves from immediate emotional reactions, individuals can more objectively assess their behavior and make rational decisions. This process encourages a broader, more critical examination of one's actions, helping individuals confront aspects of themselves they might otherwise avoid.

The effectiveness of perspective taking is supported by research in positive psychology. Brain studies have suggested that merely changing self-talk from the first-person ("I am upset") to the third-person ("You are upset") can have a significant impact on emotional self-regulation without having to engage cognitive control (Moser et al., 2017). This aligns with the concept of *self-distancing*, where individuals use verbal and visual self-distancing to gain a clearer, less emotionally charged view of their circumstances, enabling them to process information more effectively and with less emotional interference (Michel-Kröhler et al., 2021). Similarly, Orvell et al. (2021) found that *distanced self-talk*, where individuals refer to themselves using their name or non-first-person pronouns, helps regulate emotions by reducing emotional reactivity during reflections on negative experiences. This outcome occurred even for emotionally vulnerable individuals, regardless of the intensity of the event or its timing.

The core components that make perspective taking effective include its ability to *facilitate self-reflection* without the distortion of emotional biases, its capacity to *promote self-compassion* by allowing individuals to see themselves more objectively, and its role in *fostering critical thinking* by prompting individuals to consider their behaviors from a broader viewpoint. By taking this step back, individuals can recognize when optimism is clouding their judgment and adjust their choices accordingly, reducing the likelihood of miscalculating risks or making impulsive decisions based on an inflated sense of security.

Case Analysis

The perspective taking task suited John's psychological state, marked by delusions of grandeur and the belief that he was Jesus Christ. This extreme *self-positivity bias* prevented critical self-examination, as he considered his actions to be justified. Erickson's approach encouraged John to reflect on both his and Alfredo's behavior, helping him step outside his emotional fixation. This shift led John to recognize the absurdity of his beliefs, culminating in his breakthrough moment, "It looks to me as if we are both crazy." This realization disrupted his self-deception and initiated pragmatic problem-solving.

The nudge was effective because it leveraged John's ability to recognize patterns in others. This aligns with evidence that individuals often evaluate others' reasoning more accurately than their own, enabling corrective insight through comparison. This ability persists even in delusions. By framing John's behavior relative to Alfredo's, Erickson enabled him to view his actions more objectively. This self-distancing helped John see the absurdity of his delusion without direct confrontation.

Ultimately, John faced a choice: remain isolated in his subjective reality or embrace consensus reality. Erickson's approach provided a path for critical self-evaluation, making psychological growth and social reintegration an attractive option.

General Application

Perspective taking is a structured behavioral tactic that enables individuals to evaluate their choices from an external viewpoint, reducing emotional bias and increasing critical thinking. This tactic can be useful for individuals experiencing positivity bias. This bias is often expressed as excessive pride, ambition, or an idealized vision of one's plans. Perspective taking counter-balances overly optimistic assumptions by fostering *self-distancing* and objectivity. As argued by Kahneman (2011), when someone is deeply invested in a goal or belief, they may overlook practical limitations, fail to anticipate challenges, or dismiss contrary evidence. By adopting a third-person perspective, individuals create psychological distance, allowing them to assess their commitments and strategies more realistically.

This nudge can take various forms across collaborative problem-solving contexts. One common approach involves perspective contrast, where a person first describes their behavior from their own viewpoint and then considers how it might appear to an outside observer. Research in cognitive restructuring supports this technique, showing that shifting perspectives can help individuals recognize inconsistencies in their reasoning (Beck, 1976). Another method developed by Angela Duckworth and her colleagues involves mental simulation exercises, where individuals analyze past events or future plans from the viewpoint of an external observer. Studies on such exercises have documented enhanced metacognition and emotional regulation as a result (White et al., 2019).

Role-playing is another powerful tool where the client takes on the role of another person (e.g., a spouse or coworker) while the therapist or a group member role-plays the client. This experiential shift forces a re-evaluation of self-perceptions, often leading to new insights.

A simpler, self-guided approach is to encourage *third-person self-talk*. This linguistic distancing has been found to improve self-regulation and decision-making by promoting cognitive detachment (Kross et al., 2014). Similarly, *temporal distancing* can be achieved by projecting oneself into the future to view an immediate experience from a more detached, long-term perspective, reducing its emotional impact. Studies on linguistic and *temporal distancing* indicate that these strategies protect against emotional reactivity, even during repeated exposure to the same stress-inducing events. Additionally, *self-distancing* has been found to lower physiological markers of stress, such as blood pressure increases following anger-related experiences (Özlem & Kross, 2018). By encouraging individuals to analyze their emotions from a detached perspective, *third-person self-talk* facilitates cognitive restructuring, allowing for more rational decision-making and greater resilience to emotional distress.

Finally, a more advanced version of perspective taking involves tapping into critical projections, where clients reflect on the behaviors of others that frustrated them enough to still feel upset. They are then asked, "If you could give that person some advice, what would it be?" They are then asked to consider how this same advice might apply to their own actions. This method leverages *self-protective mechanisms* (projection) and *Solomon's paradox* (the tendency to give better advice to others than to oneself), helping clients uncover blind spots in their thinking. Although different in style, this is essentially the same tactic illustrated in Erickson's case study.

By systematically applying any of these forms of *self-distancing*, perspective taking helps individuals recalibrate their expectations, recognize cognitive distortions, and make more adaptive choices, ensuring their ambition is grounded in realistic self-awareness.

Case 2.3: What Are You Going to Do about It

John was admitted to a psychiatric ward for reasons we do not know. There he made a habit of telling everyone that he did not belong there. He followed the nurses, repeatedly insisting, "I'm locked up here for no reason at all. I don't belong here."

Seeking to construct an associative anchor, Erickson instructed all of the staff to respond to John's statement, "I don't belong here," with an equally simple, repetitious phrase, "But you ARE here."

For six months, John received the same reply. Then, one day he finally developed the capacity for reciprocal dialogue, replying, "I know I'm here!"

After being informed of this breakthrough, Erickson went to visit him.

John: I don't belong here.
Erickson: But you ARE here.
John: I know I am here.
Erickson: That's right. You are here. Now that you are here, what do you want to do about LEAVING here?

With this shift in focus, John began taking steps toward greater self-determination. Within nine months, he was discharged, secured a job as a manual laborer, and started supporting his sister's college education while contributing to his family's well-being.

Implementation Intentions

Implementation intentions, a key behavioral tactic in ECA, involve forming concrete plans to overcome obstacles by linking goal-directed actions to specific cues. This approach is grounded in extensive research demonstrating that cue-linked action planning significantly increases goal follow-through. It is one form of cue-based planning in which specific actions are pre-linked to triggers, ensuring that goal-directed behaviors are automatically activated when the relevant situation arises. Research on implementation intentions (Gollwitzer, 1999b) demonstrates that individuals are more likely to follow through with goals when they frame their intentions in *if–then* statements (e.g., "If I feel stuck, then I will ask for help"). By preloading a response to anticipated obstacles, this approach bypasses the cognitive effort required for decision-making in the moment, increasing the likelihood of goal adherence. Additionally, studies on automaticity in behavioral adaptation (Bargh et al., 2001) highlight that when these cue-action pairings are mentally rehearsed, they become reflexive, reducing the energy cost of the new adaptive behavior.

This method directly addresses the *intention-behavior gap*. This is the common tendency for individuals to set goals but fail to act on them due to distractions, lack of preparation, or uncertainty about the next steps. Studies have shown that even small nudges, such as prompting individuals to write down their plans privately, can significantly increase follow-through rates, as seen in a 13% increase in vaccination rates (Milkman et al., 2011). Similarly, planning prompts have been used to increase voter turnout by 9% (Nickerson & Rogers, 2010), highlighting their broad applicability.

A related challenge in goal execution is the *planning fallacy*, a cognitive bias in which individuals underestimate the time, effort, and potential obstacles required to complete a task. This overconfidence often leads people to set overly ambitious deadlines or assume they can achieve goals without setbacks. Implementation intentions help counteract this bias by requiring individuals to think through the specific logistical steps involved in execution, thereby reducing the risk of procrastination or failure due to unrealistic expectations. This connects to another bias: the *illusion of explanatory depth*, which is the tendency to believe one understands a topic more deeply than they do. While people tend to be more accurate in assessing procedural knowledge (how to do something), they often overestimate their explanatory knowledge (why it works). Research by Nickerson and Rogers (2010) has shown that simply prompting individuals to explain how they will accomplish a goal reveals gaps in understanding, increasing their awareness of what preparation is truly needed.

Additionally, *implementation proposals* are a variation of cue-based planning that shift responsibility back onto the external agent making a demand. This approach was extensively discussed by former FBI hostage negotiator Chris Voss. It involves asking questions, such as "How am I supposed to get my hands that much money?" to force others to consider logistical constraints and implicit obstacles. Voss notes that this tactic is useful in both high-stakes negotiations and everyday commitments, as it helps reveal underlying ambivalence. Whether assessing the seriousness of a violent threat or a commitment to voting, the presence of concrete implementation details, such as specific times (when they will kill the hostages), locations (where it will happen), and methods (how they will do it) serves as a key indicator of genuine intent (Voss & Raz, 2016, p. 118). Without these details, people are more likely to stall in a deliberation mindset instead of transitioning into an implementation mindset.

The core components of implementation intentions in ECA include *formal commitment*, *salience*, *automaticity*, and *motivation*. *Formal commitment* involves framing plans as "If X happens, then I will do Y," establishing a preloaded response to recurring challenges. *Salience* requires the cue to be specific, visible, and cognitively prominent, as the likelihood of goal achievement increases when the cue is detailed and concrete (Gollwitzer, 1999b). *Automaticity* refers to the mental rehearsal of the cue-action linkage, which reduces the need for conscious decision-making at the critical moment and enhances follow-through. *Motivation* ensures that the chosen action aligns with personal values, thereby increasing *intrinsic motivation* and making progress feel meaningful. By embedding these mechanisms into nudges, ECA practitioners help individuals bridge the gap between intention and action, transforming obstacles into prompts for adaptive decision-making. Whether applied to mental health recovery, negotiation, or everyday goal-setting, implementation intentions offer a structured yet flexible approach to adjusting expectations and promoting follow-through.

Case Analysis

John's rigid belief that he "didn't belong" in the psychiatric ward reflected an overly optimistic view of his social functioning and kept him from engaging reality in a way that would support progress. Erickson did not confront this belief directly. Instead, he used John's repeated claim, "I don't belong here," as a cue for redirection, replying, "But you ARE here." This bypassed diagnostic arguments, instead anchoring John to a concrete reality. Over time, John shifted from denial ("I don't belong here") to acknowledgment ("I know I am here"), creating the turning point that allowed Erickson to introduce a solution-focused frame: "Now that you are here, what do you want to do about LEAVING here?" This structured linkage redirected John from confrontation to actionable planning and ultimately facilitated his transition out of the ward. Accordingly, studies show that individuals who set specific, actionable goals are more likely to follow through than those who remain focused on their emotional state (Gollwitzer, 1999b).

If we dissect Erickson's use of implementation intentions, we can see that it contained several key elements. The first was the use of an *if–then contingency*. The staff's consistent response, "But you ARE here," laid the groundwork for John to eventually reason, "If I am here, then what can I do about it?" The second element was *goal-directed thinking*. Once John acknowledged his reality, Erickson posed a future-oriented question, "Now that you are here, what do you want to do about LEAVING here?" This framed progress as a personal decision. Rather than feeling trapped by circumstances outside his control, John was guided toward recognizing the choices available to him, which led to his eventual employment and to becoming a vital contributing member to his family.

General Application

Implementation intentions link specific actions to predetermined cues, ensuring that goal-directed behaviors are activated automatically when the relevant situation arises. By framing intentions as "If X happens, then I will do Y," individuals create a structured response to obstacles, reducing hesitation and emotional pushback. Research shows that this approach enhances follow-through by making goal pursuit more automatic, minimizing the need for in-the-moment decision-making (Gollwitzer, 1999a).

For individuals who overestimate progress or underestimate challenges (positivity bias), implementation intentions help ground their aspirations in concrete, actionable steps. In therapy, a client prone to believing they are improving simply because they feel motivated might be encouraged to set an explicit plan, "If I go a day without practicing my coping strategies, then I will journal about what got in the way." In coaching, an entrepreneur with an overly optimistic outlook could pre-plan corrective actions, "If my business proposal is rejected, then I will seek feedback from two experts before submitting the next one." By tying behavior to clear triggers, implementation intentions ensure that motivation translates into action, helping individuals with positivity bias balance optimism with practical, measurable progress.

Case 2.4: Doing Things Slowly

The parents of a boy named Jimmy reported that he exhibited intolerable sluggishness. From Jimmy's perspective, his behaviors were beyond reproach because he did as he was told, eventually. For example, he would eat all his breakfast—after two hours had passed. He would put on the socks his mother set out for him, but only after two full hours of delay.

Despite their repeated pleas for him to hurry, there was no change in Jimmy's behavior.

In a private discussion, Erickson recommended that the parents spend a week framing Jimmy's behavior in positive terms. They were advised to emphasize that Jimmy was simply a boy who liked to eat slowly. They were also instructed to stop trying to correct him.

At the end of that week, Erickson told the parents to prepare very small pancakes for Jimmy, serving them one at a time, beginning with 15-minute intervals between each tiny pancake. They were instructed to insist that this method was the perfect solution for someone who liked to eat slowly but still wanted his pancakes hot. Erickson explained that the intervals between his bite-sized pancakes should gradually increase until Jimmy became frustrated and began insisting that they hurry.

Under these conditions, it took less than a week for Jimmy to decide that he did not like eating his food slowly. Now, he consistently finished his breakfast before anyone else in the family.

The following week, Jimmy was invited to a party. Erickson advised his mother to lay out some socks with holes in them for Jimmy to wear. As expected, Jimmy took two hours to put on the socks. Just before the party, his mother insisted that he change into new socks without holes but also told him he would need the same two hours to put them on.

Jimmy pleaded with his mother, saying, "I want to put my socks on faster. I don't want to miss the party!" However, following Erickson's instructions, his mother remained firm. She calmly responded, "I believe you enjoyed dressing slowly this morning, and I still believe that now." She added, "Tomorrow, you might tell me something different and I might believe you," and there was no further discussion about the party.

The next day, Jimmy told his mother that he now liked to dress quickly. She accepted his new preference but reassured him that he was under no obligation to dress fast, if he didn't want to.

Permissive Destabilization

Permissive destabilization, as employed in ECA, is a behavioral tactic that leverages strategic non-interference to encourage self-initiated growth. It does not apply pressure or impose corrective measures, such as punishment or criticism. Instead, it allows an individual's own behaviors and patterns to naturally lead to discomfort or unsustainable conditions, ultimately fostering a self-motivated adaptation. This is achieved by deliberately removing or withholding the usual resistance, constraints, or counter-balance that individuals rely on to regulate their behavior.

This tactic reflects findings that self-generated consequences produce more durable behavioral change than externally imposed correction. It aligns with psychological theories of *intrinsic motivation* and behavioral self-regulation, wherein individuals are more likely to modify their behavior when they perceive the need for change themselves versus when it is externally imposed (Deci & Ryan, 2008). A comparable application can be found in Foster Cline and Jim Fay's (2020) parenting philosophy, which emphasizes natural consequences as an essential means of character development for children, thereby teaching them how to think responsibly.

This tactic is best suited for relationship dynamics where one partner unintentionally enables destructive behavior in the other. As an example, a man attending couples therapy refused to choose between his devoted wife and his 24-year-old mistress, believing the latter fulfilled a deep emotional need. With the support of the therapist, his wife employed permissive destabilization.

Instead of pleading for his love, she "allowed" him to leave the house and move in with his mistress. Without the stabilizing force of his wife's attention and dedication (which had enabled *his* overconfidence), he quickly experienced the natural consequences of his decision. After two weeks in a filthy apartment, away from his children, and disillusioned with the immaturity of the younger woman, he begged his wife to take him back. However, from her new position of power, she set her own terms: He had to remain faithful or she wanted a divorce. Previously, she had been willing to do whatever it took to save the marriage. This was an enabling pattern that had shielded him from experiencing the true weight of his choices.

The design and implementation of permissive destabilization requires the identification of two key elements: *their* personal responsibility and *your* over-protection (enabling). For example, while consulting with a 70-year-old woman who was unhappy about paying all the bills for her 50-year-old son, I asked, "What is it that your son is doing that you con sider to be irresponsible?... And, why is it a problem?" After securing a firm commitment to the identified problem, my next question was, "What things are you doing to help sustain this irresponsible behavior?" This led her to suspend her proactive caretaking, allowing her son to do as he chose but without external stabilization. As a result, he became much more responsible.

This type of critical reasoning and enhanced self-awareness is helpful for the agent (e.g., parent, spouse, supervisor) who must implement the permissive destabilization outside your office. For the target of permissive destabilization, it is different. There is no explanation or negotiation. The success of the operation depends instead on the strategy of *redirection*, or more specifically, pattern interruption. In other words, natural consequences serve as direct feedback, reinforcing the impact of their actions without imposed correction. Ideally, the experience fosters *self-regulation* and *awareness*, as individuals come to recognize their own limits and the necessity of behavioral adaptation. Because the natural consequences become harder to ignore, the irresponsible party begins to ask, "What am I giving up by pursuing this path, and is it worth it?" thereby engaging in a deeper cost-benefit analysis of their behavior.

By integrating these elements with an awareness of opportunity costs, permissive destabilization not only exposes individuals to the reality of their choices but also equips them with the insight and motivation necessary for sustainable growth.

Case Analysis

Erickson's *nudge* addressed Jimmy's sluggishness by subtly redirecting his behavior toward self-regulation. Rather than labeling his behavior as passive-aggressive defiance, Erickson reframed the delays in eating breakfast and putting on socks as personal preferences. This allowed Jimmy to feel ownership of his choices, which is a key component of responsibility.

Jimmy began reconsidering his behaviors after recognizing that his parents' acceptance of his sluggishness could be very frustrating and even costly for him. Over time, the nudge guided him toward progress by allowing him to recognize the benefits of efficiency without feeling coerced.

If we dissect Erickson's use of permissive destabilization, we can see that it contained several key elements. One was *empathy and acceptance.* Jimmy's parents did not become angry or punitive. Instead, they voiced support for his preferences and demonstrated that support in subtle but meaningful ways, such as cooking very small pancakes so he would always have a warm bite available. Another key element was *autonomy and self-reflection.* The nudge respected Jimmy's autonomy by allowing him to experiment with new behaviors on his own terms. Adaptation was framed not as something imposed on him, but as a natural shift that could emerge through self-observation and reflection. A final essential element was that there could be *no escape from consequences.* The strategy depended on the consistent implementation of naturally occurring outcomes. If Jimmy had been allowed to talk his way into going to the party, despite his delay, the affordance would have lost its effectiveness. Avoiding such enabling behaviors was critical to preserving the integrity of the approach. Finally, the nudge did not rely on insight or discipline. It simply made slowness less appealing and efficiency more rewarding.

General Application

Permissive destabilization is a strategic approach that promotes self-motivated growth by allowing individuals to experience the natural consequences of their own choices. Rather than attempting to control the person, this method focuses on shaping the environment by removing artificial reinforcements and withholding unnecessary support. This is particularly useful for individuals with a positivity bias, as they may habitually downplay risks, overestimate their abilities, or dismiss potential negative outcomes. By stepping back and letting reality impose its own lessons, permissive destabilization helps correct overly optimistic assumptions without direct confrontation.

When consulting with an executive who is frustrated with a partner who consistently overcommits to investors and takes unnecessary risks, the business coach might ask, "How are you helping make his behavior possible?" If the answer is, "I clean up his messes," then the next question is, "Under what conditions would you be willing to stop cleaning up his messes?"

Sometimes, the problem is a client's willingness to take advantage of the consultant, such as coming late to meetings and running over. This time-related accountability can be addressed by simply accepting lateness without reprimand. A therapist might respond to a client's habitual tardiness with, "There's no need to explain why you are late. Come whenever you feel comfortable. You are paying for the full hour so I have no reason to complain." Of course, the session needs to be ended precisely at the scheduled time. This mirrors the famous response by an assistant to Leonard Bernstein's habitual tardiness to his own concerts. Without sarcasm, his assistant assured Bernstein, saying, "It's okay, we'll just start without you."

Similarly, in a classroom setting Erickson's use of a deep salaam bow to a chronically late student (prompting the entire class to stand and bow as she awkwardly searched for a seat) was a nonconfrontational yet powerful way of letting natural consequences take effect. This girl had previously been threatened by the dean and rebuked by all her professors for routinely disrupting class. After Erickson's nudge, she became the first student to arrive in class thereafter (Rosen, 1982). By refraining from immediate correction, permissive destabilization allows discomfort and reality to drive meaningful, self-directed behavioral adaptation.

Designing an Optimal Choice Environment (OCE) for Positivity Bias

Designing an *optimal choice environment* for individuals dominated by a positivity bias requires structuring clients' decisions in ways that align with their preference for optimism while subtly guiding them toward better outcomes. Alignment ensures that available choices resonate with the individual's values and aspirations, making them more likely to engage with the decision-making process. Research on motivated reasoning (Kunda, 1990) suggests that people are more likely to accept information that aligns with their preexisting beliefs, meaning that choice environments should be congruent with their worldview. Experiential congruence further enhances this by ensuring that choices "feel right" based on an individual's lived experience, reducing cognitive dissonance and increasing the likelihood of follow-through.

To facilitate effective decision-making, the choice environment should prioritize processing ease, presenting options in a way that is intuitive and easily comprehensible given the individual's expectations and beliefs. Research on cognitive fluency (Alter & Oppenheimer, 2009) indicates that people prefer choices that are easier to process, as these options feel more natural and reliable. Implicit guidance can also be used to shape behavior without triggering pushback, subtly directing individuals toward beneficial outcomes that align with their internal logic. This can be reinforced through resonant framing, where language, metaphors, and narratives match the individual's meaning structures, making new choices seem like natural extensions of their existing beliefs. A positivity bias optimal choice environment does not fight against the individual's optimism but instead leverages it to promote growth, happiness, and well-being, ensuring that positive expectations are met with equally positive realities.

Thought Exercise

Next, you will have the opportunity to apply your design skills. When creating an optimal choice environment for someone with a positivity bias, remember that this environment can include mental landscapes such as imagery, beliefs, and goals, or changes to their physical surroundings. The only requirement is that you respect their right to maintain a hopeful or optimistic outlook about their needs, wants, or aspirations.

For this thought exercise, imagine speaking with a client who was recently released from jail for engaging in non-consensual viewing of women undressing (voyeurism). This man has already been in therapy for this same issue but the more he talked about the urge, the greater his need became for this type of experience, until he finally acted on the impulse and got caught.

Signs of a positivity bias in this case include either a false confidence in his ability to control his impulses, or an exaggerated belief in the effectiveness of his previous therapy, or (most likely) an unrealistic expectation that he could fulfill his need for human contact through secretive, non-consensual sexual observation.

Before reading further, consider how you would respond to this man. What would you say or do to design an optimal choice environment that recognizes his positive motivation toward goal pursuit while also guiding him to evaluate potential obstacles to reintegrating into society as a valued, contributing member?

***

Erickson described a case (2.5 in the case index) involving these same circumstances. After being released from jail the man came to Erickson and said, "I think the analyst is wrong. I'm quitting him. What's your advice on voyeurism?"

In response, Erickson asked the man to describe exactly what he wanted to see. The man provided a highly detailed description of a female body, including the type of clothing she would wear and how she would undress.

Erickson had the man reiterate this fantasy approximately a dozen times. Then he asked, "Where will you find this girl?" The man confessed, "She doesn't exist. She's just my idea." Erickson then asked, "Do you think you'll go out and try to find her?" The man emphatically replied, "Hell no."

Erickson explained this affordance by stating that the man needed to explore his voyeuristic impulses. By guiding him through mental simulation, Erickson allowed the man to vividly visualize, articulate, and reflect on his fantasies, helping him evaluate their meaning and value. As the client imagined himself performing these actions, he implicitly became an outside observer to his behavior (perspective taking). This self-distancing helped redirect the man's behavior and alter his goals. As the client put it, "She doesn't exist. She's just my idea."

Conclusion

In examining the nuances of positivity bias, we have explored its psychological underpinnings, its impact on decision-making, and its implications for personal and social well-being. From cognitive heuristics that favor optimism to the subtle ways in which positive framing influences choices, this chapter has illustrated how this bias shapes our perceptions and actions in profound ways.

A key takeaway from this discussion is that positivity bias is not merely a distortion of reality but a functional adaptation that can serve individuals and societies alike. By focusing on positive outcomes, people may sustain motivation, bolster resilience, and cultivate an outlook that promotes well-being. However, as we have seen, unchecked optimism can also lead to overconfidence, miscalculations, and a failure to prepare for realistic challenges.

The overarching message of this chapter is that awareness of positivity bias allows for a more nuanced engagement with its effects. Rather than viewing it as wholly beneficial or wholly detrimental, we can strive for a balanced approach by leveraging optimism when it fosters growth while remaining vigilant against its potential pitfalls.

By using tactics such as anchoring high, perspective taking, implementation intentions, and permissive destabilization, ECA practitioners guide positive tendencies toward realistic growth, critical reflection, purposeful action, and greater self-correction (Table 2.1). By recognizing the conditions under which positivity bias serves us well and when it may lead us astray, we can refine our decision-making processes, enhance our psychological resilience, and cultivate a mindset that is both hopeful and grounded in value-aligned outcomes.

Quick-Reference Tactic Map

Table 2.1 Tactics Suited for *Positivity Bias* and the Broader Architecture of Strategic Influence

If Client...	*Then Use...*	*Because*
Is overconfident yet under-performing	*Anchoring high*: Setting performance objectives slightly above performance capabilities to encourage growth.	*Primes* higher internal standards and focus without negating optimism.
Becomes emotionally self-absorbed, defensive, or feels victimized	*Perspective taking*: The act of perceiving a situation or understanding a concept from an alternative point of view, such as that of another individual.	Activates *critical thinking* by reducing egocentric appraisal and expanding the range of interpretable meanings.
Enthusiastic but impractical; ignores obstacles	*Implementation intentions*: Strengthening follow-through by linking a goal-directed action to a specific cue or obstacle using an if–then plan.	*Commitment* converts optimism into cue-based action, increasing the likelihood that intention becomes behavior.
Dismissive of feedback or immune to correction	*Permissive destabilization*: Deliberately removing or withholding the usual resistance, constraints, or counter-balance that individuals rely on to regulate their behavior.	*Redirection* occurs when natural consequences prompt self-correction and responsibility.

References

Alter, A. L., & Oppenheimer, D. M. (2009). Uniting the tribes of fluency to form a metacognitive nation. *Personality and Social Psychology Review*, *13*(3), 219–235. https://doi.org/10.1177/1088868309341564

Armor, D. A., & Taylor, S. E. (2002). When Predictions Fail: The Dilemma of Unrealistic Optimism. In *Heuristics and Biases: The Psychology of Intuitive Judgment* (pp. 334–347). Cambridge University Press. https://doi.org/10.1017/CBO9780511808098.021

Bandura, A. (2000). Exercise of human agency through collective efficacy. *Current Directions in Psychological Science*, *9*(3), 75–78. https://doi.org/10.1111/1467-8721.00064

Bargh, J. A., Gollwitzer, P. M., Lee-Chai, A., Barndollar, K., & Trötschel, R. (2001). The automated will: Nonconscious activation and pursuit of behavioral goals. *Journal of Personality and Social Psychology*, *81*(6), 1014–1027. https://doi.org/10.1037/0022-3514.81.6.1014

Beck, A. T. (1976). *Cognitive Therapy and the Emotional Disorders*. International Universities Press.

Carver, C. S., & Scheier, M. F. (2001). *On the Self-Regulation of Behavior*. Cambridge University Press.

Cline, F., & Fay, J. (2020). *Parenting with Love and Logic: Teaching Children Responsibility*. NavPress.

Deci, E. L., & Ryan, R. M. (2008). Self-determination theory: A macrotheory of human motivation, development, and health. *Canadian Psychology / Psychologie Canadienne*, *49*(3), 182–185. https://doi.org/10.1037/a0012801

Duckworth, A. L., Kirby, T. A., Tsukayama, E., Berstein, H., & Ericsson, K. A. (2011). Deliberate practice spells success: Why grittier competitors triumph at the national spelling bee. *Social Psychological and Personality Science*, *2*(2), 174–181. https://doi.org/10.1177/1948550610385872

Dweck, C. S. (2006). *Mindset: The New Psychology of Success*. Random House Publishing Group.

Gollwitzer, P. M. (1999a). Deliberative versus Implemental Mindsets in the Control of Action. In S. Chaiken & Y. Trope (Eds.), *Dual-Process Theories in Social Psychology* (pp. 403–422). Guilford Press.

Gollwitzer, P. M. (1999b). Implementation intentions: Strong effects of simple plans. *American Psychologist*, *54*(7), 493–503. https://doi.org/10.1037/0003-066X.54.7.493

Hmieleski, K. M., & Baron, R. A. (2009). Entrepreneurs' optimism and new venture performance: A social cognitive perspective. *Academy of Management Journal*, *52*(3), 473–488. https://doi.org/10.5465/amj.2009.41330755

Kahneman, D. (2011). *Thinking, Fast and Slow*. Farrar, Straus and Giroux.

Korn, C. W., Sharot, T., Walter, H., Heekeren, H. R., & Dolan, R. J. (2014). Depression is related to an absence of optimistically biased belief updating about future life events. *Psychological Medicine*, *44*(3), 579–592. https://doi.org/10.1017/S0033291713001074

Kross, E., Bruehlman-Senecal, E., Park, J., Burson, A., Dougherty, A., Shablack, H., Bremner, R., Moser, J., & Ayduk, O. (2014). Self-talk as a regulatory mechanism: How you do it matters. *Journal of Personality and Social Psychology, 106*(2), 304–324. https://doi.org/10.1037/a0035173

Kruger, J., & Dunning, D. (1999). Unskilled and unaware of it: How difficulties in recognizing one's own incompetence lead to inflated self-assessments. *Journal of Personality and Social Psychology, 77*(6), 1121–1134. https://doi.org/10.1037/0022-3514.77.6.1121

Kunda, Z. (1990). The case for motivated reasoning. *Psychological Bulletin, 108*(3), 480–498. https://doi.org/10.1037/0033-2909.108.3.480

Langer, E. J. (1975). The illusion of control. *Journal of Personality and Social Psychology, 32*(2), 311–328. https://doi.org/10.1037/0022-3514.32.2.311

Michel-Kröhler, A., Kaurin, A., Heil, L. F., & Berti, S. (2021). Self-distancing as a strategy to regulate affect and aggressive behavior in athletes: An experimental approach to explore emotion regulation in the laboratory. *Frontiers in Psychology, 11*. https://doi.org/10.3389/fpsyg.2020.572030

Milkman, K. L., Beshears, J., Choi, J. J., Laibson, D., & Madrian, B. C. (2011). Using implementation intentions prompts to enhance influenza vaccination rates. *Proceedings of the National Academy of Sciences, 108*(26), 10415–10420. https://doi.org/10.1073/pnas.1103170108

Moore, D. A., & Healy, P. J. (2008). The trouble with overconfidence. *Psychological Review, 115*(2), 502–517. https://doi.org/10.1037/0033-295X.115.2.502

Moser, J. S., Dougherty, A., Mattson, W. I., Katz, B., Moran, T. P., Guevarra, D., Shablack, H., Ayduk, O., Jonides, J., Berman, M. G., & Kross, E. (2017). Third-person self-talk facilitates emotion regulation without engaging cognitive control: Converging evidence from ERP and fMRI. *Scientific Reports*, 7(1), 4519. https://doi.org/10.1038/s41598-017-04047-3

Nickerson, D. W., & Rogers, T. (2010). Do you have a voting plan?: Implementation intentions, voter turnout, and organic plan making. *Psychological Science, 21*(2), 194–199. https://doi.org/10.1177/0956797609359326

Orvell, A., Vickers, B. D., Drake, B., Verduyn, P., Ayduk, O., Moser, J., Jonides, J., & Kross, E. (2021). Does distanced self-talk facilitate emotion regulation across a range of emotionally intense experiences? *Clinical Psychological Science*, 9(1), 68–78. https://doi.org/10.1177/2167702620951539

Özlem, A., & Kross, E. (2018). In D. de Ridder, M. Adriaanse, & K. Fujita (Eds.), *The Routledge International Handbook of Self-Control in Health and Well-Being: Concepts, Theories, and Central Issues* (pp. 374–376). Routledge.

Rosen, S. (1982). *My Voice Will Go with You: The Teaching Tales of Milton H. Erickson, M.D.* W. W. Norton & Company.

Rosenthal, R., & Jacobson, L. (1968). Pygmalion in the classroom. *The Urban Review, 3*(1), 16–20. https://doi.org/10.1007/BF02322211

Tversky, A., & Kahneman, D. (1974). Judgment under Uncertainty: Heuristics and Biases. In L. C. MacLean & W. T. Ziemba (Eds.), *Handbook of the Fundamentals of Financial Decision Making, Part I* (pp. 261–268). World Scientific Publishing Co. Pte. Ltd. https://ideas.repec.org//h/wsi/wschap/9789814417358_0015.html

Voss, C., & Raz, T. (2016). *Never Split the Difference: Negotiating as If Your Life Depended on It.* HarperCollins.

Vygotsky, L. S. (1978). *Mind in Society: The Development of Higher Psychological Processes*. Harvard University Press.

White, R. E., Kuehn, M. M., Duckworth, A. L., Kross, E., & Ayduk, Ö. (2019). Focusing on the future from afar: Self-distancing from future stressors facilitates adaptive coping. *Emotion*, *19*(5), 903–916. https://doi.org/10.1037/emo0000491

Chapter 3

It Is What It Is

Status Quo Bias

It Is What It Is: *Status Quo Bias*

A conservative Indian couple came to me for help as the man was deeply depressed, suffered from chronic headaches, and could not sleep at night. He expressed hope that hypnosis might provide relief. His wife had remained silent since entering the office, but I sensed she had much on her mind. Wanting to hear her perspective, I told the husband that I would like to know more about his wife's observations. He turned to her and nodded, signaling that it was okay for her to speak freely.

His wife had keenly observed that his physical distress began around the same time his relationship with their adult daughter became strained. She explained that they were no longer speaking, and it was breaking her heart. She described her husband as a good man and a loving father but also stubborn and deeply rooted in his conservative Hindu beliefs. She noted that he disapproved of their daughter's choices, her adoption of American clothing, her use of American slang, and, most troubling to him, her desire to date whomever she chose without seeking his permission. As she spoke, he sat rigidly on the couch, staring forward as if into the abyss, his turban wrapped with meticulous precision.

I asked him for his thoughts on his wife's assessment of the situation. He admitted that she was probably right. He then added that he blamed himself entirely, as he had made the decision to move their family to America, an irreversible choice he now deeply regretted.

I confessed that I did not know enough about Hinduism to work as precisely as needed, so I asked him to educate me on the three highest ideals in the Hindu faith. He listed Dharma, the ethical and moral principles that guide a person's actions; Artha, the pursuit of economic security; and Seva, selfless service to others. He explained that these ideals had driven his decision to move his family to America, but he had never anticipated such disastrous consequences. When I asked him what he had envisioned before the move, he shook his head and simply replied, "I don't know."

DOI: 10.4324/9781003797876-4

When I enquired if he was ready for hypnosis, he questioned whether hypnosis was like meditation. I assured him that it was. He explained that he was most accustomed to meditating while sitting on the floor with his legs crossed, so I invited him to assume that posture.

Once he was ready with his eyes closed, I told him that he would remain in trance and not rise from the floor until he had experienced three profound visions. In each vision he would see his daughter many years into the future, wearing American clothing, speaking like an American, and perhaps standing beside an American husband. But these were only superficial appearances. I explained that in the first vision, he would see his daughter living out the true meaning of Dharma. In the second, he would see her embodying the values of Artha, ensuring economic security for his grandchildren. In the third, he would see her dedicating her life to Seva, selfless service to others. Having said that, I left him in meditative silence.

After approximately 20 minutes, he opened his eyes, smiled, and wiped a tear from his cheek. As he returned to the couch, I asked how his body felt. He responded that he felt tremendous relief throughout his entire body.

I told him that if he experienced further issues with depression, headaches, or insomnia, he should call me and we would determine what else needed to be done. However, I never heard from them again.

In this case, the word *hypnosis* is a distraction. It does not clarify the contextual dynamics at play any more than simply saying we had a meaningful interaction. More precisely, my approach was to create a vision of the future that would help the man rationalize and validate an irreversible choice made in the past. More specifically, I guided the man through a process of strategic *choice justification*, in which people justify those choices that are deliberate (conscious decisions) in terms of personal integrity and moral identity. My aim was to strengthen his commitment to his daughter's ability to thrive. This was achieved without asking him to change his deeply held values or his plans for the future. For those who make an irreversible decision but fail to achieve choice justification, regret is likely to intensify as time passes (Walster & Walster, 1970). This overarching methodology (behavioral adaptation without change) is unique to Ericksonian Choice Architecture (ECA) and will be defined and explored in greater detail throughout this chapter.

Recognizing Status Quo Bias in Ericksonian Choice Architecture

Status quo bias is a well-documented cognitive tendency where individuals prefer to maintain their current state rather than embrace change, even when the alternative may be beneficial (Samuelson & Zeckhauser, 1988).

In the vignette above, the father's distress was amplified by an irreversible disruption of the prior status quo (Indian family culture). The *nudge* made his decision to move to America feel acceptable by using future-focused images that highlighted his core values of Dharma, Artha, and Seva. This allowed him to view his daughter's American life as a continuation of those values rather than a loss of them. This preference for keeping things as they are may result from fear of loss, difficulty changing familiar patterns, or feeling unable to make a different choice. In the realm of ECA, recognizing this bias is crucial because it allows practitioners to employ strategic nudges that work within the individual's natural inclinations. Erickson demonstrated a profound ability to navigate this bias, utilizing indirect methods (nudges) that accommodated this state of mind while subtly guiding decision-making toward adaptive modifications.

Erickson did not oppose the need for status quo. Instead, he worked within its boundaries. This chapter explores some of Erickson's casework and then identifies concrete tactics that can be applied broadly in contextualized care for status quo bias. The key takeaway is that one does not need to imitate Erickson's methods precisely, but rather, understand why his tactics were effective and how they can be adapted.

Erickson's Casework and the Application of Tactical Nudges

Understanding status quo bias is essential, but recognizing its presence is only the beginning. Left unexamined, this bias can keep individuals locked in familiar but unproductive patterns, resisting change even when it serves their best interests. What ECA seeks to do is to work with psychological inertia, designing nudges that make change feel like a natural extension of the individual's existing state.

By leveraging techniques such as *bounded choice*, *yes-oriented contingency*, *choice justification*, and *default participation*, Erickson created optimal choice environments that subtly guided individuals toward adaptive modifications. Instead of forcing abrupt shifts, he structured decisions in a way that preserved autonomy while increasing the likelihood of progress.

The following case reviews illustrate how these tactics were applied across various contexts. Whether helping clients reclaim personal agency, guiding individuals through behavioral adjustments, or shaping interactions in leadership and negotiation settings, these examples demonstrate how subtle nudges can help individuals regain a sense of control over their circumstances. This is achieved not by changing their fundamental nature but by repurposing their cognitive tendencies into tools for growth.

Case 3.1: Three-Day Headache

A compelling example of Erickson's nuanced approach to status quo bias is the case of a woman suffering from severe headaches lasting three days each week. Describing his approach, Erickson stated, "The first thing I made clear to her is that she undoubtedly has those headaches for a reason." Instead of suggesting outright elimination, Erickson acknowledged and validated the headaches' existence.

Erickson continued,

> Next, I asked how many of those headaches she needs for that unknown reason. Does she really need them every week, or every two weeks? Does she really need to have them last for three days?...Or, since she has some unknown reason for headaches, is it necessary for her to have the headaches at an inconvenient time? Could that reason be satisfied by having the headaches at a time most convenient for her and for the shortest length of time that satisfies the reason?

By framing progress as a small, reasonable adjustment, he supported the woman's ability to choose while respecting her innate aversion to transformative change. As Erickson stated, "Thereby I emphasized that she has the headaches, that she can KEEP the headache, the duration, the severity."

After four weeks of being free from pain, she returned to the office and told Erickson that she was going to have a headache. Disrupting her black-and-white thinking, Erickson presented a range of options, asking,

> When would be the most convenient time to have the headache? Would it be possible for her to precipitate the headache a few hours in advance, or even a day in advance? Or could she delay it a few hours or even a day?

Her reaction was, "It might as well be just the usual headache." Erickson did not show any signs of approval or disapproval rather he waited for her to continue. She then decided that her headache might as well last the usual three days and it might just as well occur unexpectedly, the way it usually did. In other words, she was expressing her preference for the status quo.

Erickson stated, "That would be a sensible thing, because a month from now you might want to alter it...a month from now you can put into force any special alterations you want to make." This statement illustrates the concept of *autonomous stability*, her exercising her right to remain as she is, without pressure, while also maintaining the freedom to change on her own terms. Erickson reported that after that headache, she went another three weeks headache free. Before meeting Erickson, there had been no limitations on the intensity, duration, or frequency of her headaches.

Following a skillful series of negotiations, her choices became bounded (limited) without the woman experiencing any loss of freedom.

Bounded Choice

This approach reflects *bounded choice*, which retains familiar elements while guiding individuals toward more favorable outcomes. More specifically, bounded choice means carefully limiting the available options to guide a decision while still allowing the person to feel in control of the choice. This tactic is particularly useful for meeting the needs of individuals exhibiting status quo bias.

Psychological research on macro-level choice architecture supports this approach, showing that structuring and limiting options can reduce decision fatigue and increase compliance (Thaler & Sunstein, 2009). While it's often assumed that people prefer having more choices, evidence suggests otherwise. For example, one study explored whether making a personal choice is always rewarding. Although participants expected to feel better simply from choosing, they were only more satisfied when their options were genuinely appealing (Botti & lyengar, 2004). Instead of treating bounded choice as something people must be persuaded to accept, it may be more accurate to view limits on negative options as inherently appealing, especially for those who struggle to perceive positive alternatives.

Case Analysis

In traditional psychotherapeutic literature, this case has been described as an example of symptom prescription (O'Hanlon & Hexum, 1990). Similarly, other instances of Erickson using bounded choice have been labeled as symptom displacement or symptom substitution. However, these terms do not align with *choice-centric care*, which prioritizes leveraging existing behaviors as entry points for adaptive progress.

We should recognize that Erickson's use of bounded choice provided the woman with a sense of control, allowing her to moderate her phenomenological experience on her own terms. If we dissect this approach, we can identify several key elements. First, Erickson *validated* the status quo by stating, "The first thing I made clear to her is that she undoubtedly has those headaches for a reason." This affirmation acknowledged her experience without attempting to immediately change it, which helped preserve her sense of agency. Next, he *introduced small modifications*, a stratagem often referred to as *pattern interruption*. Instead of questioning whether she should stop having headaches altogether, Erickson asked, "How many of those headaches does she need for that unknown reason? Does she really need them every week, or every two weeks? Does she really need to have them last for three days?" Nudging her toward more manageable options, he asked her if that reason could be satisfied by having the headaches at a more convenient time and for the shortest length of time that satisfies the reason. As Erickson explained, "I put it in such a way that she is not going to confront me with the idea, 'But I can't get rid of the headache!' I am just suggesting a modification, and she can accept that."

Another critical element was *strategic proximity*. Erickson did not propose eliminating the headaches altogether; instead, he limited the scope of change by suggesting she "keep the headache, the duration, the severity," and only adjust the frequency. This positioning created a sense of longing by placing a slightly improved state within sight but just beyond reach, thereby increasing her motivation to pursue it. As Erickson noted, "I am being too conservative...She wants me to be less conservative but it is her want, not my insistence." By framing it this way, the environment for choice was optimized at unconscious levels.

Finally, Erickson structured the nudge to include the possibility of future adaptation by inviting the woman's future self into the decision-making process. He framed her current acceptance of the headaches as a reasonable choice, adding, "That would be a sensible thing because a month from now you might want to alter it. A month from now you can put into force any special alterations you want to make." In doing so, he preserved her autonomy while planting a seed for growth over time.

While not every instance of bounded choice will follow the sequence illustrated by Erickson, there are four key elements that characterize this tactic. Most importantly, *a limited set of options* is presented to avoid argument, decision fatigue, or choice paralysis (curated options). These options are then framed as minor modifications or anchored to the status quo (framing and anchoring). Also, by bounding choices, complexity is reduced, making it easier for individuals to evaluate and decide (simplification). Despite all these constraints, autonomy is maintained ensuring that individuals feel a sense of control and satisfaction over their decisions to change or not change. By integrating these elements, bounded choice creates an environment where adaptation is more desirable and seamlessly integrated into existing habits.

General Application

Bounded choice allows familiar behaviors to continue while subtly limiting the ways they can be expressed (e.g., decreasing the size, intensity, frequency, duration, or limiting the context of a problematic behavior). These modifications occur incrementally, ensuring that established behaviors are not eliminated outright but rather gradually reshaped. This subtractive approach facilitates change without overwhelming the individual. Recent research by Adams et al. (2021) demonstrates that individuals systematically default to seeking additive transformations while frequently overlooking subtractive ones. This means that while many people could reduce the severity of problematic behavior, they do not independently think to do so. While an overtly additive approach is most suitable for individuals exhibiting an implicit change bias (Neroni et al., 2024), those with a status quo bias may respond more favorably to a subtractive approach (one that reduces options rather than introducing new ones) since it is less likely to be experienced as threatening.

As an illustration, consider the problem of procrastination, which often involves avoiding decisions and delaying action even when the person knows that taking action would be beneficial (Steel, 2007). Instead of confronting procrastination head-on, bounded choice allows for subtle adjustments by working within the individual's existing patterns. Instead of asking them to stop procrastinating, one might ask, "How long does your procrastination need to last?" or "What amount of time could you reduce your procrastination by without really noticing the difference?" (duration). Similarly, one could explore, "Do you need to procrastinate daily, or would once a week be enough?" (frequency), "How much effort do you need to put into procrastinating? If you were lazy about procrastinating, what would that look like?" (intensity), or "In which workspace are you least likely to procrastinate?" (context). By subtly reshaping procrastination, bounded choice shields the collaborative relationship from conflict and transforms avoidance into a structured pathway toward action.

Case 3.2: The Childless Couple

Erickson often oriented people toward the future, using this perspective to clarify both the nature of the problem and possible solutions. One example of this approach can be seen in his work with a childless couple. As Erickson stated, "They were very happily married, so far as they understood...They said they didn't want children." The problem was that the husband, Edward, was torn between his love for his wife and his loyalty to his domineering mother, who lived with them. As Erickson put it, "she really governed that household." Having reached the end of her patience, Edward's wife delivered an ultimatum, "Either mother goes or I go. There can't be two of us under one roof."

This man loved his wife and did not want to lose her. But he also loved his mother and did not feel able to kick her out of the only home she had. He did not know how to choose the choice that had to be chosen.

Rather than offering advice or engaging in confrontation, Erickson created a choice preview by guiding Edward into a deeply reflective state and asking him to imagine it was six years in the future. Then Erickson asked,

"Can you tell me how did it happen that you finally decided that your mother should leave your home and live by herself? Explain to me just how it came about and how she got along." The man replied, "You know, back in 1959 I didn't want to kick my mother out, but she made me. And, it was a most fortunate thing"..."I knew she was a very, very capable woman... always managing things in the best way possible." This exercise allowed Edward to justify a necessary decision by attributing it to circumstances.

The man continued with his choice preview, "Somehow my life with Jeanie also changed after my mother left our home. I can't exactly describe these changes, but our life changed for the better." Before the couple left the office, Erickson told Edward to go home and speculate with his wife and mother about their situation and to arrive at a nice conclusion.

During the discussion between the three of them, Edward's mother decided on her own that she should move into a place that she could call her own. As expected, his mother made a successful transition to independent living, and unexpectedly, Edward and his wife's relationship flourished in new ways. They later decided to have children, something they had not previously considered. This nudge demonstrates how *prospective choice justification* (mentally simulating future decisions and their positive outcomes) can facilitate change while preserving an individual's sense of agency.

Choice Justification

Another useful tactic for creating an optimal choice environment for status quo bias is choice justification, which involves helping individuals evaluate, explain, or simulate the outcomes of a decision that was made in the past or that needs to be made in the future. This process helps clients align the decision with their values and goals. A primary function of this tactic is to reinforce commitment to a chosen path. Beyond shaping long-term behavior and self-perception, choice justification can also reduce internal conflict, a phenomenon known as post-decision dissonance (Knox & Inkster, 1968).

When individuals justify a conscious decision, they align that choice with their self-concept, reinforcing their sense of identity. If a person sees continuity between their present and future self, they are more likely to justify deliberate decisions that involve long-term benefits. By strengthening perceived connectedness (through narrative framing, goal-setting, or highlighting past consistencies) ECA practitioners can help individuals make future-oriented decisions that align with their broader, future-oriented goals. Studies that explore the connection between a person's present and future-self show that people are more likely to choose short-term rewards over long-term benefits when they feel disconnected from their future-self

(Urminsky, 2017). These findings highlight the importance of designing choice environments that make future-focused decisions feel personally relevant and meaningful in the present moment.

Ironically, choice justification can also transform the past. For example, back in 1994, I met with a man who physically assaulted his girlfriend in front of their two young daughters. His violence was so bad that a judge terminated all his parental rights. The children were secretly relocated out of state with their mother. The judge told my client he would never see his daughters again. After telling me this story, and with a look of immense pain, he said, "My girls will grow up remembering me as a monster. There's nothing I can do to make it up to them or set things right. I'll spend the rest of my life regretting what I did." Having made this confession, he hung his head forward, staring at the ground in shame.

I decided to utilize his suffering and help him see how this choice, to carry the pain, may serve a meaningful purpose. After leaving him alone with his thoughts for a little while, I asked, "How do you feel about your actions?" Without hesitation, he responded, "I feel like a piece of shit!" My reply was,

> Good. That means you have a conscience. With the right amount of therapy, this conscience of yours could really be valuable in the next relationship. You will be able to do for the next woman what you did not know how to do for your daughter's mother.

To be clear, it was not his violent behavior that was justified but rather his choice to feel intense remorse and to seek out professional help. The use of choice justification shifted the client from self-loathing to recognition of remorse as a form of moral integrity. This case illustrates how the reinterpretation of one's own choices can convert shame into responsibility and future-oriented commitment. Erickson frequently employed similar approaches, helping clients discover meanings that supported adaptive action rather than paralysis.

Case Analysis

In the case above, Erickson applied the concept of choice justification by helping Edward, a man torn between his loyalty to his domineering mother and his love for his wife, to mentally simulate future outcomes that align with his values. The central issue is Edward's inability to make a difficult decision: whether to satisfy the needs of his wife or to maintain the status quo by continuing to host his mother. Psychological research on post-decision dissonance (Knox & Inkster, 1968) highlights that people often experience internal conflict after making difficult decisions. Erickson's approach was effective because it empowered Edward to mentally justify his choice before making it, aligning the decision with his core values and alleviating the psychological burden of internal conflict (choice justification). This helped minimize dissonance, allowing Edward to embrace the decision and reduce feelings of regret or internal conflict. Erickson's nudge helped facilitate a decision while preserving his client's sense of agency and self-consistency.

If we dissect this approach, we can identify three key elements. One is the *validation of emotional conflict.* Erickson acknowledged the conflicting emotions and values Edward was experiencing. This response reinforced Edward's autonomy in the decision-making process. Erickson did not push Edward to choose between his wife and mother immediately, but instead created a space for thoughtful reflection.

A second key element was the use of *choice preview.* Erickson helped Edward mentally simulate a future scenario in which the decision has already been made. By asking, "Can you tell me how did it happen that you finally decided that your mother should leave your home and live by herself? Explain to me just how it came about and how she got along," Erickson invited Edward to project himself six years into the future. This allowed Edward to evaluate the decision from a distance, gain clarity about its benefits, and make sense of it as if it were already resolved. The intent was not to dictate the choice but to enable Edward to retrospectively justify it, reinforcing a sense of agency and appropriateness in the imagined outcome.

A third element is *prospective justification.* This prospective version of choice justification is applied before making a significant decision that carries the potential for regret. By guiding Edward through an imagined future, Erickson allowed him to mentally legitimize the decision to have his mother move out. This process naturally introduces *progress bias* as it encourages individuals to focus on the broader trajectory of their future. For example, within the context of the mental simulation Edward confessed, "You know, back in 1959 I didn't want to kick my mother out, but she made me. And, it was a most fortunate thing..." From research we know that people are more willing to make choices today, which may benefit them in the years to come, when this future-self shares similarities with the present-self, when it is viewed in vivid *and* realistic terms, and when it is seen in a positive light (Hershfield, 2011). Thus, prospective justification helps shift attention away from temporary discomfort and toward the enduring benefits of a well-considered decision. It also seems that this nudge helped bring previously unconscious emotional needs into conscious awareness. As Erickson later observed, Edward and his wife's relationship flourished in new ways, eventually leading them to consider and pursue having children, something they had not envisioned before.

In some cases, such as the one described at the beginning of this chapter (the conservative, immigrant father), the decision has already been made, and the individual is navigating its aftermath. In these instances, *retrospective justification* serves as a strategy to reinforce commitment to the chosen path by emphasizing how the outcome aligns with personal expectations, values, or long-term goals. Rather than prompting deliberation about what to do next, this process engages *critical thinking* at an implicit level, consolidating the meaning of what has already been chosen. For individuals who do not wish to pursue further change, this process affirms the status quo by framing it as a deliberate and meaningful choice. Additionally, retrospective justification enhances the intrinsic appeal of the decision by reducing post-decision dissonance and increasing psychological ownership over the chosen course of action. Research suggests that individuals who perceive their past decisions as self-concordant (that is, aligned with their personal values) experience greater satisfaction and long-term motivation (Sheldon & Elliot, 1999). By reinforcing the perceived value of the current circumstances, retrospective justification not only solidifies commitment but also fosters engagement in productive and fulfilling ways.

General Application

Choice previews involve imagining or simulating potential outcomes associated with a given decision, whether that decision is to act or to remain inactive. By framing both action and inaction as choices, individuals can better evaluate their consequences and avoid defaulting to passive decisions. The general application of choice justification, across a variety of concerns, is the most appropriate tactic when a person is struggling with decision inertia or feeling trapped by the perceived risks of change.

Consider the phenomena of *regret asymmetry*: when a person regrets trying and failing more than they regret sticking with a negative status quo. This can understandably discourage their initiative or participation in progress-focused activities. However, the dynamic can quickly shift by having the person role-play their future self in an impromptu style, explaining to their present self the value of a rewarding status quo that emerged because of an outcome initially framed as failure. It is remarkable how much insight people can self-generate when asked to explore a poignant prompt within the context of role-play.

In addition to status quo bias, discomfort with solution-oriented action can also be influenced by *omission bias*, a psychological tendency wherein people judge harmful actions as more morally blameworthy than equally or even more harmful inactions. For example, if a doctor fails to administer a life-saving drug due to its experimental nature, a pool of jurors may perceive this omission as less negligent than if the doctor had used the drug and it caused irreversible damage.

This can lead to regrets of omission. These are missed opportunities, paths not taken, or actions left undone. Researcher Daniel Pink (2022) explains that while people can often rationalize or make amends for mistakes they actively made, they struggle more with inaction because they are left wondering what could have been. For these situations prospective choice justification is useful. For example, "Imagine a future version of yourself doing something really spectacular, something that would not have been possible if you had married that French girl." This gently guides the individual back into a future filled with possibility.

Another common area where choice previews are useful is the avoidance of difficult conversations, conflict, or condemnation. When facing a difficult conversation, individuals may instinctively hesitate, fearing discomfort or negative repercussions. A useful image for countering this avoidance might be evoked by saying, "See the future outcome that justifies having this difficult conversation. See how the situation improves with honest communication, and how proud you feel for having done it." This prompt for future simulation is not to be confused with reason-based discussions about the same topic. Verbal logic does not influence emotional states to the same degree as vivid imagery and a virtual experience.

Case 3.3: Becoming Christ-Like

An early example of Erickson's novel communication approach involved a man at Worcester State Hospital who believed he was Jesus Christ.[1] Before getting into the details of this case, it is important to learn more about the context in which it took place.

The design of the Worcester State Hospital, built in 1856, followed the principles of the Kirkbride Plan. Dr. Thomas Story Kirkbride's philosophy emphasized the connection between the physical environment and mental health. The key elements of this philosophy centered on creating a physical environment that promoted healing and well-being for patients. Therapeutic architecture played a crucial role, with buildings thoughtfully designed to include large windows that brought in natural light and fresh air, both of which were believed to have a calming and restorative effect. The hospitals were also set on expansive, picturesque grounds featuring gardens, walking paths, and farms to encourage physical activity and connection to nature. Additionally, the design supported the moral treatment philosophy by providing patients with clean, comfortable, and aesthetically pleasing surroundings, aiming to inspire hope and dignity.

It was in this inspiring setting that Erickson first began to experiment with *micro-level choice architecture*. Thus, when assigned to a patient who had the delusional belief that he was Jesus Christ, Erickson looked for ways to inspire hope and restore the man's dignity. Erickson described the situation this way, "And here was this patient, wrapped up in a sheet, walking around communicating with God." A centerpiece of hospital policy was to encourage patients to engage in productive life activities, such as farming or carpentry. So, while walking across the hospital grounds, discussing the goodness of God's creation and the importance of using the skills and abilities God has given us, Erickson stopped at the dirt tennis courts and made an important observation.

There Erickson noticed some uneven spots on the dirt court and declared that surely God did not want the doctors playing tennis on an uneven court. Erickson asked if the man might be able to help by leveling the courts. After all, as Jesus, it was his mission to serve humankind. The man accepted this logic and said he would certainly try. After completion, Erickson studied the man's work and let him know that he was an excellent tennis court grounds keeper.

Next, Erickson noticed that the psychology lab wanted a handyman to build some bookcases. While talking about this with the man, Erickson mentioned the fact that Jesus Christ grew up as a carpenter. The man decided that he was probably up for the task so he built the bookcases, eventually becoming the psychology department's handyman. The man eventually came to embrace his new identity as someone who is fully human, and a valued contributing member to his community.

Instead of confronting the patient's belief, Erickson expanded upon it in a way that facilitated engagement and personal growth. Therapy outcome research supports this approach, indicating that affirming an individual's current state while embedding new, complementary behaviors can increase collaborative engagement and reduce client and practitioner discordance (Hayes et al., 2003).

Yes-Oriented Contingency

Yes-oriented contingency in ECA is a tactic that facilitates change by integrating new actions as natural extensions of existing behaviors. By emphasizing continuity over change, this approach makes adaptation feel effortless and nondisruptive. Instead of challenging current beliefs or behaviors, it affirms and validates an individual's existing state, reducing the discordance between client needs and the practitioner's initiatives. New options are framed as enhancements that are aligned with familiar patterns to encourage receptivity.

Importantly, this tactic leverages *intrinsic motivation* by linking new actions to an existing mindset, making engagement feel like a seamless progression rather than a fundamental shift. By preserving habitual behaviors or emotional patterns, while introducing transformative elements, yes-oriented contingency encourages gradual identity shifts. Furthermore, anchoring change within familiar contexts allows individuals to perceive transitions as an organic evolution versus an imposed disruption and increases the likelihood of lasting adoption.

Case Analysis

In traditional psychotherapeutic literature, this case has been categorized as behavioral task assignment, reframing, and utilization (O'Hanlon & Hexum, 1990). Similar approaches by Erickson have also been described in the same textbook as utilization of behavioral patterns or symptom prescription. While these terms capture the mechanics of the operation, they do not specify when or why it should be applied. Yes-oriented contingency provides a more precise framework by linking this methodology to situations where a status quo bias is present, offering clearer guidance on its practical use.

In the case above, we can see that Erickson's use of yes-oriented contingency provided the man with a sense of personal dignity, allowing him to evolve his identity on his own terms rather than feeling forced to change his beliefs. If we dissect this approach, we can identify several key elements. The first was the affirmation of the status quo. After accepting the patient's preferred identity (as Jesus Christ), Erickson entered the patient's belief system and engaged in conversations about God's creation. This approach reduced defensiveness and fostered open dialogue, making the patient more receptive to Erickson's guidance.

The second element involved introducing additive solutions. Erickson presented work opportunities as natural extensions of the patient's divine role. For example, when they came across an uneven tennis court, Erickson reframed the task of leveling it as a mission aligned with the patient's sacred duty, saying, "Surely God wouldn't want the doctors playing tennis on an uneven court." This framing encouraged the patient to take action while supporting his chosen identity. Similarly, when the psychology lab required bookcases, Erickson invoked the idea that Jesus Christ was a carpenter. This alignment between the task and the patient's identity allowed for a seamless adoption of the new role. Over time, the patient became a valuable contributor to the hospital community, embracing his identity as a skilled handyman.

Finally, Erickson leveraged intrinsic motivation by linking new actions to an expression of the patient's existing self-concept. The patient was not asked to abandon his belief but was instead given opportunities to enact purpose-driven behavior through tangible contributions. This method utilized the unconscious preference for maintaining the status quo while subtly guiding the patient toward new accomplishments, making adaptation feel natural and self-initiated.

This case shows how carefully preserving familiar parts of a person's identity can turn them into paths toward engagement rather than barriers to change. Instead of challenging the man's core beliefs, Erickson created an easy path that allowed him to carry familiar roles into new, socially constructive settings. The success of this approach lies in its quiet alignment: Meaningful actions were presented as natural extensions of existing narratives, turning identity preservation into a source of contribution. What we learn here is that sustainable behavioral pivots often emerge not from confrontation, but from the strategic layering of purpose onto preexisting frameworks. Yes-oriented contingencies honor the past while quietly redesigning the future.

General Application

A yes-oriented contingency preserves an individual's habitual behaviors while incorporating a transformational element. This approach affirms the status quo and then ties it to a growth-oriented action. For instance, when working with individuals struggling with anxious obsessions, a therapist might say, "Yes, you will probably spend a lot of time worrying about what could go wrong, and you can learn a lot about good contingency planning each time you become anxious." Or, "Yes, fear and anxiety are sometimes warranted, especially when felt at the right time, in the right place, and for the right reasons." Another example might be, "You should allow enough anxiety to motivate you to carefully pursue your values and goals." Similarly, the therapist might say, "Yes, it's not so easy to stop worrying on our own. Who do you know that offers the best encouragement?" or

> Yes, you may get overly anxious, and, if you pause to take a single breath before reacting, then next time you may be able to take two deep breaths. Work your way up to three deep breaths and you will be surprised by the benefits.

By embedding a small but constructive action within a familiar habit, yes-oriented contingency fosters incremental progress without creating feelings of pressure or coercion. This leads to incremental progress by attaching change to established routines, making the next step easier, more repeatable, and more likely to endure (Clear, 2018).

Case 3.4: Wasting Time in Therapy

Erickson briefly described a case involving a woman who weighed 255 pounds and wanted help with the problem of obesity. She had been in therapy before but it was not successful. She described herself as being resistant to any attempts by men to manipulate her.

When it became apparent to Erickson that she did not want to talk about issues that were relevant to weight loss, he decided to be forthright, saying, "I believe that no matter what I do, you will continue to insist on wasting the therapy hour." She did not reject this statement but instead continued to waste time.

Before the hour ended, Erickson acknowledged that she was indeed manipulating him. He also pointed out that it was a privilege that came with a price. She could continue wasting his time, but only if she demonstrated some gradual improvement in her overall condition. In other words, if she wanted Erickson to witness and validate her ability to defy authority figures, she would have to commit to some other means of making progress. Opting out of therapy was an unappealing option for someone determined to maintain the status quo. Faced with this paradox, she might have felt that failure to commit would require change (a new therapist) whereas progress could be achieved doing the same as before (wasting time). Ironically, her progress was made contingent on her maintaining existing behaviors.

Default Participation

While *utilization* is one of the most celebrated skill sets in Ericksonian therapy, its broad application and varied manifestations indicate that utilization is a general strategy rather than a concrete technique. In other words, there are many types of utilization with differing tactical applications. The type of utilization described in the preceding case is more precisely described as the design and incorporation of default participation.

In macro-level choice architecture, default participation (or *default option*) refers to automatic enrollment in a service or decision unless the individual actively opts out. Defaults, which are preselected options that take effect without proactive choice, are increasingly common. A familiar example is signing up for a free online service, where users are automatically enrolled in marketing emails unless they uncheck a box before submitting. Since people often default to inaction, or avoid making decisions, leveraging a default position can be a reliable form of influence.

To provide for the welfare of the public, governments need a means of influencing their citizen's behavior. This is why opt-in and opt-out designs are becoming important components in policy development and legislation. For example, research has shown that organ donation rates are significantly higher in countries where citizens are automatically enrolled as donors by default, compared to countries requiring active enrollment (Johnson & Goldstein, 2003). Another study showed that automatic enrollment in 401(k) plans significantly increases participation rates (86% vs. 37%) and leads most contributors to invest in money market funds, demonstrating its positive influence on savings behavior and its role in narrowing demographic disparities (Madrian & Shea, 2001). The conclusion of these and numerous other studies is that default participation is an effective form of guidance.

To further make this point, one study that manipulated the default electricity provider (gray versus green electricity sources) found that both the default option and how strongly people felt about their choices influenced what they decided. However, having a strong opinion did not seem to weaken the power of the default option. People still tended to go with the default, even if they had contrary beliefs (Vetter & Kutzner, 2016).

Within the context of ECA, default participation is defined as any design that makes progress contingent on existing behavioral tendencies (such as a habit, compulsion, or personality trait), so that non-participation requires actively opting out. While this tactic has broad application across various mental states, it is highlighted in this chapter because research shows that individuals with a status quo bias are especially likely to stick with default options (Jachimowicz et al., 2019; Samuelson & Zeckhauser, 1988). However, defaults are not always chosen due to status quo bias alone. They may also be preferred because they require less cognitive effort (*effort reduction bias*), are perceived as official recommendations or endorsements (*authority bias*), or, in some cases, enable individuals to resist external influence while still maintaining the status quo (*reactance*).

Case Analysis

This latter possibility (reactance) is evident in Erickson's interactions with the woman who did not wish to be manipulated. Her case illustrates the occasional overlap of biases, in this instance status quo bias and reactance. In other words, when a person defiantly decides to "stand their ground," they are, in effect, fighting to preserve a status quo. As explained by Weinberger and Stoycheva (2019), *heuristics* are arational (use different rules than conscious logic). Thus, it was irrelevant that the woman actively sought help from male therapists. She remained unwilling to let a man manipulate her.

The essential point to recognize is that Erickson's use of default participation provided the woman with a sense of control, allowing her to moderate her phenomenological experience on her own terms. If we dissect Erickson's use of default participation, we can see three essential elements. The first was validating the status quo. Erickson stated, "I believe that no matter what I do, you will continue to insist on wasting the therapy hour," thereby acknowledging her current behavior without attempting to directly challenge it.

The second element involved introducing small modifications. In this case, the subtle shift was Erickson redirecting her focus away from her body and toward her interactions with him. This allowed her to preserve her need for control by continuing to engage in non-productive dialogue throughout their sessions (essentially maintaining a version of the status quo) while moving away from using her obesity as the defining reference point. Erickson facilitated this change by framing her presence in his office as a privilege she paid for by making progress.

The third element was the *opt-out contingency*, also known as a passive contingency. Although Erickson did not articulate this explicitly, the structure of the therapy made it clear: The woman's progress would continue automatically unless she disrupted the status quo. That disruption could come either by engaging in meaningful dialogue, which would lead to further positive outcomes, or by quitting therapy. Unlike active contingencies, which require deliberate action to produce a result, passive contingencies operate through inertia. People remain in the default state unless they actively choose to *opt out*.

In doing these things, Erickson leveraged default participation, ensuring that her need to resist was met while also automatically enrolling her in a program of self-directed reform. This approach was successful because it aligned with her immediate emotional needs.

Within the context of ECA, default participation involves making progress contingent on an individual's immediate motivations, established habits, or personality traits. As an example of default participation, a client who was nervously pacing back and forth across Erickson's office was told that each movement from one side of the room to the other could make him feel more relaxed and more ready to enter a therapeutic trance. Similarly, in the introductory chapter to this book, Erickson described how he might utilize a client's refusal to speak by saying, "As you sit there in conscious silence, let your unconscious mind work." By embedding therapeutic progress within the client's operational tendencies, a default participation design increases accessibility and fosters seamless engagement. This approach, known as *frictionless design*, was a hallmark of Erickson's methods. It also aligns with research showing that reducing decision friction increases cooperative engagement (Williams et al., 2020).

General Application

Although default participation is widely used, it can be difficult to recognize within the context of ECA because its effects occur in the mental landscape versus the external world. There, it silently shapes various aspects of mental processing, including thoughts, emotions, attitudes, motivations, memory, and perception. That said, its application across different concerns can be surprisingly simple—make a status quo behavior the default for progress.

As an example of designing default participation, a college student came to me with a problem he was too ashamed to name. After some tentative guesswork, I said, "You are worried that something is horribly wrong with you because you are now in college and yet you have never kissed a girl." He nodded yes, flushed with emotion, and explained that all his friends now had girlfriends. He could not imagine how he would ever get married and have a family because he was too shy to kiss a girl.

To engage his shyness as the default option rather than as a barrier, I said,

> I know several beautiful girls who have been burned by charming guys and now avoid anyone who seems overly self-confident. The next time you are at a social gathering, be more obvious about your shy nature and notice who smiles at you.

He was encouraged by this idea but still unsure what to do if a girl seemed attracted to him. So, I explained,

> Just do not reject her. If she smiles at you, smile back. If she walks toward you, walk toward her. If she tells you her name, tell her yours. If she looks into your eyes, look into hers. If she leans toward you, lean toward her. Given enough of this, your lips will eventually collide.

In other words, I framed the interaction as something that could unfold on its own, unless he actively chose to *opt out*.

At the opposite end of the spectrum, consider the possibility of a trainee under your supervision who exhibits a *confirmation bias* in the form of the *Semmelweis effect* (a reflexive tendency to reject new information that contradicts established beliefs). This can make teaching challenging, as these individuals only engage with what they already know. In this case, you make their pushback the opt-out contingency, by saying, "It's important that you voice every disagreement that comes to mind; otherwise, I won't know where your understanding is incomplete. If you are debating me, I'll know you're genuinely engaged in learning." Ironically, to *opt out* of learning, they must agree with the new information that you are presenting.

For those who are wishing to better understand the difference between default participation and yes-oriented contingency, it is a matter of active versus passive engagement. A yes-oriented contingency actively invites participation through an additive process, making the new behavior feel like a natural extension of the person's existing identity or routine. In contrast, default participation passively encourages progress by establishing it as the default option, where progress emerges unless actively contested or opted out of. Thus, the crucial difference between yes-oriented contingencies and default participation in the context of ECA lies in how engagement is structured and initiated.

Designing an Optimal Choice Environment (OCE) for Status Quo Bias

The mission of a choice architect is to empower individuals to make optimal choices for themselves while preserving personal liberty. Instead of enforcing change, the goal is to create an environment that naturally supports beneficial choices. This is particularly important when working with individuals who exhibit a status quo bias—those who prefer maintaining their current state, even when better alternatives exist.

An *optimal choice environment* supports an individual's best interests, values, and long-term goals while minimizing cognitive, social, and emotional barriers. Research on cognitive load theory suggests that simplifying choices and aligning them with existing beliefs can significantly increase cooperative exchanges (Sweller, 2011). ECA optimizes this process by acknowledging the existing state, introducing attractive choices, and reinforcing autonomy. By focusing on incremental modifications versus direct confrontation or pressure to change, individuals can be guided toward adaptive behaviors in a way that feels intuitive and non-threatening. This approach is particularly effective for those who find comfort in their current preferences and habits, allowing them to explore alternatives without feeling coerced.

A well-structured optimal choice environment includes several key features. *Empowerment* ensures that individuals maintain a sense of autonomy while being gently guided toward beneficial outcomes. *Reflective readiness* helps engage higher cognitive functions and flexible motivational states, making adaptation more accessible. *Alignment* matches individual preferences with available choices, reducing friction in decision-making. Finally, *salience* ensures that options are cognitively accessible and easy to process, preventing decision fatigue.

Thought Exercise

Next, you will have the opportunity to apply your design skills. When creating an optimal choice environment for someone with a status quo bias, remember that this environment can include mental landscapes such as imagery, beliefs, and goals, or involve the adaptive reconstruction of their physical surroundings. The only requirement is that you respect their right to maintain their status quo.

For this thought exercise, imagine speaking with a male client who tells you that he spends every day sitting alone in his room, doing nothing. Notably, he does not ask for help changing this behavior; he simply presents it as an unfortunate reality. When you ask what he has tried to do to change this pattern, his body stiffens and he looks visibly uncomfortable. Instead of offering helpful information, he merely shakes his head. You recognize that his current state of mind reflects a status quo bias.

Before reading further, consider how you would respond to this person. What would you say or do to design an optimal choice environment that acknowledges his need for stability while gently inviting the possibility of improved quality of life?

***

Erickson described a case (3.5 in the case index) involving a man who complained of wasting all his time sitting alone in his room every day. In response, Erickson asked, "Can't you waste time elsewhere? ...How about wasting time at the library?" When the man accepted this possibility as a viable option, Erickson pointed out that the library had a comfortable sitting area surrounded by magazine racks.

The man began visiting the library daily to read magazines. During one visit, another patron noticed him reading about cave spelunking and asked if it was something he enjoyed. The man admitted he had never tried it, prompting the patron to invite him to join a group of cave explorers. This experience eventually led the man to meet another group of people who enjoyed downhill skiing in the mountains near Flagstaff, Arizona. Through his time at the library, he gradually learned how to connect with others who shared his interests.

Erickson's approach exemplified a yes-oriented contingency, where the discovery of new opportunities was made contingent on the man's existing habit of wasting time. Instead of asking him to change his behavior, Erickson simply altered the physical context in which that behavior occurred. Once the man established a routine of reading magazines at the library, his social progress became a matter of default participation. He would have needed to stop going to the library altogether to *opt out* of further progress.

When designing an optimal choice environment for individuals with a status quo bias, it is essential to prioritize stability over abrupt change. Rather than attempting to disrupt existing patterns, the goal is to create an environment that feels safe and familiar while gently expanding possibilities. Erickson's approach demonstrates how subtle modifications to the choice environment (such as embedding bounded choice, yes-oriented contingencies, choice justification, and default participation) can encourage progress without triggering psychological pushback. By working within the individual's existing framework ECA facilitates natural, self-directed adaptation.

Conclusion

The integration of behavioral economics within ECA highlights how deeply ingrained biases (such as status quo bias) shape decision-making, implicit choices, and social interactions. When a strong status quo bias goes unnoticed by the practitioner, collaboration and shared success become unlikely. Recognizing this bias allows ECA practitioners to work with psychological inertia, increasing the likelihood of meaningful progress.

Rather than directly challenging an individual's current state, ECA techniques (such as bounded choice, yes-oriented contingency, choice justification, and default participation) subtly guide individuals toward adaptive modifications (Table 3.1). These small, well-timed prompts create an environment where change feels both natural and personally driven. This framework extends beyond therapy into fields like coaching, counseling, education, negotiation, and democratic governance. These are areas where influencing decision-making without coercion is essential. Whether guiding a client through personal growth, encouraging employees to embrace innovation, or structuring negotiations for mutually beneficial outcomes, ECA provides a roadmap for leveraging existing cognitive patterns.

Quick-Reference Tactic Map

Table 3.1 Tactics Suited for *Status Quo Bias* and the Broader Architecture of Strategic Influence

If Client...	*Then Use...*	*Because*
Is affected by secondary-gain(s) or suppression leads to ironic-rebound	*Bounded choice*: Achieving partial control by altering the onset, context, frequency, duration, or intensity of unwanted behavior.	*Redirects* the size and scope of the distressing behavior, restoring agency, building awareness, and creating a bridge to self-regulation.
Denies any possibility for new choices	*Choice justification*: Simulating the outcomes of a difficult decision, which was made in the past or which needs to be made in the future, to catalyze incubated cognition.	Focusing on beneficial outcomes activates *critical thinking* in the form of implicit re-evaluation and unconscious goal-setting.

(*Continued*)

Table 3.1 (Continued)

If Client...	*Then Use...*	*Because*
Signals the inevitability of status quo behavior	*Yes-oriented contingency*: The status quo is embraced, and an additive solution is introduced that expands or enhances the existing behavior.	*Utilizes* existing behavior and then expands or adds growth opportunity onto it.
Values stability over change and has established strong routines	*Default participation*: Making progress contingent on existing behavioral tendencies (such as a habit, compulsion, or personality trait), so that non-participation requires actively opting out.	*Utilizes* existing behavioral momentum by making participation the path of least resistance.

Note

1 Erickson encountered multiple men who fixated on this idea.

References

Adams, G. S., Converse, B. A., Hales, A. H., & Klotz, L. E. (2021). People systematically overlook subtractive changes. *Nature*, *592*(7853), 258–261. https://doi.org/10.1038/s41586-021-03380-y

Botti, S., & lyengar, S. S. (2004). The psychological pleasure and pain of choosing: When people prefer choosing at the cost of subsequent outcome satisfaction. *Journal of Personality and Social Psychology*, *87*(3), 312–326. https://doi.org/10.1037/0022-3514.87.3.312

Clear, J. (2018). *Atomic Habits: An Easy & Proven Way to Build Good Habits & Break Bad Ones*. Avery.

Hayes, S. C., Strosahl, K. D., & Wilson, K. G. (2003). *Acceptance and Commitment Therapy: An Experiential Approach to Behavior Change*. Guilford Publications.

Hershfield, H. E. (2011). Future self-continuity: How conceptions of the future self transform intertemporal choice. *Annals of the New York Academy of Sciences*, *1235*(1), 30–43. https://doi.org/10.1111/j.1749-6632.2011.06201.x

Jachimowicz, J. M., Duncan, S., Weber, E. U., & Johnson, E. J. (2019). When and why defaults influence decisions: A meta-analysis of default effects. *Behavioural Public Policy*, *3*(2), 159–186. https://doi.org/10.1017/bpp.2018.43

Johnson, E. J., & Goldstein, D. (2003). Do defaults save lives? *Science*, *302*(5649), 1338–1339. https://doi.org/10.1126/science.1091721

Knox, R. E., & Inkster, J. A. (1968). Postdecision dissonance at post time. *Journal of Personality and Social Psychology*, *8*(4, Pt.1), 319–323. https://doi.org/10.1037/h0025528

Madrian, B. C., & Shea, D. F. (2001). The power of suggestion: Inertia in 401(k) participation and savings behavior. *The Quarterly Journal of Economics*, *116*(4), 1149–1187. https://doi.org/10.1162/003355301753265543

Neroni, M. A., Crilly, N., & Brandimonte, M. A. (2024). Unveiling the associative mechanisms underlying the additive bias: Using an implicit association test to gain insight into people's preference for additive actions. *The Journal of Creative Behavior*, *58*(3), 388–411. https://doi.org/10.1002/jocb.660

O'Hanlon, B., & Hexum, A. L. (1990). *An Uncommon Casebook: The Complete Clinical Work of Milton H. Erickson*. Norton.

Pink, D. H. (2022). *The Power of Regret: How Looking Backward Moves Us Forward*. Penguin.

Samuelson, W., & Zeckhauser, R. (1988). Status quo bias in decision making. *Journal of Risk and Uncertainty*, *1*(1), 7–59. https://doi.org/10.1007/BF00055564

Sheldon, K. M., & Elliot, A. J. (1999). Goal striving, need satisfaction, and longitudinal well-being: The self-concordance model. *Journal of Personality and Social Psychology*, *76*(3), 482–497. https://doi.org/10.1037/0022-3514.76.3.482

Steel, P. (2007). The nature of procrastination: A meta-analytic and theoretical review of quintessential self-regulatory failure. *Psychological Bulletin*, *133*(1), 65–94. https://doi.org/10.1037/0033-2909.133.1.65

Sweller, J. (2011). Chapter Two - Cognitive Load Theory. In J. P. Mestre & B. H. Ross (Eds.), *Psychology of Learning and Motivation* (Vol. 55, pp. 37–76). Academic Press. https://doi.org/10.1016/B978-0-12-387691-1.00002-8

Thaler, R. H., & Sunstein, C. R. (2009). *Nudge: Improving Decisions About Health, Wealth, and Happiness*. Penguin.

Urminsky, O. (2017). The role of psychological connectedness to the future self in decisions over time. *Current Directions in Psychological Science*, *26*(1), 34–39. https://doi.org/10.1177/0963721416668810

Vetter, M., & Kutzner, F. (2016). Nudge me if you can—How defaults and attitude strength interact to change behavior. *Comprehensive Results in Social Psychology*, *1*(1–3), 8–34. https://doi.org/10.1080/23743603.2016.1139390

Walster, G. W., & Walster, E. (1970). Choice between negative alternatives: Dissonance reduction or regret? *Psychological Reports*, *26*(3), 995–1005. https://doi.org/10.2466/pr0.1970.26.3.995

Weinberger, J., & Stoycheva, V. (2019). *The Unconscious: Theory, Research, and Clinical Implications*. Guilford Publications.

Williams, L., Buoye, A., Keiningham, T. L., & Aksoy, L. (2020). The practitioners' path to customer loyalty: Memorable experiences or frictionless experiences? *Journal of Retailing and Consumer Services*, *57*, 102215. https://doi.org/10.1016/j.jretconser.2020.102215

Chapter 4

Change Is the Only Constant

Change Bias

Change Is the Only Constant: *Change Bias*

In 2000, while working as a school psychologist, I was approached by concerned parents who asked me to evaluate their teenage son for Special Education services due to a severe emotional disturbance. During the interview, they expressed frustration and despair that their son never studied, was failing several subjects, and avoided eating dinner with the family, instead taking food to his room to play video games. The father stated that he felt ashamed that his son entirely ignored his grandfather, who had recently moved in with them, choosing instead to remain in his bedroom. He stated that he could not imagine doing such a thing and that as a boy he had looked for ways to spend time with his father. Despite multiple attempts at constructive criticism, the father saw no efforts by the teen to change and concluded that his son did not care about the family.

The parents were fundamentally kind people who had been attempting to parent without any meaningful consequences for poor choices. Therefore, I suggested some at-home strategies to try before considering Special Education testing. First, I advised the mother not to offer any food to their son unless he came to the table to eat with the family. I also encouraged her to use similar powers of persuasion to convince him that he wanted to help set the table while she prepared dinner. For the father, I recommended removing the video game console from the boy's bedroom and placing it in the family room. He was to tell his son that work comes before play, so he had to finish homework before he was allowed to play video games. I also suggested mentioning to his son that sometimes work can turn into another form of fun. I explained that I would not be willing to pursue Special Education as an option unless they first tried increasing the structure at home, thereby modeling the same motivational approach they needed to implement with their son. I then invited them to return by the end of the semester for a follow-up.

DOI: 10.4324/9781003797876-5

Before the follow-up meeting, I gathered feedback from the boy's teachers who reported significant improvements. He was now sitting at the front of the class, participating in discussions, and his grades had improved from mostly D's to mostly B's, and a couple of C's. When the parents returned, I expected them to also share some good news. However, when asked how things were going at home, they complained that NOTHING had changed. Confused, I placed the paper with his current grades in front of them. I then pointed to another page showing how different the grades were just two months ago. They acknowledged that there was some progress, but they were dissatisfied that he still had not earned a single A. I explained that given the boy's estimated intelligence and the difficulty of the classes he was taking, a B-grade represented good earnest effort.

I then asked the mother if her son was still avoiding family meals. She blushed slightly and admitted that he was eating dinner with the family every night and even helped prepare the meal the night before. I then asked the father if his son was still ignoring his grandfather. The father confessed that his son had been working with his grandfather to build a fence around the yard. He was delighted to see them laughing and really enjoying their time together.

In a playful tone I asked, "Are you absolutely certain there have been no changes in your son's behavior?" After a moment of reflection, the parents acknowledged that their expectations had been too high, realizing that their son's future might not align with their own achievements (they were both lawyers who had graduated from Yale Law School). They recognized the need to accept his progress at his own pace. After that meeting, there were no further reported problems.

Recognizing *Change Bias* in Ericksonian Choice Architecture

Change bias is the cognitive tendency to perceive change as inherently positive, often associating it with growth, empowerment, and self-improvement. While this bias can enhance motivation and adaptability, it may also cause individuals to overlook risks or undervalue the benefits of stability. However, a more nuanced understanding reveals that change bias is not a single phenomenon but rather a state of mind that can take different forms depending on how individuals perceive progress. Specifically, change bias can manifest as a *false-positive* or *false-negative*, each with distinct psychological implications.

A false-positive involves overestimating change, often driven by wishful thinking, limited self-awareness, or misattribution of cause and effect.

This bias may lead individuals to perceive progress where little or none exists, resulting in premature satisfaction and neglecting areas that require further improvement. A common contributor to false-positive is *motivated reasoning*, where individuals mistake intention for implementation. By indulging in fantasy or procrastination, they generate a false sense of accomplishment that diminishes motivation to take concrete steps toward change. The pursuit of change becomes more about satisfying the desire to act than producing meaningful results, creating a cycle of superficial engagement without real progress.

In contrast, a false-negative involves failing to recognize genuine progress when it occurs, leading to frustration, discouragement, and the erroneous belief that efforts are ineffective. In the vignette above, the parents first said that "nothing had changed," even though his grades improved, the family began eating dinner together, and he reconnected with his grandfather. This reflects a false-negative judgment: the gradual gains were easy to overlook, while the high standard of "all A's" made real progress seem inconsequential. This bias is often associated with *change blindness*, where small, incremental changes spread over time go unnoticed. Because gradual improvements are less noticeable, people may overlook them or dismiss them as unimportant, creating the false impression that nothing is changing. In the example with the teenage boy's parents, they remained blind to his progress (it did not have salience) because of their unrealistic expectations.

Similarly, *maladaptive perfectionism* can drive a false-negative change bias by creating an unrelenting need to achieve more, causing individuals to overlook their own progress. The unending pursuit of mastery and the belief that it is essential to live to one's full potential can ironically leave individuals feeling very unfulfilled. This *escalating commitment* can make people feel obliged to take responsibility for a life they haven't yet lived, resulting in feelings of inadequacy and persistent dissatisfaction as earned success is continually redefined as "not enough."

Change bias often appears as the pursuit of change for its own sake or the tendency to undervalue gradual progress in favor of dramatic breakthroughs. Emotional states like frustration, impatience, guilt, or demoralization can amplify this bias, particularly when individuals perceive their progress as insufficient or misaligned with their expectations. A common theme in stress-management programs is that individuals who received too little attention or approval in childhood may pursue self-improvement relentlessly yet still feel dissatisfied because their expectations outpace their observable progress. Addressing this pattern requires more than encouraging change. It involves helping individuals ground their perceptions of progress in concrete, verifiable experience. This is important because, when people can recognize and appreciate incremental gains, motivation becomes more resilient and less dependent on dramatic, often unrealistic transformation. For those who lacked validation in childhood, it can be especially helpful to share their evidence of progress with a respected other.

The problem of a fixation on change bias can sometimes be compounded by an *action bias*, which describes a tendency to favor action over inaction. When individuals feel compelled to act for the sake of acting (particularly when fueled by frustration or impatience) they may engage in misguided efforts that neither produce meaningful outcomes nor enhance their sense of competence. This automatic and sometimes desperate drive to act can undermine well-being, especially when it leads to repeated failures or increasing feelings of inadequacy. Research suggests that taking action can reduce discomfort during uncertainty or intense emotion, even when the action is unlikely to improve the situation (Sunderrajan & Albarracín, 2021). The challenge, then, is to utilize the energy produced by change or action bias in a way that directs motivation toward sustainable, adaptive growth.

Recognizing and managing change bias within Ericksonian Choice Architecture (ECA) is essential because it allows practitioners to balance enthusiasm for transformation with realistic assessments of progress and sustainability. The goal is not to suppress the desire for change but to harness it effectively, channeling motivation toward adaptive, meaningful growth. Unlike common approaches to *macro-level choice architecture*, which emphasize stabilizing behavior through attractive defaults, ECA's approach to change bias focuses on empowerment, competence building, and strategic pacing. These elements work together to create environments where progress feels both attainable and meaningful, thereby enhancing resilience and motivation.

The following sections will explore four key tactics that reflect Erickson's approach to managing change bias: *temporal self-comparison*, *self-monitoring*, *mental contrasting*, and *injunctive contingency*. These methods provide structure and clarity to the change process, validating the individual's desire for growth while enhancing the likelihood of sustained, meaningful progress. More than merely replicating Erickson's methods, this chapter aims to distill core principles that can be adapted to contemporary contexts, showing how choice architecture can engage the desire for change while preserving ECA's broader focus on meaningful choice and sustainable follow-through.

Erickson's Casework and the Application of Tactical Nudges

Recognizing the distortions created by change bias is important, but insight into one's own misperceptions does not by itself guarantee progress.

Whether individuals overestimate their growth due to wishful thinking (false-positive) or fail to see real improvements and become discouraged (false-negative), both tendencies can distort motivation and decision-making. Without strategic nudges, people may either abandon meaningful efforts prematurely or chase illusions of progress that lack real substance.

This is where ECA becomes a powerful tool. Instead of forcing individuals to adopt a rigid definition of progress, ECA leverages change bias itself using tactics, such as temporal self-comparison, self-monitoring, mental contrasting, and injunctive contingency, to shape an environment where opportunity is perceived constructively. By making incremental growth observable, tying actions to meaningful consequences, and aligning aspirations with causal reality, these tactics help individuals engage with the ongoing adaptive process as an expression of choice rather than a static endpoint that denotes "real change."

The following case reviews illustrate how Erickson applied these principles to empower those who previously felt "stuck." By designing choice environments that provided tangible proof of progress and structured opportunities for self-reflection, he transformed distorted perceptions of *change* into a source of motivation. This helped individuals not only recognize but also sustain meaningful growth.

Case 4.1: Bedwetting and Handwriting

A mother and her 12-year-old son came to Erickson for help because the boy was wetting his bed every night. His mother wanted to help him with this problem, but the father did not. Erickson described the father as a harsh and cold man who accused his wife of "babying the brats too much." Erickson was told that when the boy went to his father for help, he would get shoved aside. Thus, another unstated problem was that the boy needed help learning to believe in himself.

The boy wanted to *change* the bedwetting but he had an antagonistic attitude toward his mother, perhaps displaced from a father who was too unavailable to be angry at. As Erickson put it, "it was apparent that Johnny was utterly hostile toward his mother about this bed wetting. He was angry and in a struggle with her about it." Given the existing power struggles, Erickson believed that pressuring the boy to stop wetting his bed would be ineffective. So, Erickson said to the boy, "I have a solution for you but you're are not going to like it and your mother is going to like it even less." After disarming both the mother and son with a *preemptive devaluation* of the solution, Erickson focused the boy's energies on a volitional task (improving his handwriting) and told him that this effort would automatically resolve the bedwetting issue (a tactic described later in this chapter as injunctive contingency).

The way this assignment was structured was that anytime the boy's sheets were wet, his mother would wake him early to practice handwriting by copying a certain number of pages from a book of his choice. She was instructed to sit with him from 5 a.m. to 7 a.m., attentively observing his progress. The task was meant to be disagreeable but it was also avoidable. As Erickson put it, "It sounded unpleasant to have Mother sit there watching him improve his script, yet he only had to do it on the mornings when his bed was wet."

At the same time, the boy needed his mother's loving attention. Erickson explained that as the mother sat watching her son improve his handwriting, she was able to take pride in his accomplishment. This helped increase the probability that the boy would notice and take pride in his own progress.

Over time the frequency of his bedwetting decreased, occurring only every five days, then every ten days, then once a month, until it eventually stopped altogether.

During treatment Erickson asked the boy to bring in his writing samples, which Erickson arranged in chronological order. At first, the boy only saw failure, describing his previous work as "awful." However, as Erickson guided him through the pages, pointing out the beauty of specific letters and acknowledging his progress, the boy became increasingly pleased. By the time they reached his most recent samples, the boy felt genuinely proud of his improvement. Following this exercise, the boy's grades improved, his social interactions flourished (eventually leading to his election as captain of the baseball team), and he consistently earned A's and B's instead of D's and F's.

Temporal Self-Comparison

Temporal self-comparison is a process of comparison that focuses on a single individual. This tactic is supported by temporal comparison theory, which studies the effects of the same individual comparing themself at two different points in time (Albert, 1977). This process of self-evaluation is meant to identify progress, growth, or change over time. By making gradual improvements more apparent, it effectively counters the tendency to overlook ongoing change (false-negative), thereby reinforcing the potential for further development. This approach enhances self-concept clarity by making personal growth tangible and fostering temporal self-continuity, which is the sense of being the same person despite change. As a result, temporal self-comparison contributes to a more coherent and stable self-concept, promoting higher self-esteem and motivation as individuals become increasingly aware of their achievements and progress (Wolff & Möller, 2022).

In contrast, *social comparison* involves evaluating oneself against others, which can boost self-esteem through downward comparison (I am better than them) or diminish it through upward comparison (they are better than me). While social comparison may provide valuable information about personal standing and inspire motivation, it often undermines self-concept clarity by prioritizing external benchmarks over intrinsically valued growth (Kedia et al., 2014). On the other hand, temporal self-comparison offers a more reliable pathway to building resilience and adaptive self-regulation by centering attention on personal development versus external validation. It is particularly effective for individuals aiming to overcome a false-negative change bias, enhance motivation, or rebuild confidence following perceived failures. By highlighting genuine progress, temporal self-comparison makes change more salient and accessible, providing a powerful tool for reinforcing personal growth and fostering a more positive outlook on future challenges.

Case Analysis

In traditional psychotherapeutic literature, this case has been described as an example of a behavioral task assignment (O'Hanlon & Hexum, 1990). While that description is accurate, it leaves important questions unanswered: "Why this task for this person?" and "Why was it helpful? What psychological effects contributed to this outcome?" Rather than assuming any randomly assigned task might work, it is essential to maintain focus on the central mission of ECA, which is to provide *choice-centric care*. In this case, the overarching choice opportunity was success versus failure, across multiple domains (e.g., at home, in class, on the playing field).

Using temporal self-comparison, Erickson guided the boy to focus on the progress he had made in handwriting, linking this self-improvement to gaining mastery over bedwetting. By emphasizing his writing improvements, Erickson cultivated a sense of accomplishment, effectively shifting the boy's attention from perceived failure to genuine progress. This mirrors evidence showing that visible progress strengthens motivation by reinforcing perceived competence. It counters a false-negative change bias by making gradual progress visible and tangible. The boy desired change, and now he could see that, although slow, change was genuinely occurring.

Examining Erickson's use of temporal self-comparison reveals several key elements that contribute to its effectiveness. One of the most important elements is the emphasis on highlighting positive change. By drawing attention to measurable improvements, this technique counters the perception that no progress has been made. In the case example, Erickson guided the boy through a review of his handwriting, pointing out the beauty of specific letters and acknowledging the improvement he had achieved. This helped the boy recognize his own development, reinforcing a sense of movement toward success.

Another essential element is the use of visual or physical evidence. Concrete artifacts such as past work or photographs make progress undeniable. Erickson demonstrated this principle when he said, "Bring in your writing samples so that we can examine them." By looking at tangible proof of change, the boy was able to see the difference for himself, making the experience of progress less abstract and more real.

Additionally, reinforcing agency and self-efficacy is a core component of this approach. Linking progress to the individual's own efforts helps to enhance self-belief. While the literature does not explicitly mention Erickson doing this in the handwriting case, it is consistent with his general approach to the use of affordances. Similarly, the technique often involves normalizing struggles as necessary parts of growth. Furthermore, reframing past difficulties as essential steps in the journey promotes a *growth mindset*. Although this aspect is not specifically documented in this case, Erickson was known for encouraging clients to view their setbacks as integral to eventual success.

Essentially, Erickson curated a choice environment that made success more visible and attainable. By guiding the client toward a temporal self-comparison, Erickson shifted the boy's attention away from repeated failure and toward a meaningful, achievable path to progress. This approach illustrates how to structure choice moments that highlight agency, leverage change bias, and satisfy an innate need to develop personal skill sets.

General Application

Choice architects can effectively utilize the tactic of temporal self-comparison by guiding clients to assess their progress through tangible evidence collected over time. This can also include observing evidence of their children's progress, as described in the vignette at the opening of this chapter. This approach allows individuals to shift their focus from self-criticism to acknowledgment of growth, promoting greater self-confidence and reducing negative self-talk. By actively drawing attention to personal achievements and improvements, practitioners help clients counteract a false-negative. Temporal self-comparison can also enhance motivation and resilience by making change more apparent and accessible, particularly when clients feel stuck or demoralized by perceived stagnation.

Temporal self-comparison works because feedback loops enable individuals to calibrate effort based on visible results. The nudge can be anything that enables an individual to compare the present to the past to highlight change or lack of change. Encouraging clients to review old journal entries or write about past challenges they have overcome can highlight their growth and ability to persist through difficulties. Visual evidence, such as old photos, academic records, or creative work, provides concrete proof of improvement and transformation over time. Additionally, comparing past feedback, such as performance reviews or compliments, with recent assessments can reveal areas of growth that might otherwise be overlooked. By systematically guiding clients to collect and compare evidence of progress, practitioners can help them develop a more balanced and accurate perception of their journey, strengthening their capacity for adaptive self-regulation and goal-directed behavior.

Case 4.2: Bilateral Arm Paralysis

Another compelling example of Erickson's nuanced approach to change bias is the case of a preadolescent girl who took the initiative to call Erickson herself, stating, "I had infantile paralysis and I have forgotten how to move my arms. Can you hypnotize me and teach me?" Clearly, she was looking to introduce change into her life.

Erickson had the girl's mother bring her in for a medical examination and observed that for a 12-year-old, she had rapidly developing breasts, with the right breast having migrated under her arm. He instructed the girl, "For three times a day you ought to sit in front of a mirror, nude to the waist, and make faces at yourself."

This seemingly playful instruction was in fact a sophisticated nudge designed to reintroduce volitional control and awareness over her upper body. Research on motor learning shows that small voluntary movements often reactivate broader movement patterns through neural generalization (Krakauer et al., 2006). By directing her attention to making exaggerated facial expressions, Erickson was encouraging subtle activations of the platysma muscle and associated neural pathways extending to her chest and shoulders. As Erickson explained,

> This started her exercising the muscles in her chest... When you start one muscle moving, there is a tendency for that to spread to other muscles. You try to move just one finger. You start to spread the movement, unintentionally.

Erickson's approach echoes principles described by Moshé Feldenkrais (1981), a world-renowned rehabilitation physiologist. Feldenkrais emphasized that breaking rigid, habituated patterns through gentle, exploratory actions allows the nervous system to discover new, more efficient ways of functioning. Improving voluntary control over one area of the body, according to both Erickson and Feldenkrais, enhances the brain's capacity to stimulate muscle activations and reestablish neural connections in areas where movement has been impaired.

Importantly, the use of a mirror meant that the girl was actively engaging in a self-monitoring exercise. The mirror provided immediate visual feedback, helping her track subtle changes in her movements and recognize progress she might have otherwise ignored. This ongoing feedback loop likely reinforced her sense of agency and mastery.

Erickson also paid careful attention to the choice environment, ensuring the girl felt ownership of her change process. When she asked, "Do I have to sit in front of a mirror?" Erickson replied, "Where would you like to sit?" The girl responded that she would like to imagine a TV program. Without hesitation, Erickson accommodated her wish, suggesting that three times a day she sit and watch an imaginary program on an imaginary TV.

During a later visit, the girl reported that she enjoyed "watching the imaginary TV while making faces." More importantly, she also observed that her arms had begun to move. This observation was made possible by her own self-monitoring and heightened awareness. As her body reconfigured itself, her right breast migrated toward a more symmetrical positioning. Erickson's approach not only activated underused neural pathways but also empowered the girl to recognize and build upon her own progress, reinforcing her growing sense of agency and control.

Self-Monitoring

Self-monitoring is a self-regulation tactic that involves drawing attention to personal patterns in real time or retrospectively to enhance decision-making, self-regulation, and performance. Rooted in the benefit of creating feedback loops, self-monitoring is most effective when it provides accurate, immediate feedback, which serves as a *prime*. Because motivation increases engagement, it is also important to align the monitored task with an individual's *intrinsic motivation* and personal goals. For example, asking a child to make funny faces in a mirror aligns with a child's need to be playful. A crucial element of self-monitoring is the use of clear metrics—well-defined criteria that are specific, relevant, and actionable. These metrics may include measurable behaviors (e.g., time spent on a task), emotional states (e.g., stress levels), or cognitive patterns (e.g., frequency of negative self-talk), allowing individuals to recognize trends and make targeted adjustments (Vohs & Baumeister, 2011).

Consistent tracking and reflection are fundamental to this process, as they help individuals identify meaningful patterns over time.[1] Studies show that regular self-monitoring can improve self-regulation and goal adherence, particularly when combined with structured reflection (Carver &

Scheier, 2001). External cues and prompts, such as alarms, visual reminders, or social accountability, further enhance self-monitoring by reducing reliance on internal motivation alone and increasing follow-through.

For example, when I was teaching a graduate course on brief therapy, I would assign students to choose a concrete behavior they wanted to change and create a self-monitoring system to track their progress. While nearly everyone reported some benefit, a quarter of the students would enthusiastically report that the assignment had changed their lives.

For instance, there was a student who struggled to drink enough water throughout the day, resulting in painful headaches and low energy. Her doctor attributed these problems to dehydration. She asked me whether she needed to use rewards or punishments to motivate herself. I told her that wasn't necessary. Instead, I suggested placing her favorite jar, filled with the full amount of water she needed to drink, in a visible location. Her task was to chart how much water she had consumed by the end of each day.

A week later, she was consistently drinking the required amount of water and was astonished by the simplicity and effectiveness of the technique. This outcome reflects findings that tracking behavior alone often increases adherence without requiring additional incentives. Unlike mainstream approaches where self-monitoring often relies on external devices (e.g., fitness trackers), ECA emphasizes making the act of observation intrinsically meaningful and personally relevant by tapping into people's immediate values and underserved interests, such as a favorite jar or the joy of watching imaginary TV.

Another useful detail is to focus on additive solutions (adding a new skill) versus subtractive ones (stopping an undesirable habit). Instead of trying to count the number of instances of not doing something, it's more effective to introduce a positive behavior that is incompatible with the undesirable behavior. The brain learns new patterns more easily than it unlearns established ones, so replacing a bad habit with an enjoyable positive action will diminish the unwanted behavior. For example, many people struggle with excessive self-criticism. Once they recognize it as a problem, they may begin criticizing themselves for being too self-critical. Recently, while eating pizza at a public gathering, a college student sitting next to me confessed to struggling with this downward spiral. I asked whether he knew what self-compassion is. He did not, so I explained that it involves reflecting on one's shortcomings with the same kindness and forgiving attitude that one would show a total stranger. In saying this, I was addressing him as a stranger, who was modeling the type of kindness he needed to direct inward. Later that evening, the young man approached me and thanked me for talking with him. Recent research by Neroni et al. (2024) found that people generally perceive additive actions as safer and more functional than subtractive concepts. Also, individuals are more likely to internalize growth when it builds upon their existing habits (Botti & Iyengar, 2006), such as adding self-compassion onto a tendency toward self-consciousness.

Case Analysis

Erickson's case of a girl using a mirror to monitor her progress has been described elsewhere as an example of a behavioral task assignment (O'Hanlon & Hexum, 1990). This label tells us nothing about the specifics of the methodology, the reasons for its use, or the research associated with this effect. Self-monitoring on the other hand addresses all these questions. In this case, the client was literally instructed to watch herself. Erickson guided the developing girl to become aware of her body's needs and abilities by providing clear metrics for progress (arm movement). The nudge was not about forcing change but about enhancing awareness of progress already taking place. This approach demonstrates how self-monitoring can reveal gaps between intention and action, making new opportunity available.

If we dissect Erickson's use of self-monitoring, we can see that it contained several key elements. One of these was motivational relevance. The act of self-monitoring must align with personal goals and intrinsic motivation. In this case, the girl was keenly interested in her changing body and what it might be capable of doing.

Another element was the use of clear metrics, which serve as a motivational prime. Self-monitoring requires specific, relevant, and actionable criteria. In this case, bodily movement served as the metric. Erickson did not immediately instruct the girl to monitor her arm movements. Instead, he began by having her make faces at herself in the mirror, a humorous activity that likely animated her entire body, especially if she began to laugh at herself. This indirect approach paved the way for more intentional physical observation.

A third element was temporal self-comparison. It is essential to establish a baseline and then track progress over time. While there is no indication that the girl kept a written record of her physical changes or received systematic feedback from her mother, such data would have theoretically enhanced the effect. Nonetheless, the passage of time and the girl's repeated mirror interactions likely helped her perceive subtle improvements.

Finally, external cues and prompts played a role. Reminders, social accountability, or environmental triggers can support self-monitoring. In this case, the presence of a large mirror in the girl's bedroom would have served as a daily prompt, subtly encouraging her to observe her muscle movement and reinforcing the habit of self-awareness.

This case highlights how thoughtfully designed self-monitoring can serve as a powerful nudge. Rather than prescribing behavior change directly, Erickson created an environment where the client could notice and reflect on her own progress in a personally meaningful way. By aligning the monitoring task with her intrinsic motivation and using a mirror as both a tool and environmental cue, he enabled her to generate evidence of change from within. This approach reduced reliance on external validation and encouraged internal agency. By making progress observable, relevant, and self-driven, choice-centric care fosters greater autonomy, insight, and momentum for behavioral adaptation.

General Application

Modern applications of self-monitoring have significantly evolved since Erickson's time, integrating technology and refined methodologies to enhance self-awareness and facilitate behavior change. Digital tools, such as smartphone applications and wearable tracking devices, allow real-time data collection and feedback, improving outcomes across various domains. For example, combining self-monitoring apps with health coaching has shown significant improvements in weight loss, waist circumference, triglyceride levels, hemoglobin A1c, and daily caloric intake among individuals struggling with obesity (Lee et al., 2018). The ability to track dietary intake, physical activity, and other metrics provides both clients and coaches with valuable insights, enhancing accountability and support.

Studies have demonstrated that when coaches have access to clients' self-monitoring data, outcomes improve as personalized feedback can be provided based on concrete observations (Butryn et al., 2024). Furthermore, structured self-monitoring techniques are essential in behavior modification strategies, allowing clients to gain insights into patterns that may hinder their goals and empowering them to take proactive steps toward improvement. Very recently, the potential for *cognitive* self-monitoring has emerged after integrating artificial intelligence (AI)–powered chatbots to analyze and monitor not only explicit cognitive patterns, such as negative self-talk, but also implicit biases and heuristics that can be discerned in speech patterns. These advancements in self-monitoring contribute to more personalized and effective nudges, promoting sustained personal and professional growth.

Case 4.3: Overcoming Bedwetting with Good Handwriting (4.1 Continued)

Earlier in this chapter, I described the case of a mother and her 12-year-old son who came to Erickson for help with bedwetting. As you may recall,

Erickson created an opportunity for success and greater self-confidence by having the boy practice his handwriting. He was not alone in this task; his mother was present to celebrate his progress, providing social validation and encouragement. Perhaps even more importantly, Erickson himself witnessed and validated the boy's improvement using handwriting samples to conduct a temporal self-comparison, allowing the boy to see his progress over time.

However, this was not the only tactic involved, and perhaps not the most important. Research on placebo effects and modern hypnosis suggests that non-volitional behaviors are particularly responsive to expectancy effects. More specifically, if a response expectancy is established (where engaging in task-X is believed to lead to changes in non-volitional behavior-Y) then the transformation tends to occur automatically once the prescribed actions are implemented (Kirsch, 1990). In this case, the boy's handwriting practice was framed as a means of ending his bedwetting, creating an expectancy that this voluntary action would lead to effortless, unconscious transformation.

Another finding from placebo research is that the individual's own motivation to improve can enhance the placebo response, especially when they are actively seeking relief or a solution to their problem. Additionally, placebos tend to be more effective when they involve a structured or ritualistic process, such as engaging in a therapeutic routine that feels purposeful and relevant. As argued by Jerome Frank, in an influential co-authored book, *Persuasion and Healing*, effective psychotherapy often involves structured rituals that provide clients with a sense of order, purpose, and expectation (Frank & Frank, 1961).

When considering urinary tract control as a process of bodily learning, it becomes evident why the handwriting assignment may have felt intuitively relevant. Effective handwriting requires several complex skills, including fine motor control, bilateral and visual–motor integration, motor planning, in-hand manipulation, proprioception, visual perception, sustained attention, and sensory awareness. Each of these elements contributes to a broader sense of bodily control and coordination.

Furthermore, the placebo response is strengthened when patients believe a trusted authority figure endorses the treatment (Colloca & Miller, 2011). In this case, both Erickson and the boy's mother provided crucial social validation by encouraging his progress and supporting the prescribed ritual. This combination of motivation, ritualistic engagement, and social validation created an optimal environment for activating this expectancy-based response.

Injunctive Contingency

Often, Erickson would make the point that people need to be able to do something about their problems. However, this seemingly straightforward principle becomes challenging when the issue involves a non-volitional behavior (something the individual feels powerless to control). In such cases, the ECA tactic known as injunctive contingency proves especially useful.

Broadly defined, injunctive contingency is a form of behavior regulation rooted in expectation and embodied cognition. This formulation is supported by placebo and expectancy research demonstrating that belief-linked voluntary action can trigger involuntary physiological changes. It operates as a form of *cue-based planning* in which a volitional action becomes an implicit cue for the regulation of non-volitional processes. The formula is: When X is a problem (e.g., depression), do Y (e.g., take a pill) to achieve Z (e.g., relief from depression). Consistent with Haley's (1973) analysis of standard hypnotic procedure, effective directives typically proceed in two stages: First, individuals are asked to perform actions they can voluntarily control (e.g., sitting comfortably, focusing attention, eye closure); second, these voluntary actions function as gateways to spontaneous or involuntary changes, such as shifts in mood, sensation, or physiological regulation. Importantly, the aim is not mechanical compliance but autonomous participation, where individuals follow directives while experiencing emergent changes as self-generated rather than imposed.

As placebo research illustrates, the voluntary act need not share a direct causal relationship with the outcome beyond expectancy effects. For this reason, directives should focus on behaviors under voluntary muscle control (striated muscles) rather than attempting to command autonomic functions governed by smooth muscle activity, such as sleep, appetite, or emotional states. This avoids internal power struggles over processes outside conscious control and instead channels effort toward actions that can be intentionally enacted while allowing desired involuntary adjustments to arise indirectly.

As Paul Watzlawick et al. (1967), a prominent figure in communication theory and psychotherapy, pointed out, language can be either indicative or injunctive, each carrying distinct implications. While indicative language is factual and descriptive, conveying information without implying directives or obligations, injunctive language involves an implicit or explicit expectation about what should or should not be done.

If a person feels they have no viable options for addressing unwanted behaviors or experiences, providing an injunctive contingency can feel like an expansion of possibilities. However, if the individual already has their own ideas about how to address the problem, a prescribed injunctive contingency may be perceived as an infringement on their personal freedom. Therefore, the effectiveness of injunctive contingency depends on the client's state of mind, specifically their motivation to expand personal agency and whether they believe other options are available.

Case Analysis

Erickson's use of injunctive contingency in this case was multifaceted. By prescribing a volitional task (handwriting practice) with an embedded expectancy for resolving a non-volitional problem (bedwetting), Erickson skillfully activated an automatic, unconscious process of transformation. His approach was further strengthened by social validation, ritualistic engagement, and the perceived relevance of the handwriting task to bodily control.

The essential point to recognize is that Erickson's use of injunctive contingency provided both the mother and her son with a means of working together to do something about the unwanted behavior. It is as much a story about loving attachment and shared joy as it is about personal growth.

Dissecting Erickson's use of injunctive contingency, we can see four essential elements that contributed to its effectiveness. The first is the *framing* of volitional action as a pathway to non-volitional opportunity. Erickson assigned the boy the task of practicing his handwriting, an activity the boy could consciously control. By presenting this volitional behavior as a method for addressing his non-volitional issue (bedwetting) Erickson created an expectancy effect, linking intentional action with desired but seemingly involuntary outcomes.

The second element involved establishing expectancy through ritualistic engagement. The handwriting assignment functioned as a structured and purposeful ritual. Such ritualistic practices can enhance placebo effects, especially when the individual believes that adhering to the process will lead to the desired outcome. In this case, the boy was encouraged to view his consistent engagement with handwriting practice as a way to gain greater control over his body.

A third essential element was the use of authority and suggestion. Erickson's role as a trusted authority figure strengthened the expectancy effect by lending credibility to the nudge. Additionally, the supportive presence of the boy's mother reinforced the legitimacy of the task and provided emotional encouragement, which likely increased the boy's motivation and belief in the process.

Finally, the handwriting task had symbolic relevance to the boy's original issue. It engaged skills directly related to bodily control, such as fine motor coordination, motor planning, sensory awareness, and sustained attention. Improving these abilities may have contributed to the boy's unconscious sense of increased bodily regulation (the *domino effect*), allowing the task to feel meaningfully connected to the bedwetting issue he sought to overcome.

General Application

Modern applications of injunctive contingency have evolved to address non-volitional behaviors by framing their regulation as a byproduct of prescribed volitional actions. This approach focuses on tasks involving voluntary muscle control versus autonomic functions, thus enhancing agency and avoiding futile power struggles over uncontrollable experiences. Practitioners can refine this approach by aligning behavioral prescriptions with clients' existing motivations, allowing them to influence non-volitional experiences without demanding unrealistic levels of self-regulation.

For example, a woman who wants to manage her anxiety and enjoys being in nature can be urged to spend 20 minutes walking in green spaces at least three times a week (Braçe et al., 2020). Her expectations for a positive outcome can be enhanced by explaining that the exercise's effectiveness will increase if she focuses on the beauty of nature during her walk and allows herself to experience feelings of awe (Bai et al., 2021). This approach is an ideal injunction because it aligns with her personal preferences while also being evidence-based, with research suggesting that spending time in green spaces can even reduce mortality (Gascon et al., 2016). This example highlights how injunctive contingency can be effectively applied by tailoring nudges to an individual's interests and framing them as accessible, enjoyable activities. By linking voluntary actions to automatic progress, practitioners enable the self-regulation of behaviors once thought impossible.

Case 4.4: Getting Ready for a Wedding

This next case study illustrates how a false-negative change bias was resolved using a future-oriented fantasy to highlight implicit choices. This woman was experiencing severe anxiety along with deep depression, withdrawal, and dependency patterns. Although hypnotherapy initially showed success, she became increasingly rigid as therapy continued. While she actively engaged in intellectual discussions about her problems and needs, she struggled to achieve recognizable changes in her daily life.

For instance, she acknowledged the intolerable conditions of her parental home but continued living there despite real difficulties and opportunities to leave. She expressed bitter resentment toward her job yet refused a readily available promotion. Though she recognized the need for social interaction, she actively avoided all opportunities. She often spoke about her desire to read but refused to enter the library she passed daily, despite repeatedly promising herself to do so. As her frustration grew, she demanded that Erickson take decisive action to force her into doing what she knew was necessary but could not bring herself to do. Her hope was that achieving just one desired goal would give her the motivation needed to accomplish others.

Accepting her statement at face value, Erickson induced a deep hypnotic trance. In this state, the woman was instructed to visualize a series of crystal balls, each depicting significant experiences from different stages of her life. She was to compare, contrast, and notice the continuity of various elements across these scenes. The purpose was to allow a constellation of ideas to form unconsciously, eventually manifesting in another, larger crystal ball. This larger crystal ball would show her a desirable future scenario where she had overcome the obstacles to success and was feeling happy, fulfilled, and actively engaged in life.

Erickson reported that the woman spent about an hour deeply immersed in the imaginary scenes, occasionally glancing around the room as if searching for the larger crystal ball. Finally, she located it and began eagerly describing the scene within. She vividly detailed a wedding scene involving a lifelong family friend that was not scheduled to occur for over three months. She saw herself in "close-ups" looking beautiful, dancing, and even being asked on a date by a man named Ed. She repeatedly commented on how happy she appeared and how starkly this contrasted with her current appearance.

Ending the session, Erickson instructed her to retain all her visualized experiences unconsciously, leaving her with a suggestion to consciously forget the trance experience while drawing motivation from it. The patient attended only two more sessions, each brief and focused on deepening the previous experience. She asked to be hypnotized both times to enhance her memory of the wedding scene. After each session, she left with silent determination, ending therapy entirely after her third visit.

Three months later, the woman returned to Erickson's office, feeling compelled to share recent developments. She explained that following the last session she felt driven to prepare for the upcoming wedding.

> I've come to tell you about Nadine's wedding. I have an odd feeling that you know all about it and yet don't know a thing. But I do know that I have to give you an explanation for some reason.

She elaborated that she and Nadine and the bridegroom had been lifelong friends and that their families were intimate friends.

The woman continued, "Some three months ago, following a therapeutic session, I felt compelled to discontinue therapy and to devote my energies to getting ready for that wedding." After being asked to be a bridesmaid, she decided to make her own dress, which required her to accept a promotion at work to obtain better hours. She also moved to an apartment in town to avoid the long commute. Eagerly participating in the wedding preparations, she went on shopping tours with friends, helped select presents, and arranged various bridal showers. Her conclusion was, "All in all, I have been exceedingly and happily busy."

The wedding itself proceeded much as she had foreseen (unconscious goal implementation). When Erickson asked if she had danced with Ed, she was startled at his detailed knowledge. She admitted she had danced with him but had turned down his invitation for a date, finding him below her standards. Instead, she accepted a date from another dancing partner.

When reminded of her original purpose in seeing Erickson, she simply replied, "I was a pretty sick girl when I first came to see you. I was horribly mixed up, and I'm grateful to you for getting me straightened out in time so that I could get ready for the wedding." She remained unaware that her efforts to prepare for the wedding were directly linked to her recovery. Erickson reports that later encounters with her confirmed that she was happily married and the mother of three children, which was an ideal outcome in the culture of the time.

Mental Contrasting

Mental contrasting, as applied within ECA, is a behavioral tactic that involves vividly imagining a desired future while simultaneously acknowledging the current obstacles standing in the way of that goal. This process creates a psychological contrast between the envisioned future and the present reality, enhancing motivation by highlighting the discrepancy between where one is and where one wants to be. Grounded in Gabriele Oettingen's research, mental contrasting enhances commitment to goals by making the necessary actions more accessible and urgent thereby strengthening the association between desired outcomes and the actions required to achieve them (Oettingen & Mayer, 2002). Mental contrasting also helps people decide which goals are worth pursuing by changing how they view their current situation. When success seems likely, present difficulties become challenges to overcome. When success seems unlikely, those difficulties provide less motivation to keep striving (Kappes et al., 2013). This adaptive mechanism helps individuals allocate their cognitive and motivational resources more efficiently, disengaging from unattainable goals while fully committing to realistic and achievable ones.

Mental contrasting functions through two core components: *positive visualization* and *goal analysis*. The positive visualization aspect involves generating a detailed and appealing mental representation of a desired future. This vivid mental imagery serves to activate positive feelings and energize motivation. In contrast, the goal analysis aspect involves acknowledging present obstacles that stand in the way of achieving that desired future. This type of *critical thinking* clarifies what needs to be addressed and prompts a readiness to take actionable steps. This effect is further strengthened when individuals use implementation intentions to specify concrete strategies for addressing obstacles, ensuring that motivation translates into sustained action (Duckworth et al., 2011).

Case Analysis

The case of the woman who struggled with profound anxiety and severe depression illustrates how Erickson effectively applied a form of mental contrasting to facilitate psychological growth and behavioral adaptation. In traditional psychotherapeutic literature, this technique has been described as an example of future projection (O'Hanlon & Hexum, 1990), which is accurate but lacking in nuance. More than the mental simulation of a future-self, Erickson's design of an *optimal choice environment* addressed her psychological state of dependence and self-limitation by activating latent motivations and intrinsic desires.

Before guiding her through a vivid and emotionally appealing vision of the future, Erickson had her spend a full hour creating a stark contrast, using her status quo as a backdrop. According to the theory of mental contrasting, imagining a desired future activates positive feelings and increases motivational energy, but this must be paired with an awareness of current obstacles to prompt effective action (Marquardt et al., 2017). In this case, the woman's own admission that "if she could achieve even one of the desired things, she would then have the impetus and firmness of intention to achieve the others," demonstrates a change bias that Erickson could build upon through mental contrasting.

The nudge proved helpful because it created a dynamic tension between her present stagnation and a desirable, achievable future. Instead of attempting to confront her directly about her self-limiting behavior, Erickson allowed her unconscious mind to reconcile the contrast between her immediate limitations and the fulfillment depicted in the wedding scene. This resonates with research showing that mental contrasting not only enhances motivation but also strengthens the cognitive associations between desired outcomes and the instrumental actions required to achieve them (Oettingen & Mayer, 2002).

If we dissect Erickson's use of mental contrasting, we can see that it contained several key elements. One of the first was mental simulation. By evoking imagination and creativity in a way that felt automatic and natural, the woman was led to envision competing versions of herself. This helped create a cognitive space in which multiple possible outcomes could coexist.

Another important element was temporal self-comparison. The nudge prompted her to contrast her current, unhappy state with a vividly appealing future as depicted in the imagined wedding scene. This contrast heightened her awareness of the gap between where she was and where she wanted to be, thereby enhancing her motivation to change.

In addition to this, Erickson facilitated the construction of a future identity. By vividly visualizing herself at the wedding, the woman was given an opportunity to project herself into a version of who she wanted to become. This future self then became a concrete motivational target. It provided something to reach for rather than just an abstract hope.

Finally, the visualization activated a range of implicit goals, such as social acceptance, autonomy, and engagement. These goals were not externally imposed but arose naturally from within the woman's own desires, which made her motivation to pursue them more sustainable and personally meaningful.

Essentially, Erickson created a structured opportunity for the woman to witness a meaningful gap between her current limitations and a compelling, achievable future. This contrast served as a nudge to make change feel necessary and desirable from within. The woman's eventual behavioral shift was not externally enforced, but emerged from a reorganized sense of what was possible and preferable.

General Application

Mental contrasting has gained considerable attention in modern problem-solving contexts due to its robust empirical support and adaptability to various domains of personal and professional growth. While the technique has its roots in cognitive-behavioral and motivational theories, it has been increasingly integrated with technological advancements to enhance engagement and improve outcomes.

One of the most prominent contemporary applications of mental contrasting is in the field of coaching, particularly goal-setting and performance enhancement. Coaches frequently employ mental contrasting to help clients clarify their goals and identify potential obstacles that may hinder progress. By juxtaposing a desired future state with current limitations, clients can better formulate actionable plans and enhance their commitment to achieving their objectives. Studies have demonstrated that mental contrasting is especially effective when combined with implementation intentions, a technique known as MCII (*Mental Contrasting* with *Implementation Intentions*), which links the desired outcome with specific actions to overcome anticipated obstacles (Oettingen, 2012).

Therapeutic applications of mental contrasting have also evolved, with practitioners using this approach to address issues such as depression, anxiety, and emotional regulation. For example, therapists working with clients experiencing depressive symptoms may guide them through a process of visualizing a positive future and then contrasting it with their current emotional state. This approach can help clients identify specific barriers contributing to their depression and develop concrete strategies for improvement. Additionally, mental contrasting has been used to enhance resilience and promote adaptive coping, particularly in individuals struggling with chronic stress or trauma.

In counseling, mental contrasting has proven valuable for clients dealing with career transitions, relationship difficulties, and self-esteem issues. Counselors may employ this technique to help clients visualize desired relationship dynamics or professional achievements while acknowledging and preparing for the challenges that may arise along the way. The resulting clarity often leads to a greater sense of agency and motivation, empowering clients to take proactive steps toward their goals.

Technological advancements have further refined the application of mental contrasting, making it more accessible and customizable. Digital platforms, including smartphone apps and virtual coaching tools, have been developed to guide individuals through structured mental contrasting exercises. These tools often incorporate interactive features, such as personalized feedback, progress tracking, and adaptive prompts that respond to user input. For instance, the WOOP (Wish, Outcome, Obstacle, Plan) app is based on MCII principles and provides a user-friendly interface for applying mental contrasting to daily life challenges.

Research supports the efficacy of digital formats using mental contrasting. Studies have shown that individuals who use apps designed for mental contrasting and implementation intentions report higher levels of goal attainment and improved well-being compared to those who rely solely on traditional goal-setting techniques (Oettingen & Mayer, 2002). These findings suggest that technological integration can enhance the reach and impact of mental contrasting, particularly for individuals who may lack access to traditional in-person resources.

Looking ahead, the continued integration of mental contrasting with emerging technologies, such as virtual reality and AI, holds promise for creating even more immersive and personalized nudges. As researchers and practitioners continue to explore these possibilities, mental contrasting is likely to remain a powerful tool for enhancing motivation, resilience, and overall well-being in a wide range of collaborative problem-solving contexts.

Designing an Optimal Choice Environment (OCE) for Change Bias

The mission of a choice architect is to empower individuals to make optimal choices for themselves while preserving personal autonomy. Therefore, an optimal choice environment for change bias should emphasize self-efficacy and the perception of progress, fostering a sense of autonomy while subtly guiding individuals toward competence-building goals. Research suggests that self-efficacy is a key driver of motivation and persistence in goal pursuit (Bandura, 2000), making it essential to design choice structures that reinforce confidence and skill acquisition. *Associative anchoring* (framing choices in relation to an individual's existing strengths, preferences, or unfulfilled aspirations) can help facilitate smoother transitions by making progress feel self-directed (Deci & Ryan, 2008). Strategic pacing is also crucial; introducing choices gradually and in alignment with an individual's readiness prevents overwhelming disengagement while maintaining momentum toward self-determined action (Prochaska & DiClemente, 1983). Furthermore, embedding freedom within the decision-making process supports an *internal locus of control*, which has been linked to greater motivation and long-term commitment to ongoing progress (Rotter, 1966). By integrating these elements, an optimal choice environment for change bias fosters empowerment and sustainable transformation while ensuring individuals retain a sense of ownership and discovery in their choices.

Thought Exercise

Next, you will have the opportunity to apply your design skills. When creating an optimal choice environment for someone with a change bias, remember that this environment can include mental landscapes, such as goals (what they hope to accomplish) and intentions (their reasons for pursuing these goals). In some cases, adaptation involves revisiting proven options. For example, when Coca-Cola introduced "New Coke" (a marketing disaster) and then pivoted by reintroducing "Coca-Cola Classic" (a marketing triumph). The key is to honor each individual's right to innovate and creatively participate in the ongoing flux of life.

For this thought exercise, imagine talking to a distressed couple who tells you they are deeply in love but have stopped having sex and feel unable to regain the fulfilling, frequent sex life they once enjoyed. Both partners are highly focused on their careers and time spent with each other, so they decided early on that they never wanted children, which led them to routinely use contraception.

One day, a friend conducting sperm research asked the husband, a college professor, for a sperm sample. Knowing the couple's decision not to have children, the friend cheerfully reported that the husband's sperm count was essentially zero. At first, the husband and wife were relieved they no longer needed contraception. However, over the next few months they grew increasingly irritated with each other and their sex life became so unsatisfying that they eventually stopped having sex altogether. Clearly, the couple wants to return to the way things were (the current status quo is unacceptable) making this an interesting example of a change bias.

Before reading further, consider how you would respond to this couple. What would you say or do to design an optimal choice environment that acknowledges their need to attain something that now seems unattainable?

***

Erickson described a case (4.4 in the case index) with these same details. His initial move was to interview each partner privately so that they could speak freely. While interviewing the husband, Erickson learned that he felt something was lacking during sex because he didn't have sperm in his semen. After meeting with the wife, Erickson found that she had a similar underlying feeling.

Next, Erickson saw them together and explained that their bodies might have psychosomatically altered their gonadal functioning as a form of protection against potential pregnancy. Erickson suggested they resume using contraception, which would likely restore their fulfilling sex life (an injunctive contingency). His explanation, which was long and filled with impressive medical and psychological terminology, sounded intelligent so they agreed to follow his advice.

At their follow-up appointment a month later, they reported that they had resumed using contraception and their sex life had returned to normal. At that time, the husband commented on the common human tendency, regardless of intelligence, to draw broad conclusions from insufficient data in one area and apply them extensively to unrelated fields. In other words, there was no logical reason for their sex life to have been disrupted.

This case highlights how sex, heavily influenced by psychological factors, can be deeply affected by our beliefs, perceptions, and everyday routines. This aligns with evidence showing that expectations and perceived conditions strongly influence subjective physiological experiences. It illustrates how an injunctive contingency can leverage a false-positive change bias (they imagined change where none had occurred) by prescribing an action that created the illusion of resolution (psychologically undoing the imagined change). This way Erickson enabled the couple to perceive meaningful improvement even though physiologically nothing substantial had changed between them.

Conclusion

The cases discussed throughout this chapter demonstrate how ECA effectively addresses the complexities of change bias by channeling its motivational energy toward adaptive growth. Change bias can manifest in two primary forms: false-positive and false-negative. While false-positive involves overestimating progress due to wishful thinking or unrealistic expectations, false-negative involves the failure to recognize genuine progress, leading to frustration, discouragement, and the mistaken belief that one's efforts are ineffective.

The tactics reflected in Erickson's work: self-monitoring, temporal self-comparison, injunctive contingency, and mental contrasting serve as new environmental designs that accommodate a change bias by providing tangible, structured opportunities for individuals to perceive progress accurately (Table 4.1). For instance, self-monitoring and temporal self-comparison address false-negative by making incremental improvements observable and undeniable, thereby enhancing self-efficacy and motivation. Conversely, injunctive contingency and mental contrasting help counter false-positive by transforming vague aspirations into concrete, meaningful actions aligned with personal values and intrinsic motivations. Research underscores the importance of grounding perceptions of progress in concrete evidence rather than idealistic aspirations. Studies indicate that consistent self-monitoring paired with structured reflection significantly improves self-regulation and goal adherence (Carver & Scheier, 2001).

The central thesis of this chapter is that ECA does not classify change as a goal to be achieved; rather, it treats change as a pervasive life process found in all forms of nature from which meaningful growth can potentially emerge. While individuals may be hindered by phenomena such as *change blindness* or *maladaptive perfectionism*, recognizing the influence of change bias allows practitioners to guide them toward discovering progress that feels both attainable and authentic.

Quick-Reference Tactic Map

Table 4.1 Tactics Suited for *Change Bias* and the Broader Architecture of Strategic Influence

If Client...	*Then Use...*	*Because*
Blind to progress or believes change is nonexistent	*Temporal self-comparison*: Highlighting development by comparing current performance to past baseline, rather than to other people.	*Frames* progress within a growth trajectory.
Difficulties are private, variable, or internally experienced	*Self-monitoring*: Directing individuals to track behavior or outcomes so automatic patterns become visible, measurable, and easier to adjust.	Builds awareness and accountability (*commitment*) by converting vague internal experience into observable patterns.

(*Continued*)

Table 4.1 (Continued)

If Client...	*Then Use...*	*Because*
Behavior is involuntary or if attempts at direct regulation fail	*Injunctive contingency*: Framing the regulation of non-volitional behavior as a byproduct of a volitional action (When X is a problem, do Y to achieve Z).	Establishes a plan (*commitment*) indirectly by linking a difficult-to-control behavior to a voluntary regulatory action.
Dreams big without anchoring in realistic steps	*Mental contrasting*: Juxtaposing positive fantasies about a desired future with the present reality's obstacles that may impede achieving that future.	Tightens goal analysis (*critical thinking*) at preverbal levels by emotionally weighting and evaluating possible outcomes.

Note

1 The use of temporal contrast is an essential subcomponent of all *self-monitoring* systems, though *temporal self-comparison* is not meant to serve as a system of tracking, nor is it meant to be as precise or elaborate as formal *self-monitoring* systems.

References

Albert, S. (1977). Temporal comparison theory. *Psychological Review*, *84*(6), 485–503. https://doi.org/10.1037/0033-295X.84.6.485

Bai, Y., Ocampo, J., Jin, G., Chen, S., Benet-Martinez, V., Monroy, M., Anderson, C., & Keltner, D. (2021). Awe, daily stress, and elevated life satisfaction. *Journal of Personality and Social Psychology*, *120*(4), 837–860. https://doi.org/10.1037/pspa0000267

Bandura, A. (2000). Exercise of human agency through collective efficacy. *Current Directions in Psychological Science*, *9*(3), 75–78. https://doi.org/10.1111/1467-8721.00064

Botti, S., & Iyengar, S. S. (2006). The dark side of choice: When choice impairs social welfare. *Journal of Public Policy & Marketing, 25*(1), 24–38. https://doi.org/10.1509/jppm.25.1.24

Braçe, O., Garrido-Cumbrera, M., Foley, R., Correa-Fernández, J., Suárez-Cáceres, G., & Lafortezza, R. (2020). Is a view of green spaces from home associated with a lower risk of anxiety and depression? *International Journal of Environmental Research and Public Health*, *17*(19), Article 19. https://doi.org/10.3390/ijerph17197014

Butryn, M. L., Miller, N. A., Hagerman, C. J., Arigo, D., LaFata, E., Zhang, F., Spring, B., & Forman, E. (2024). Coach access to digital *self-monitoring* data: An experimental test of short-term effects in behavioral weight-loss treatment.

Obesity (Silver Spring, MD), *32*(11), 2111–2119. https://doi.org/10.1002/oby.24138

Carver, C. S., & Scheier, M. F. (2001). *On the Self-Regulation of Behavior*. Cambridge University Press.

Colloca, L., & Miller, F. G. (2011). Role of expectations in health. *Current Opinion in Psychiatry*, *24*(2), 149. https://doi.org/10.1097/YCO.0b013e328343803b

Deci, E. L., & Ryan, R. M. (2008). Self-determination theory: A macrotheory of human motivation, development, and health. *Canadian Psychology / Psychologie Canadienne*, *49*(3), 182–185. https://doi.org/10.1037/a0012801

Duckworth, A. L., Grant, H., Loew, B., Oettingen, G., & Gollwitzer, P. M. (2011). Self-regulation strategies improve self-discipline in adolescents: Benefits of mental contrasting and *implementation intentions. Educational Psychology*, *31*(1), 17–26. https://doi.org/10.1080/01443410.2010.506003

Feldenkrais, M. (1981). *The Elusive Obvious: The Convergence of Movement, Neuroplasticity, and Health*. Meta Publications. https://www.alibris.com/search/books/isbn/9781623173340

Frank, J. D., & Frank, J. B. (1961). *Persuasion and Healing: A Comparative Study of Psychotherapy*. JHU Press.

Gascon, M., Triguero-Mas, M., Martínez, D., Dadvand, P., Rojas-Rueda, D., Plasència, A., & Nieuwenhuijsen, M. J. (2016). Residential green spaces and mortality: A systematic review. *Environment International*, *86*, 60–67. https://doi.org/10.1016/j.envint.2015.10.013

Haley, J. (1973). *Uncommon Therapy: The Psychiatric Techniques of Milton H.* Erickson, MD. W.W. Norton & Company.

Kappes, A., Wendt, M., Reinelt, T., & Oettingen, G. (2013). Mental contrasting changes the meaning of reality. *Journal of Experimental Social Psychology*, *49*(5), 797–810. https://doi.org/10.1016/j.jesp.2013.03.010

Kedia, G., Mussweiler, T., & Linden, D. E. J. (2014). Brain mechanisms of social comparison and their influence on the reward system. *Neuroreport*, *25*(16), 1255–1265. https://doi.org/10.1097/WNR.0000000000000255

Kirsch, I. (1990). *Changing Expectations: A Key to Effective Psychotherapy* (pp. xviii, 231). Thomson Brooks/Cole Publishing Co.

Krakauer, J. W., Mazzoni, P., Ghazizadeh, A., Ravindran, R., & Shadmehr, R. (2006). Generalization of motor learning depends on the history of prior action. *PLoS Biology*, *4*(10), e316. https://doi.org/10.1371/journal.pbio.0040316

Lee, J.-A., Choi, M., Lee, S. A., & Jiang, N. (2018). Effective behavioral intervention strategies using mobile health applications for chronic disease management: A systematic review. *BMC Medical Informatics and Decision Making*, *18*(1), 12. https://doi.org/10.1186/s12911-018-0591-0

Marquardt, M. K., Oettingen, G., Gollwitzer, P. M., Sheeran, P., & Liepert, J. (2017). Mental contrasting with implementation intentions (MCII) improves physical activity and weight loss among stroke survivors over one year. *Rehabilitation Psychology*, *62*(4), 580–590. https://doi.org/10.1037/rep0000104

Neroni, M. A., Crilly, N., & Brandimonte, M. A. (2024). Unveiling the associative mechanisms underlying the additive bias: Using an implicit association test to gain insight into people's preference for additive actions. *The Journal of Creative Behavior*, *58*(3), 388–411. https://doi.org/10.1002/jocb.660

Oettingen, G., & Mayer, D. (2002). The motivating function of thinking about the future: Expectations versus fantasies. *Journal of Personality and Social Psychology, 83*, 1198–1212. https://doi.org/10.1037/0022-3514.83.5.1198

O'Hanlon, B., & Hexum, A. L. (1990). *An Uncommon Casebook: The Complete Clinical Work of Milton H. Erickson*. Norton.

Prochaska, J. O., & DiClemente, C. C. (1983). Stages and processes of self-change of smoking: Toward an integrative model of change. *Journal of Consulting and Clinical Psychology, 51*(3), 390–395. https://doi.org/10.1037/0022-006X.51.3.390

Rotter, J. B. (1966). Generalized expectancies for internal versus external control of reinforcement. *Psychological Monographs: General and Applied, 80*(1), 1–28. https://doi.org/10.1037/h0092976

Sunderrajan, A., & Albarracín, D. (2021). Are actions better than inactions? Positivity, outcome, and intentionality biases in judgments of action and inaction. *Journal of Experimental Social Psychology, 94*, 104105. https://doi.org/10.1016/j.jesp.2021.104105

Vohs, K. D., & Baumeister, R. F. (2011). *Handbook of Self-Regulation: Research, Theory, and Applications* (2nd ed.). Guilford Press.

Watzlawick, P., Beavin, J. H., & Jackson, D. D. A. (1967). *Pragmatics of Human Communication: A Study of Interactional Patterns, Pathologies, and Paradoxes*. Norton.

Wolff, F., & Möller, J. (2022). An individual participant data meta-analysis of the joint effects of social, dimensional, and temporal comparisons on students' academic self-concepts. *Educational Psychology Review, 34*(4), 2569–2608. https://doi.org/10.1007/s10648-022-09686-1

Chapter 5

Make My Day

Reactance

Make My Day: *Reactance*

A mother contacted me by phone to request that I work with her 18-year-old daughter who had just been discharged from the hospital following lethal, self-inflicted wrist injuries. Over the past three years, the teenage girl had experienced periods of violent acting-out, anxiety, and severe depressive episodes. After her stay at the hospital, she was assigned a label of bipolar disorder. When I agreed to work with her, the mother expressed concern that her daughter would reject therapy. During an argument with her mother, she had insisted that she would refuse to speak to any therapist. I told the mother that there was no need to debate the issue. If she could get her daughter to my office, I assured her that I would take care of the rest.

When the teenage girl marched in, agitated and defiant, I gestured toward a large chair and verbally invited her to make herself comfortable. She did so by sprawling out, arms and legs extended in opposite directions, forming a double-X with her four limbs. I had seen adults signal a guarded mental stance by crossing their arms. However, I had not previously seen such a full-body expression of emotional barricade. Her forearm was lined with metal piercings and long fringe dangled from her hippy-style leather boots. Fixing her gaze on me, she declared that she was not willing to speak to any therapist. I nodded and said, respectfully, that her mother had already told me as much and I reassured her that she would not need to say a word since, fortunately, "I enjoy listening to myself talk."

Next, I told her that she did not need some therapist talking at her. After which, I repositioned my chair next to hers, facing the same direction so that I was no longer in the spot where she had initially projected her anger. I explained that this new position would allow me to speak more softly and that there was no need to listen to what I had to say. I added that if she wanted, she could even go to sleep. As I softened my voice and talked about the goodness of her mind and her right to happiness and self-respect, she responded by closing her eyes and listening in a relaxed, peaceful state for approximately 30 minutes.

DOI: 10.4324/9781003797876-6

After this ego-strengthening exercise, she spontaneously started sharing information about her struggles at home and school. For her next visit, she returned on a day and time she had chosen and our conversations deepened. Eventually, she described hearing voices and experiencing intense feelings of fear and suspicion. I asked when these experiences had begun. "At fifteen," she said. Given her style of clothing and cultural mannerisms, I felt confident that I knew her preferred means of rebellion. I asked if she had spent any extended time away from home. She recalled visiting her grandparents' farm the summer she turned sixteen. I took a guess that she was not suicidal or paranoid during those two months. Her surprised expression confirmed I was right. Curious, she asked how I knew. This summer getaway had been the only exception to her emotional turmoil.

I said I had one more guess to make, asking, "Did you start smoking marijuana routinely around age fifteen?" Still perplexed, she admitted I was right again. I then offered my explanation, "It looks like your biological system reacts badly to cannabis. For some reason, THC triggers anxiety, paranoia, and even suicidal thinking, for you."

She sat motionless connecting the dots in her mind, decided that I was correct, and exclaimed, "Fuck! All that time in the hospital...and having other kids think I am some crazy freak...It was all avoidable! Fucking hell!" The idea that her struggles were not a reflection of who she was, but rather how her brain responded to a specific substance, was a huge relief. She stopped using marijuana that day. Soon, her mood lifted, her thinking cleared, and she remained drug-free for five months, until April 20. That evening marked the start of a smoking binge that ended in another crisis. She was arrested after running through a distant neighborhood nude in a state of confusion and panic, followed by another hospitalization.

After a period of recovery, she went out of state for college, committed to complete abstinence, and continued therapy with someone new. Two years later, I received an email from her mother saying her daughter had adjusted well to college life following her fresh start in a new social environment.

This case shows how verbal and environmental design can defuse confrontation. Instead of opposing her defiance, I incorporated it into our interaction by telling her I enjoyed listening to myself and was fine with her closing her eyes and drifting off. This affirmed her self-protective disengagement as a valid choice and preserved three key freedoms: She did not have to act, choose, or agree. This effect aligns with *reactance* research showing that interpersonal struggles diminish when individuals perceive their autonomy is preserved rather than challenged. By respecting her autonomy and subtly reshaping the context, I created space for engagement to emerge on her terms. In time, she reorganized her life on her own terms.

Recognizing Reactance in Ericksonian Choice Architecture

Reactance is the emotional and cognitive response individuals experience when they perceive that their ability to choose freely among options is being limited or taken away (Brehm, 1966). In the vignette above, her opening declaration that she "was not willing to speak to any therapist" signaled an autonomy threat. My nudge defused her reactance by explicitly preserving freedom (she didn't have to talk, listen, act, choose, or agree) and by repositioning the interaction so engagement could emerge as her decision rather than as compliance. In all cases, perceived threats to autonomy generate an unpleasant emotional state (reactance), motivating the individual to restore their freedom. This motivation can manifest in various ways, such as defying the restriction, reasserting control, or valuing the restricted option more highly. The trigger may be subtle, like persuasive messaging, or overt, like mandates or commands. This threat elicits a strong urge to defy external pressure and reassert control. At its core, reactance is not without merit. It serves as a psychological safeguard against coercion.

Operationally, reactance manifests in behaviors such as rapid rejection of advice, heightened interest in discouraged options, or reframing neutral choices as declarations of independence. Emotionally, it may surface as anger, sarcasm, or defensiveness. Cognitively, it often includes black-and-white thinking, selective attention, and memory biases that exaggerate the controlling nature of past authority figures. Socially, it can take the form of non-cooperation, backlash behavior, or a drive to "win" trivial disputes to reassert autonomy.

Reactance may also appear as principled nonconformity or resistance to group consensus. This opposition is driven more by the desire to assert individuality than by reasoned content disagreement. While this impulse can foster creativity and independent thought, it can also lead individuals to reject beneficial guidance merely to resist external influence.

Whether reactance is adaptive or counterproductive depends on context. In its constructive form, it defends against manipulation, reinforces core values, and fuels independent thinking. It becomes an asset when directed at oppressive norms or deceptive influence. For example, Christopher Bryan et al. (2016) demonstrated that when adolescents were presented with healthy eating as a form of rebellion against manipulative food marketing, they responded by making significantly healthier food choices. Framing health behaviors as acts of defiance activated their intrinsic values (justice, autonomy, and fairness) leveraging the same motivational state that might otherwise lead to less advantageous choices. Similarly, research by Al-Khouja et al. (2021) demonstrated that when women are made aware of oppression toward other women, they are more motivated to express themselves. This recontextualization (i.e., the mistreatment of women) transformed nonconformity into an empowered form of self-expression. This shows how reactance can be a positive force when aligned with *intrinsic motivation* and social identity.

However, when activated within a fundamentally safe context, reactance may block collaboration, blind individuals to useful feedback, or undermine trust. Individuals in a state of reactance often display hostile attribution bias, interpreting neutral intentions as threats, or assume others act purely from external incentives (i.e., they do not truly care). These distortions, particularly in situations involving negative transference or a perceived power imbalance, can magnify everyday interactions into perceived battles for control. This often leads to unproductive conflict or emotional withdrawal.

Reactance is often categorized by the specific type of freedom that feels threatened (Wicklund, 2024). One form involves freedom of belief or opinion, as in "My thoughts are being undervalued," which often produces an automatic rejection of others' ideas. This type of reactance can be addressed with tactics such as *preemptive devaluation* or *strategic surrender*, which signals that the threat to autonomy has ended. A second form centers on decision freedom, as in "I can't choose for myself," and aligns with tactics such as a *no-oriented proposition*. A third involves threatened freedom of action, for example, "I can't do what I want," which is closely related to the tactic of *injunctive reversal*. Across all three forms, effective collaborative design does not fight for control; it clarifies rights and responsibilities. Identifying the specific type of reactance makes it easier to design choice environments that honor the client's implicit values, allowing adaptive engagement to emerge naturally rather than through external pressure.

Erickson's Casework and the Application of Tactical Nudges

Now that we've explored how to recognize the cognitive and emotional signs of the reactance bias, we can begin to see how Erickson worked not by confronting defiance, but by designing environments where opposition became unnecessary. Rather than attempting to overpower those who felt cornered, coerced, or powerless, Erickson created contexts where these individuals could reexperience agency in subtle but meaningful ways. This reflects evidence showing that restored perceptions of agency increase willingness to engage and cooperate.

This next section presents clinical examples where Erickson used principles of choice architecture to support autonomy, preserve dignity, and invite engagement without triggering defensiveness. These are *not* merely clever interventions, they are carefully structured encounters that demonstrate how optimal choice environments can disarm reactance by affording clients a path back to self-direction.

Case 5.1: What Kind of an Ass Are You Going to Make of Yourself

A 24-year-old woman had been diagnosed with paranoid schizophrenia after exhibiting both auditory and visual hallucinations, along with growing antagonism toward her parents and siblings. She had previously been hospitalized in several psychoanalytically oriented facilities, where multiple psychiatrists attempted treatment, without success. The patient consistently mocked their efforts, placing the doctors on the defensive. Eventually, her doctors deemed her "untreatable" and recommended electroshock therapy. However, neither the woman nor her family was willing to pursue that option, so she was discharged and brought to Erickson by her parents.

Upon meeting Erickson, the woman assumed a mocking posture and said sarcastically, "My family thinks you can hypnotize me into being sane. I'd like to see what kind of ass you're going to make of yourself." Erickson replied politely, "I hope not to make an ass of myself, although I suppose I have the potential. All I really intend to do is bore you for the next two hours."

Amused by his candor, the woman remarked that most psychiatrists tried too hard to be interesting. Erickson then began reading aloud a dry academic article on working with resistant patients, which included an extended hypnotic induction. He invited her to listen with resentment, emphasizing that the boredom she would experience should help her stay awake, also adding, "Just don't fall asleep out of spite."

With a scornful expression, she sat through the reading until, to her surprise, she noticed her right hand beginning to lift involuntarily in response to the suggestions embedded in the script. This spontaneous movement bypassed her conscious opposition and introduced a low-friction pathway for engagement. What began as self-protective reactance shifted subtly into active participation, not through confrontation, but through the design of an experience that was implicitly appealing.

Over time, her psychotic behavior dissipated. She re-enrolled in college and developed improved relationships with her family. Importantly, she continued therapy with Erickson even after her hallucinations had ceased, a sign that her engagement had shifted from defiance to genuine trust.

Preemptive Devaluation

In Ericksonian Choice Architecture (ECA), the behavioral tactic known as preemptive devaluation involves deliberately revealing a personal flaw, limitation, or self-deprecating remark early in an interaction to leverage a predisposition toward disagreement. This technique is disarming because it neutralizes anticipated criticism, diffuses aggression by showing vulnerability or humility, and invites collaboration, as opposed to triggering power struggles. It draws on the *pratfall effect*, a phenomenon in social psychology where individuals who display a small, relatable imperfection are perceived as more likable and trustworthy. By modeling humility or welcoming criticism, the speaker *redirects* the impulse to oppose into a less adversarial and more affiliative form of engagement.

In the context of high-stakes negotiation, former FBI hostage negotiator Chris Voss describes a tactic that he calls an accusation audit, which closely resembles what ECA refers to as preemptive devaluation. As Voss points out, by preemptively acknowledging potential criticisms or negative perceptions, the negotiator disarms the other party, reducing opposition and building trust. He also argues that this tactic demonstrates empathy and transparency, helping the counterpart feel in control and more open to dialogue. For example, saying, "You might think I'm just here to sell you something you don't need" defuses skepticism before it arises. Voss makes the point that constructive engagement becomes more likely when objections are addressed as early as possible (Voss & Raz, 2016).

Preemptive devaluation is an especially effective tactic when addressing a psychological dynamic known as *reactive devaluation*. This is a cognitive bias where people instinctively dismiss ideas simply because they originate from a source perceived as an opponent or competitor. This defensive posture often serves to protect one's intellectual autonomy or status in the face of a perceived power imbalance. Under these conditions, a listener will respond to new evidence by strengthening their previous beliefs—a phenomenon known as the *backfire effect* (Sanna et al., 2002). However, by proactively devaluing one's own authority, or offering, the speaker disrupts this defensive reflex.

On the surface, the speaker's self-negation seems to invite rejection. However, when a listener is predisposed to disagree reflexively, that negative self-assessment is often contradicted by the listener's own more favorable response, which in turn makes the listener more receptive to subsequent ideas. I first discovered the utility of this maneuver in 1993, when working with court-ordered clients who were forced to come to counseling because they had been violent or abusive. Most of my clients were older than me, from a different ethnicity or culture, and not oriented toward seeking outside counsel. During the first session, I would sometimes remark, "I am certain that the last thing you want is some book-smart kid trying to tell you how to live your life." In every instance, these clients disagreed with me, making affirming remarks such as, "That's not really right. I am sure there are some useful things that you could teach me." The only cautionary rule while using this tactic is to avoid the use of sarcasm or harsh self-devaluation. Honest humility strikes the right note.

As counterintuitive as it may seem, acknowledging one's shortcomings at the outset of a conversation can increase the sense that one is safe, humble, and unlikely to be controlling. Paul Silvia's (2006) experimental work on message framing helps explain why timing matters. He found that when a message began with a threat to autonomy, people were more likely to engage in critical scrutiny, generate opposing views, and maintain that disagreement over time. By contrast, when reactance was triggered later in the message, it was more likely to fade once the pressure subsided. This suggests that a preemptive concession at the beginning of an interaction can reduce sustained counterarguing and create space for more genuine engagement.

Building on this, recent research by Wald et al. (2024) further underscores the strategic value of modest self-disclosure in persuasive and collaborative contexts. Across ten studies, Wald found that acknowledging one's perceived lack of credibility by using phrases like "I know this may sound hard to believe" or "I'm not that smart, but..." can enhance perceptions of sincerity and self-awareness, particularly when the speaker is not already seen as highly credible. These so-called "credibility disclaimers" signal humility and transparency, qualities that can disarm skepticism and build trust. Importantly, Wald's findings suggest that such modest framing is especially effective when trying to establish rapport or influence from a non-dominant position, making it a useful complement to strategies that aim to reduce reactance and encourage collaboration. By lowering the perceived threat level from the outset, preemptive devaluation turns skepticism into curiosity and repositions influence as partnership versus persuasion.

Case Analysis

Erickson's guidance with the 24-year-old woman diagnosed with paranoid schizophrenia demonstrates the effective use of preemptive devaluation. This woman had previously exhibited significant opposition to therapy, often mocking her care providers and rejecting their authority. Erickson's tactic involved exposing his own perceived shortcomings by admitting he hoped not to "make an ass of himself," acknowledging his potential to do so. This brief comment deflated any expectations she might have had about him being a traditional, authoritative therapist, allowing her to engage without feeling the need to reject him outright.

This approach was particularly useful given the woman's psychological state. Having been labeled as "untreatable" by other clinicians and repeatedly rejecting their attempts, she had developed a defensive posture toward authority figures. Her opposition was not just to psychiatrists but more broadly a means of preserving her autonomy, which she felt was constantly under threat. Understanding this, Erickson used preemptive devaluation to neutralize her initial attack by emphasizing his own limitations.

Research on reactive devaluation (Cheung et al., 2020) suggests that when individuals feel their autonomy is threatened, they are motivated to resist helpful guidance. In this case, however, the woman's core decision was not simply whether to follow instructions, but whether to participate in the process in a way that preserved her sense of control. By *preemptively devaluing* himself (saying that he was only going to bore her) Erickson altered the relational frame. Therapy no longer appeared to be something imposed on her by a controlling authority, but something she could enter without needing to defend herself through opposition. In this way, preemptive devaluation created conditions for *dynamic reversal*: Instead of resisting the process, she could choose cooperation on her own terms. The tactic thus helped soften her defenses, making it possible for her to engage more fully and ultimately contribute to adaptive outcomes.

General Application

Preemptive devaluation is a behavioral tactic that neutralizes skepticism by strategically minimizing the significance of external influence before the person has a chance to reject it. Preemptive devaluation *uses the client's own skeptical filter as a starting point*, often by acknowledging a limitation or downside of the proposed idea before the client can do so. This bypasses defensiveness by aligning with their protective stance, restoring a sense of psychological sovereignty.

This tactic is especially effective for individuals experiencing reactive devaluation. Rather than fight this opposition, preemptive devaluation works with it, showing respect for the person's critical stance and reducing the likelihood of defensive pushback.

In clinical practice, Erickson would sometimes say, "I can be really dense at times. If I miss something important, that you want me to understand, then please say a little more so that it becomes obvious to me." In a different setting, a business coach might note, "This approach can feel formulaic. And, you may already know much of this. So please tell me if I am starting to bore you." These statements signal openness and protect the client's freedom to decline, which paradoxically makes acceptance more likely.

Supporting this method, recent studies on expectancy violation and strategic message framing (Tormala & Rucker, 2022) show that when influencers acknowledge their own limitations or potential biases up front, audiences become more open and less resistant. By addressing potential objections early, it models respect for autonomy and creates a low-pressure space for self-directed action.

Case 5.2: That Will Pay You for Your Time

A man sought out Erickson after falling into a deep depression following the tragic death of his oldest son. The loss was painful and linked to hypnosis because his son had been his first hypnotic subject. Since then, the man had been unable to use hypnosis in his clinical practice, which was a skill that had once been central to his professional identity.

When he arrived at Erickson's office, he walked in, placed a check on the desk, and said firmly, "That will pay you for your time. All I want is to have you hypnotize me, remove my block against hypnosis, and send me on my way."

Erickson noted the man's rigid posture. He sat stiffly upright in his chair, arms folded tightly across his chest, and eyes narrowed in suspicion, tracking Erickson's every movement.

First, Erickson directly invited him to relax, saying, "You may now lean back and relax."

The man replied tersely, "I am perfectly relaxed. Just go ahead and try to hypnotize me. I've given you a check large enough to pay for the next two hours of your time." The man had no awareness of the depth of his own defiance.

Erickson proceeded to use a series of hypnotic induction techniques, one after another. None were successful. After two hours of persistent effort, Erickson finally leaned back and said, without sarcasm or frustration, that he had to confess his "absolute inability to induce a trance."

To this, the man smiled politely and reassured Erickson, "It doesn't matter. I was just on my way to the Grand Canyon. I only stopped in to see if I could be hypnotized. Now that I know I can't be, I'll just drop the idea of therapy altogether."

They shook hands and Erickson wished him a pleasant trip. Then, with casual friendliness, Erickson added, "Before you go, would you like to meet my wife?" The man agreed. In another room, introductions were made. They chatted briefly about the upcoming trip, and again, Erickson said goodbye.

However, during this second farewell Erickson altered the handshake. Instead of the firm, quick gesture from earlier, he withdrew his hand in a slow, lingering, and subtly indefinite way. This secured the man's full attention and suspended his usual mental habits.

In that moment, the man slipped into a frozen state and then into a profound somnambulistic trance.

Without any disagreement, he was gently guided back to Erickson's office. Erickson told him that he had in fact accomplished what he came for. He said that the block had been removed and that he should now spend the next hour quietly reflecting on his life.

Erickson added, "You are to use me merely as a sounding board for your ideas."

The man sat silently for much of the hour, occasionally murmuring to himself. Every now and then, he asked a quiet question about using hypnosis again in his practice. Erickson offered simple, direct reassurance in response.

Eight years later, Erickson reported that the man was once again practicing hypnosis confidently. His depression had not returned, and he maintained a full and active clinical practice.

Strategic Surrender

In ECA, strategic surrender is a behavioral tactic that involves feigning surrender in a power struggle to lower the opponent's guard, creating an opportunity for a surprise counteraction. This tactic is grounded in research showing that perceived freedom restoration reduces opposition and defensiveness. By appearing to give up, the practitioner disarms the other's opposition and creates a window of opportunity for a well-timed, often subtle, counteraction. This temporary posture is not genuine defeat. It is a calculated maneuver designed to bypass psychological reactance and regain influence in a less confrontational manner.

The psychological effectiveness of strategic surrender rests on three core components. *Pseudo closure* gives the impression that the contest is over, reducing vigilance. *Tactical passivity*, where the practitioner temporarily withdraws or adopts a submissive stance, reinforces this illusion. Crucially, the resignation is *reversible*, allowing the practitioner to pivot seamlessly back into active influence once the moment of tension has passed. This requires timing sensitivity, as the maneuver must be executed precisely when the other person's guard is down and their reactive posture has relaxed.

The theoretical underpinnings of strategic surrender are grounded in research on psychological reactance. Baer et al. (1980) found that perceived threats to autonomy (not actual force) drive reactance. Publicly conceding or disengaging can therefore restore a sense of control to the individual, weakening their need to oppose. Similarly, Hannah et al. (1975) showed that *predictability* in behavior can provoke reactance ("I knew you would do that!"). Strategic surrender introduces ambiguity, preventing the client or counterpart from locking into a defensive script.

The value of this tactic is apparent when framed within the *paradox of power*, which states that the more overt pressure one applies, the more opposition it tends to generate. Strategic surrender turns that paradox inside out by *appearing* to let go of control, subtly repositioning the practitioner from a former antagonist to a subdued persona. In therapeutic contexts, this might look like a clinician saying, "Perhaps it's time I give up on trying to convince you," which shifts the burden of initiative back to the client, often prompting a spontaneous re-engagement on their part.

Case Analysis

In the case of the grieving hypnotherapist, Erickson clearly employed strategic surrender, which is the deliberate appearance of surrender in a power struggle to reduce opposition and open the door to unexpected influence. The client entered Erickson's office with a rigid posture and a transactional request, "All I want is to have you hypnotize me, remove my block against hypnosis, and send me on my way." His defensive stance reflected a deep ambivalence. He wanted help, but also needed to prove that help was beyond reach. This tension revealed his core psychological bind, which was seeking recovery while holding tightly to the belief that his trauma had rendered hypnosis, his life's work, ineffective and inaccessible.

Erickson responded with what appeared to be a doomed effort. After two hours of failed inductions, he acknowledged that he had been unable to induce trance. This apparent failure was not a retreat but strategic passivity. By mirroring the man's belief that "hypnosis won't work on me," Erickson aligned with the client's internal narrative and allowed him to make his point. Research by Baer et al. (1980) suggests that reactance is strongest when autonomy feels threatened. Erickson's admission of failure removed that threat and preserved the man's sense of control. In that moment, the client felt he had won and had nothing left to prove.

As the man stood to leave, Erickson changed the context by introducing his wife and ending with a handshake. The handshake was deliberately slow, lingering, and imprecise, capturing the man's attention after the contest had ended. This illustrates the reversibility central to strategic surrender: What looked like capitulation was only superficial, while Erickson remained ready to act when the moment opened. The client, caught off guard, entered a state that had been inaccessible. Erickson then established a sense of equality by inviting the man to use him as "a sounding board" for his own ideas. This shifted the encounter from top-down authority to collaborative exploration, thereby preserving the autonomy he needed. The question was no longer whether hypnosis worked, but whether he would re-engage with life. Eight years later, he had returned to a full professional life, used hypnosis enthusiastically, and had no recurrence of depression.

This case shows that effective influence does not require confrontation or overt persuasion. Instead, it depends on creating accessible entry points that respect autonomy, credibility, and dignity. In this instance, strategic surrender created a neutral space in which the client could step out of the power struggle without losing face. Erickson thus transformed the encounter from a contest of wills into a shared inquiry, using the client's own worldview to restore agency. By separating support from pressure and progress from obedience, he created space for increased self-efficacy and cooperative engagement.

General Application

The essence of strategic surrender lies in its ability to sidestep opposition by appearing to accept defeat, inviting the other party to lower their defenses. It is especially effective for individuals in a state of reactance where perceived threats to autonomy trigger defiance. While *ambivalence* may also be present, reactance is the primary heuristic guiding its use. By reducing pressure and momentarily removing the practitioner as a target of a power struggle, the strategy *primes* self-initiative rather than rebellion.

In practice, signaling defeat or underscoring one's own limitations removes the practitioner as a threat to the client's autonomy. This often prompts the client to reassert control not in opposition to the practitioner, but in pursuit of their own goals. For example, a counselor might signal defeat by saying, "I don't think I can convince you." By subtly drawing attention to the option being declined, the client's power is underscored. This has been shown to reduce reactance (Baer et al., 1980). In motivational interviewing, a related approach, "rolling with resistance," achieves similar results by intentionally avoiding direct persuasion to elicit internally motivated change (Rollnick et al., 2008).

Coaching applications may involve acknowledging the limits of influence, such as, "You're right, if this is not the right time, then it simply isn't. Maybe this is not something we will resolve in our work together." Paradoxically, such statements often increase commitment by positioning the decision as the client's to reclaim.

Across contexts, strategic surrender works not through dishonest manipulation but through the authentic design of scenarios in which autonomy is preserved, opposition becomes unnecessary, and the act of choosing emerges as both self-directed and self-reinforcing.

Case 5.3: Cinnamon Face

A concerned mother came to Erickson's office seeking help for her eight-year-old daughter. She described the girl as deeply hostile and withdrawn:

> She is eight years old. She hates her sister, she hates me, she hates her father, she hates her teacher, her schoolmates. She hates the mailman, the milkman, the man at the gas station. She just plain hates everybody.

> She hates herself. I've tried for a long time to get her to go to Kansas for the summer to visit her grandparents. She hates them, even though she doesn't know them.

Erickson asked, "What's all this hate about?" The mother replied, "A mass of freckles on her face. The kids at school call her 'Freckles,' and she hates those freckles terribly." Erickson then asked, "Where is the girl?" "She's out in the car," the mother said. "She doesn't want to come in. She hates you because you're a doctor and because she's got freckles." Without hesitation, Erickson instructed, "Go out and bring the girl in, even if you have to use force. And bring her into this room."

Force wasn't needed. The girl walked in on her own, fists clenched, jaw set, glaring at Erickson with open defiance. She was ready for a fight. Erickson met her glare and said firmly, "You're a thief! You steal!" Scornfully, the girl snapped, "I am not a thief! I don't steal!"

"Oh, yes," Erickson insisted. "You're a thief. You steal things. I even know what you stole. I even have proof that you stole." The girl vigorously defended her honor, "You haven't got proof! I never stole nothing!" Feeding her indignation, Erickson said calmly, "I even know where you were when you stole what you stole."

As her emotional energy rose, Erickson delivered the punchline:

> I'll tell you where you were and what you stole. You were in the kitchen, setting the kitchen table. You were standing at the kitchen table. You were reaching up to the cookie jar, which was filled with cinnamon cookies, cinnamon buns, and cinnamon rolls. And, you spilled some cinnamon on your face. You're a Cinnamon Face!

In an instant, everything shifted. The accusation, which began as an insult, turned into a nickname. It was playful, not mean. He reframed the source of her shame into something fun and affectionate.

That summer, the girl went to visit her grandparents and thoroughly enjoyed herself. She even began corresponding with Erickson, sending him smiling pictures of herself. In return, Erickson sent her whimsical letters discussing the "hidden joys of living," each letter signed by the Easter Bunny.

A little over 20 years later, I had the opportunity to interview Cinnamon Face, hoping she could share more details about her one and only face-to-face encounter with Erickson. Unfortunately, as an adult she had complete amnesia for the office visit. What she did share was the lasting significance of the letters from the "Easter Bunny," which remained among her most treasured possessions.

Fortunately, Erickson explained the logic behind his unorthodox approach:

> She was in a frame of mind to react favorably because I had intensified her hostility and anger deliberately, and then raised in her mind, literally, a vacuum. I told her I knew where she was when she stole, I knew what it was she stole, and I had proof. And so, she felt relieved at the accusation of being a thief when it didn't apply.

By building tension and then relieving it with a playful reframe, Erickson transformed the interaction:

> I was really joking with her and it became a fun situation. She liked her cinnamon rolls or buns or cookies. And, I gave her freckles a new name. ...All I did was reorient the situation. I didn't change it. I just reoriented it. Very few people know of the importance of reorientation.

For a detailed discussion of reorientation in Ericksonian therapy, see Short et al. (2005). Within ECA, emotional reorientation is understood as a type of framing.

No-Oriented Proposition

The tactic known as no-oriented proposition involves presenting an opportunity to reject influence early in the interaction, thereby safeguarding the individual's experience of autonomy and reducing psychological reactance. This is followed by strategically placing high-value options later in the sequence. This method creates space for self-assertion by offering an initial option that lacks definitive value. The refusal of this first offer not only respects the individual's need for control but also sets the stage for subsequent options to appear more attractive by comparison. The power of this tactic lies in the paradox that by designing a "no" option, the practitioner increases the likelihood of eventually receiving a freely chosen "yes." This effect reflects findings that opportunities for refusal restore autonomy and reduce resistance to later cooperation.

This approach draws support from both behavioral science and negotiation theory. Mowen and Cialdini (1980) found that people are more likely to comply with a second request if it is framed as a smaller or more reasonable version of the first, particularly when the second request remains substantial enough to avoid ceiling effects. Their research emphasized the importance of sequencing and contrast. When the first request is refused, the second is accepted more often because it seems less burdensome or fairer in comparison.

Similarly, Voss describes how eliciting a "no" gives people the feeling of safety, security, and control. He writes, "When you preserve a person's autonomy by clearly giving them permission to say 'No'...the effectiveness of the decisions go up" (Voss & Raz, 2016, p. 79). He further notes, "'No' gives the speaker the feeling of safety… You use a question that prompts a 'No' answer, and your counterpart feels that by turning you down he has proved that he's in the driver's seat" (Voss & Raz, 2016, p. 86). Across a variety of settings, whether therapeutic, educational, or negotiation contexts, allowing for early rejection levels the emotional landscape, making subsequent acceptance feel like a product of careful reasoning.

Erickson masterfully illustrated this tactic through behavioral design in clinical settings. For example, if clients announced that hypnosis probably would not work on them, Erickson would accept the overall premise and then use a tactic known as *strategic buffering* to create space for defiance. As Erickson (1944) explains, words such as "each" and "every" or "completely" and "fully" are distraction words that create an opportunity to reject the qualifying details of a task without eliminating the possibility of implementing the task in some other form. In other words, strategic buffering is the use of absolutistic terminology that invites disagreement-prone individuals to make overly fine distinctions or argue about trivial differences, while leaving the big picture idea intact.

The space to express rejection can also be achieved in concrete terms. For example, Erickson (1959) could explain to a disagreement-prone individual, "Hypnosis is not likely to work each and every time that it is attempted. It might even fail more often than it succeeds." He would then use concrete objects (such as a chair or a clock) to act as an anchor for the desired psychological reality. For example, "You can see three chairs in my office. If we were to attempt hypnosis in each chair, it would undoubtedly fail more often than it succeeds." He and the client could then test this idea in one chair, affirming the reality of the failure. Next, he would try again in a second chair, adding one more failure to the equation. Erickson then commented, "If hypnosis succeeds in the third chair, it still would have failed more often than it succeeded." And, on that third attempt the client would spontaneously enter a trance state (a behavioral "yes" to subsequent influence). This type of nudge works by leveraging *mental accounting*, which is a fast, intuitive process people use to organize choices. This allows designers to align options with implicit heuristics (unconscious rules), without relying on conscious effort.

Using this approach, Erickson allowed clients to reject his influence twice (nonverbally) before subtly aligning with him on the third and final try (their last chance). This sequence embodies a key principle of the no-oriented proposition: creating a progression in which the "yes" does not negate the earlier "no," but follows it naturally, as if chosen without persuasion.

ECA's no-oriented proposition works not just because it respects autonomy, but because it uses the psychology of contrasting, sequencing, and emotional pacing to guide clients toward cooperation without ever demanding it. By postponing high-value options and allowing the client to reject lesser ones first, the practitioner aligns with the client's natural desire to feel in control. When it comes time for "yes" it feels both safe and self-directed.

Case Analysis

In this case, Erickson used a no-oriented proposition to serve as a strategic invitation for the young girl to reclaim agency by rejecting an accusation she knew to be false. Accusing her of theft was not a suggestion but a provocation, offering the girl an opportunity to say "no" in a situation she could fully control. At a psychological level, the child had been entrenched in a pattern of self-protective disengagement fueled by deep insecurity. She perceived others' actions through a lens of antagonism. Her anger functioned as a defensive barrier; by pushing people away, she protected herself from vulnerability and rejection.

Erickson recognized this dynamic and used an unwarranted accusation to channel her oppositional energy in a new direction. According to research on no-oriented influence, the ability to reject an initial offer increases a person's sense of autonomy and reduces psychological reactance. By accusing the girl of something obviously untrue, Erickson created a psychologically safe refusal, one in which her opposition was not only expected, but also welcomed. In doing so, he reframed the interaction so that instead of being the target of unwanted attention for her freckles, she got to say "no," loudly and convincingly, to someone in a position of authority. Her sense of control was restored.

What followed was equally important. With her opposition validated, Erickson delivered the twist. The supposed "theft" was not shameful, rather it was a silly explanation for the freckles on her face. This humorous reframe not only softened her self-perception but also transformed the meaning of her freckles. Using the additional tactics of naming ("Freckle Face") and associative anchoring (her love of cinnamon), Erickson restored feelings of joyful pride in her physical appearance (identity affirmation).

This case reminds us that choice-centric care is not about delivering the right answer but about shaping the conditions under which a person can arrive at their own conclusions. By carefully designing an encounter where rejection was both safe and encouraged, he allowed her to re-engage with social influence from a position of strength versus defensiveness. In doing so, he respected the function of her opposition as a developmental asset, not a problem to eliminate. The lesson here is clear. When we treat defiance as a viable route to participation, we do not erode agency, we strengthen it. By constructing choice points that allow for meaningful refusal, practitioners create conditions for natural alignment. This way the individual not only feels in control but also begins to redefine what's worth choosing.

General Application

A no-oriented proposition is a strategic question designed to elicit a "no" response, allowing individuals to assert autonomy and release opposition without derailing engagement. This tactic is particularly effective for clients experiencing the type of reactance focused on one's freedom to decide. The no-oriented approach gives individuals a safe way to reject influence, which paradoxically increases openness by reinforcing their sense of control.

Across a variety of contexts, this tactic helps reduce defensiveness and encourages more honest reflection. For example, this effect can be achieved by asking, "Are you completely satisfied with how things are going?" This use of the qualifier "completely" invites a no response. Similarly, the question, "Do you agree with everything I'm saying?" followed by, "Well, do you disagree with everything I have said?" elicits a double "no" response while simultaneously creating space for the client to engage productively without feeling pressured or coerced. By positioning opposition as part of the process, the method fosters collaboration and gradually guides individuals toward self-directed change.

Recent innovations include layering no-oriented propositions within structured choice frameworks, offering clients more nuanced ways to engage without feeling manipulated. A clear example of recent innovation that layers no-oriented propositions within structured choice frameworks comes from the integration of motivational interviewing techniques with digital decision aids in mental health apps and behavioral health tactics. For instance, a study by Vilardaga et al. (2018) examined a mobile app designed for smoking cessation, which embedded no-oriented prompts like "Would you prefer to skip this step for now?" within guided decision pathways. These prompts allowed users to reject immediate action without exiting the change process, preserving autonomy while keeping engagement intact.

The structured framework behind this design offered multiple low-pressure entry points, allowing users to navigate toward commitment at their own pace. This combination of no-oriented phrasing and tiered behavioral options mirrors principles from *micro-level choice architecture*, where initial resistance is accepted and reframed as a valid part of the decision-making process. Such layering creates an environment in which saying "no" becomes a form of participation versus withdrawal, supporting both autonomy and momentum.

Case 5.4: The Heckler

Erickson was indirectly approached for help while demonstrating hypnosis to a group of medical students. At the outset, one student began heckling Erickson, denouncing hypnosis as fraudulent and accusing Erickson of being a charlatan. The student defiantly claimed that any demonstration involving his fellow students would be a staged hoax meant to deceive the audience.

Though Erickson initially ignored the heckling, the student's relentless interruptions made it necessary for Erickson to respond. Matching the student's emotional tone, Erickson stopped his lecture and directly engaged the student in a heated exchange.

Erickson embraced the student's need for public opposition, saying, "You must remain silent" and "You can't speak again." As the student continued to disrupt the lecture, Erickson said, "You don't dare stand up." After the student accused Erickson of fraud, Erickson insisted, "You cannot accuse me of fraud again."

After having paradoxically established the student's verbal cooperation, Erickson created the opportunity for the student to contradict him through action. In the form of a dare, Erickson said, "You're afraid to come to the front of the room" followed by, "You must do whatever I say." When the student reached the stage, Erickson added, "You're too scared to shake my hand" followed by, "You wouldn't dare sit in the volunteer chair." By this time the student had stopped speaking but continued to respond through his behavior, locked into a pattern of automatic contradiction. This illustrates how reactance can produce automatic opposition, even as the behavior transforms into cooperative engagement.

After the student began to relax, Erickson designed an opportunity for hypnotic responsiveness, saying, "You're afraid to go into a trance" and, "You couldn't even manage a light trance, let alone a deep one." Soon the student was guided into a somnambulistic trance. He then served as the demonstration subject for the remainder of Erickson's lecture. No doubt, Erickson respectfully affirmed his able demonstration of various hypnotic phenomena.

The following weekend, the student approached Erickson privately. He shared that he had been deeply unhappy and socially isolated, and he requested psychotherapy. Erickson reported that treatment progressed with exceptional speed and success.

Injunctive Reversal

Injunctive reversal is a behavioral tactic within ECA that transforms defiance into voluntary alignment with a high-value outcome. This approach draws on research showing that forbidden actions often become more attractive when autonomy feels restricted. It works by converting cooperation into an act of rebellion by explicitly prohibiting the target behavior. The effectiveness of injunctive reversal lies in designing an environment where compliance feels like an act of self-assertion, not submission.

This tactic draws from psychological reactance theory, which holds that when people sense their autonomy is threatened, they feel a strong urge to reclaim control, often by doing the opposite of what is requested. Injunctive reversal does not try to suppress this defiance; instead, it leverages the underlying motivation and redirects it. The strategy reframes oppositional momentum as a resource instead of a barrier. Rather than attempting to reduce pushback or "resistance," the tactic gives it a role to play in achieving the client's goals.

Another central component is *psychological reversal*, which reframes compliance as a rebellious or nonconforming act, while problematic behavior is subtly positioned as giving in to an undesirable influence or predictable script. The result is *autonomy activation*, which is a felt sense of self-direction and ownership over the behavior, which enhances follow-through and reduces internal conflict.

Recent behavioral research supports this dynamic. Rawal et al. (2025) found that telling participants not to buy a certain product increased attention to the product and ultimately boosted purchase intention. This aligns with the idea that reactance can be used to intensify focus and engagement, especially when the behavior is framed as off-limits or forbidden. Similarly, Ellen Hendriksen (2025) describes "demand resistance" as a form of internal sabotage where individuals avoid tasks, not because they lack desire, but because they feel pressured. This includes resisting even helpful actions due to anxiety, fear of failure, or a need for control. Injunctive reversal offers an antidote. By allowing the individual to feel they are *choosing*, it turns defiance into a vehicle for purposeful behavior.

Ultimately, injunctive reversal is not about tricking someone into doing what you want. It's about designing an environment where the *urge to resist* is honored and integrated, making room for self-determined engagement to emerge naturally.

Case Analysis

In this case, Erickson's use of injunctive reversal illustrates how a strategically designed environment can convert resistance into cooperation without triggering a loss of autonomy. The nudge began with a disruptive student who aggressively sought out Erickson's attention. Rather than attempting to silence the student, Erickson engaged him in a paradoxical interaction that leveraged the student's own psychological tendencies. Drawing on Brehm's (1966) *reactance theory*, which posits that people resist behaviors that feel externally imposed in order to restore a sense of freedom, we can see that when Erickson framed cooperative engagement as forbidden, he was utilizing the student's implicit need to oppose authority. The student's every act of contradiction (e.g., verbal disagreement, moving toward the stage, entering trance) became a defiant assertion of agency as opposed to an admission of his need for guidance.

As the student acted out his rebellion, he unknowingly pursued Erickson's help. Importantly, no one in the audience was made aware of this shift. To the student, it felt like an uninterrupted performance of resistance. To Erickson, it was the creation of an optimal choice environment—a space where autonomy could emerge not through submission, but through self-initiated movement within a restructured framework. This subtle transformation was intensified by the student's increased physical proximity to Erickson. Research by Burgoon et al. (2002) underscores how nonverbal dynamics (such as spatial distance and body orientation) affect perceptions of authority. As the student moved closer to Erickson on stage, his emotional posture reorganized, softening from antagonism to trust.

What this case teaches is that effective micro-level choice architecture does not force behavioral change; it recontextualizes behavior within a structure where individuals can reclaim authorship. Erickson did not restrict the student's freedom. Instead, he expanded it until the very behavior that once enforced disconnection (defiance) became incompatible with the emerging relational dynamic. In the end, when the student sought therapy, it was not because he had been subdued, but because he had found a pathway toward progress that felt internally authored.

General Application

Injunctive reversal transforms self-protective disengagement into engagement by making compliance feel like defiance. This tactic redirects behavior in a paradoxical direction. By framing the target behavior as off-limits, difficult, or subversive, it leverages the individual's immediate urge to oppose external control, particularly when one's behavioral freedom feels threatened.

This approach is invaluable for clients who are oppositional, avoidant, or self-sabotaging. For instance, telling a defiant client, "You're not yet ready to make this kind of progress," may trigger a subtle challenge to prove otherwise, activating effort where hesitation once ruled. Or with teens whose identities often center on courageous independence, a statement like "Most people don't have the nerve to even try this" can reframe growth as a rebellious act. Thus, injunctive reversal works by *redirecting* the client's opposition toward a worthy goal. It invites individuals to defy the very conditions that have left them feeling powerless and in doing so, offers a path forward that feels chosen, not imposed.

Designing an Optimal Choice Environment (OCE) for Reactance

Reactance emerges when a person perceives a threat to their personal liberty because of overt suggestions, persuasive appeals, or external pressure. Importantly, this state is not fixed; it can arise and recede depending on subtle contextual shifts. An *optimal choice environment* that minimizes reactance must do more than reduce friction. It must activate motivational systems in a way that is experienced as self-chosen, internally coherent, and socially meaningful. This same architecture, when properly constructed, also enhances engagement and persistence across a wide range of motivational contexts, not just those marked by defiance.

At the core of the ECA collaborative model is autonomy affirmation, which is the deliberate framing of all options as self-directed versus imposed. This aligns with evidence showing that perceived autonomy increases intrinsic motivation and sustained engagement. When individuals are reminded, implicitly or explicitly, that they retain full authorship over their actions, the likelihood of defensive pushback sharply decreases. Autonomy does not just deter defiance; it promotes deeper integration of goals and values, aligning external behavior with internal standards (personal values). This principle is especially vital when individuals are in flux (ambivalent, uncertain, or newly motivated) because in such moments, even minor cues of external control can destabilize engagement.

Supporting autonomy without triggering defiance requires subtlety. The idea of *leading from behind* involves activating motivation without overt influence. This is achieved by presenting options, defaults, or contextual cues that support adaptive behavior while allowing the individual to own their choice. A well-structured environment should suggest possibility without signaling preference (choice agnostic), creating the experience of moving forward under one's own agency. This also entails a commitment to minimal persuasion, either by avoiding the use of strong arguments, emotional appeals, or motivational language that can feel invasive. Instead, choice architects cultivate environments that highlight intrinsic motivators, such as curiosity, identity-relevance, meaningful contribution, and self-efficacy. These levers are often dormant unless deliberately utilized.

In this sense, the optimal choice environment for reactance is the gold standard for behavioral design. It models the shift away from extrinsic motivators (e.g., compliance-based tactics, explicit incentives, or corrective feedback) toward environments that prime internal motivational systems. Whether the challenge is to support behavioral adaptation, sustain long-term engagement, or reduce dropout, the architecture that engages reactance by creating space for *dynamic reversibility* will be the one most likely to sustain motivation through natural, self-reinforcing pathways.

Thought Exercise

Next, you will have the opportunity to sharpen your design skills. When creating an optimal choice environment for someone experiencing reactance, remember that this environment can include mental landscapes such as imagery, beliefs, and goals, or modifications to their physical surroundings. The only requirement is that you create a context of freedom that explicitly validates the client's ability to defy your influence.

For this thought exercise, imagine speaking with a client who enters your office and requests hypnosis to quit smoking. Because of the long drive, she indicates this will probably be her only trip to your office, meaning that this result must be achieved in a single visit. This is an older woman who, by all appearances, likes to be in charge. When asked what she does for a living, she tells you that she is a hypnotherapist who has been using hypnosis for over two decades. When you ask about her responsiveness to hypnosis, she states that she is uncertain, primarily because no one else has ever been able to get her into a trance state.

Before reading further, consider how you would respond to this person. What would you say or do to design an optimal choice environment that acknowledges her need to subvert the efforts of those who would attempt to exercise power over her, while gently inviting receptiveness to outside guidance?

* * *

These details mirror those of a client who came to my office. Reflecting on Erickson's casework, my initial response was to express regret, "I seriously doubt that I will succeed in any attempt to hypnotize you." This strategic surrender was meant to prevent reactance. Rather than looking disappointed after having driven 50 minutes to get to my office, her facial expression suggested continued engagement.

Wanting to utilize her skill sets, I continued, "The fact that you are an experienced hypnotherapist is really fortuitous." After a brief pause, I added, "I think you will be able to look over at that swivel chair next to you and see a hallucinated version of yourself." Pointing toward the imaginary figure in the chair, my gaze fixed in that direction and I said, "Just nod your head when you see her." After a moment, she nodded. Speaking slowly and emphatically, I said, "Now hypnotize her. Put her into a trance and ensure that she will quit smoking after just one session."

The woman then engaged in what I considered to be a remarkable trance induction, which lasted 30 minutes. When she was ready to address the identified problem, she chose to use aversion therapy. Her method was authoritative and domineering. Continually, she repeated the phrase, "That cigarette looks like dog shit. It smells like dog shit. It tastes like dog shit! From now on, you will be unable to smoke without feeling that you are putting dog shit straight into your mouth!" This use of direct suggestion lasted approximately 15 minutes. When she was finished, I instructed her to awaken herself from trance and to use her own best judgment as to whether or not she should suggest amnesia for the trance experience. She chose to suggest full recall. After she reoriented to the room, it was time to end our session. I made some brief remarks validating the skill of her hypnotic approach and then told her that if there was ever anything else I could do for her to give me a call. The woman left my office pleased with the experience and made no further contact.

Conclusion

Reactance, often mistaken for stubbornness or combativeness, emerges as an urgent need to preserve autonomy in the face of perceived intrusion. Through the lens of ECA, this chapter has shown that this state of mind need not be confronted or overcome. Instead, it can be viewed as an opportunity.

Reactance exemplifies the paradox of power, which is that the more forcefully someone tries to control another person's thoughts or actions, the less welcome their influence becomes. This insight underscores the value of designing environments that reduce external pressure and amplify the experience of voluntary action. As research by Patall et al. (2008) demonstrates, offering choice, even modest amounts, can increase intrinsic motivation. Therefore, making progress with reactance is not about "defusing resistance"; it is about creating optimal conditions for self-directed engagement (affordances). In this sense, the architecture designed to address reactance is not a narrow intervention. It exemplifies the broader mission of choice design, which is to replace controlling prompts with subtle nudges that activate intrinsic motivational systems.

By mapping specific types of threatened freedoms (action, decision, or belief) to corresponding behavioral tactics like injunctive reversal, no-oriented propositions, preemptive devaluation, and strategic surrender, we gain precision in how we engage another person's struggle to attain the feeling of self-determination (Table 5.1). Because these approaches are based on transparent intentions ("I want to communicate in a way that works best for you"), they do not seek to manipulate, rather they are a manifestation of honest respect. They affirm that influence without autonomy is problematic and that true collaborative engagement arises only when individuals feel free to disagree, opt out, or choose again.

Erickson's genius was not in coercing change but in crafting environments where sustained opposition became unnecessary. Each nudge, whether playful, permissive, or paradoxical, demonstrated how behavioral design can honor the client's psychological posture while subtly inviting forward movement. In doing so, he transformed opposition into participation, reluctance into readiness, and hesitation into self-chosen action.

When choice architecture is built on autonomy, dignity, and contextual intelligence, even the most entrenched forms of opposition become pliable. Reactance is not a barrier to behavioral adaptation. It is an invitation to design better conditions for it. And when those conditions are met, people often flourish, not because they must, but because they can.

Quick-Reference Tactic Map

Table 5.1 Tactics Suited for *Reactance* and the Broader Architecture of Strategic Influence

If Client...	*Then Use...*	*Because*
Feels threatened by authority or is prone to *reactance*	*Preemptive devaluation*: Disclosing a minor flaw, limitation, or self-deprecating point early to lower status threat, invite disagreement safely, and reduce reactive opposition.	*Redirects* critical disagreement aligning it with positive engagement.
Escalates control battles or withdraws entirely	*Strategic surrender*: Appearing to yield in a power struggle so defensiveness subsides and later influence becomes more possible.	*Reverse primes* the de-escalation of opposition by removing the immediate target against which defiance is organized.
Rejects proposals without consideration	*No-oriented proposition*: Providing multiple options to reject a request, while strategically placing high-value options later in the sequence.	*Reverse primes* feelings of control, making later cooperation feel self-initiated.
Turns defiance into identity or a point of pride	*Injunctive reversal*: Converting cooperation into an act of defiance by explicitly prohibiting the behavior.	*Redirects* defiance aligning it with adaptive action.

References

Al-Khouja, M., Weinstein, N., & Legate, N. (2021). Motivated to express: Salience of oppression toward other women encourages women's self-expression. *Journal of Social and Political Psychology*, *9*(1), Article 1. https://doi.org/10.5964/jspp.6757

Baer, R., Hinkle, S., Smith, K., & Fenton, M. (1980). *Reactance* as a function of actual versus projected autonomy. *Journal of Personality and Social Psychology*, *38*(3), 416–422. https://doi.org/10.1037/0022-3514.38.3.416

Brehm, J. W. (1966). *A Theory of Psychological Reactance* (pp. x, 135). Academic Press.

Bryan, C. J., Yeager, D. S., Hinojosa, C. P., Chabot, A., Bergen, H., Kawamura, M., & Steubing, F. (2016). Harnessing adolescent values to motivate healthier eating. *Proceedings of the National Academy of Sciences*, *113*(39), 10830–10835. https://doi.org/10.1073/pnas.1604586113

Burgoon, J. K., Bonito, J. A., Ramirez Jr., A., Dunbar, N. E., Kam, K., & Fischer, J. (2002). Testing the interactivity principle: Effects of mediation, propinquity, and verbal and nonverbal modalities in interpersonal interaction. *Journal of Communication*, *52*(3), 657–677. https://doi.org/10.1111/j.1460-2466.2002.tb02567.x

Cheung, S. O., Li, K., & Chow, O. Y. (2020). Reactive devaluation as a psychological impediment to construction dispute negotiation. *Journal of Management in Engineering*, *36*(4), 04020025. https://doi.org/10.1061/(ASCE)ME.1943-5479.0000787

Erickson, M. H. (1944). The method employed to formulate a complex story for the induction of an experimental neurosis in a hypnotic subject. *The Journal of General Psychology*. https://www.tandfonline.com/doi/abs/10.1080/00221309.1944.10545220

Erickson, M. H. (1959). Further Clinical Techniques of Hypnosis: Utilization Techniques. In E. L. Rossi, R. Erickson-Klein, & K. Rossi (Eds.), *Collected Works of Milton H. Erickson, Volume 1: The Nature of Therapeutic Hypnosis* (2008th ed., Vol. 1, pp. 271–306). Milton H. Erickson Foundation Press.

Hannah, T. E., Hannah, E. R., & Wattie, B. (1975). Arousal of psychological *Reactance* as a consequence of predicting an individual's behaviour. *Psychological Reports*, *37*(2), 411–420. https://doi.org/10.2466/pr0.1975.37.2.411

Hendriksen, E. (2025). *How to Be Enough: Self-Acceptance for Self-Critics and Perfectionists*. St. Martin's Publishing Group.

Mowen, J. C., & Cialdini, R. B. (1980). On implementing the door-in-the-face compliance technique in a business context. *Journal of Marketing Research*, *17*(2), 253–258. https://doi.org/10.1177/002224378001700210

Patall, E. A., Cooper, H., & Robinson, J. C. (2008). The effects of choice on *intrinsic motivation* and related outcomes: A meta-analysis of research findings. *Psychological Bulletin*, *134*(2), 270–300. https://doi.org/10.1037/0033-2909.134.2.270

Rawal, M., Torres, S., Jose, L., Bagherzadeh, R., Bhattarai, A., & Zaad, A. (2025). Do not buy this! Strategic self-anticonformity as an advertising tool to increase attention and boost purchase intention. *Journal of Global Scholars of Marketing Science*, *35*(1), 41–60. https://doi.org/10.1080/21639159.2024.2397586

Rollnick, S., Miller, W. R., & Butler, C. (2008). *Motivational Interviewing in Health Care: Helping Patients Change Behavior*. Guilford Press.

Short, D., Erickson, B. A., & Erickson-Klein, R. E. (2005). *Hope & Resiliency: Understanding the Psychotherapeutic Strategies of Milton H Erickson MD*. Crown House Publishing.

Silvia, P. J. (2006). *Reactance* and the Dynamics of Disagreement: Multiple Paths from Threatened Freedom to Resistance to Persuasion. *European Journal of Social Psychology*, *36*(5), 673–685. https://doi.org/10.1002/ejsp.309

Tormala, Z. L., & Rucker, D. D. (2022). Attitude Change and Persuasion: Classic, Metacognitive, and Advocacy Perspectives. In *APA Handbook of Consumer Psychology* (pp. 323–350). American Psychological Association. https://doi.org/10.1037/0000262-013

Vilardaga, R., Rizo, J., Zeng, E., Kientz, J. A., Ries, R., Otis, C., & Hernandez, K. (2018). User-centered design of learn to quit, a smoking cessation smartphone app for people with serious mental illness. *JMIR Serious Games*, 6(1), e8881. https://doi.org/10.2196/games.8881

Voss, C., & Raz, T. (2016). *Never Split the Difference: Negotiating as If Your Life Depended On It*. HarperCollins.

Wald, K. A., Chaudhry, S. J., & Risen, J. L. (2024). The credibility dilemma: When acknowledging a (perceived) lack of credibility can make a boast more believable. *Organizational Behavior and Human Decision Processes*, *183*, 104351. https://doi.org/10.1016/j.obhdp.2024.104351

Wicklund, R. A. (2024). *Freedom and Reactance*. Taylor & Francis.

Chapter 6

Follow the Leader

Authority Bias

Follow the Leader: *Authority Bias*

The year was 2019 and it was this man's first visit to my office. Six years had passed since the devastating death of his adult daughter, a tragic event he had still not recovered from. She had come to live with her father and stepmom after being thrown out of her biological mother's house for using drugs. During her two years in his home, he had committed himself to supporting her recovery with unconditional compassion and love. Despite all his efforts, she died from sepsis after injecting heroin with a dirty needle.

At her passing, the grieved father immediately sought counseling at a grief support group. In his first session, he asked the therapist how long this unbearable pain would last. She told him five years. Later, she revised that number upward to ten years. During his time in her group, he showed no signs of progress. He cried almost daily. He withdrew from his wife and other children, not allowing anyone to speak of the deceased. Eventually, the grief therapist ended her involvement, telling him that, "The kind of pain you are experiencing is something a parent can never recover from." Clearly, this was not a helpful suggestion.

Speaking with absolute confidence, I told him that the grief counselor was terribly mistaken—only one year was needed for daily crying. I shared that by the end of the second year; it is possible to leave grief behind and begin to develop a new type of relationship with those we have lost. Puzzled, he asked what I was saying. So, I put it bluntly, "You have grieved four years longer than was really necessary." I then placed the blame for his lack of progress on bad information.

When I asked about other therapy encounters, he mentioned that he had also tried EMDR. He acknowledged that it was probably a helpful activity, but he remained resentful about being made to focus so directly on the trauma of losing his daughter. He had no desire to return to that therapist or re-engage with any type of trauma work. I assured him that he would not need to see disturbing images while working with me.

DOI: 10.4324/9781003797876-7

Then, I inquired about the circumstances surrounding his beloved daughter's passing, focusing his attention on whether anything "strange" had occurred after this loss. I immediately added that if something happened, it would most likely have occurred within 48 hours of her death.

The question was meant to serve as a distraction, to lead him safely through the traumatic event without any horrifying imagery. In response to my question, he shared a vivid and deeply personal experience. Three days after she passed, during a visitation, he saw her sitting in the corner of his bedroom reading a book. He looked away and when he looked back, she spoke to him, saying, "Thank you." He told me that I was the first person with whom he had dared to talk about this.

Speaking again as an authority figure, I told him that he is truly fortunate and that only 15% of the population is blessed with this type of experience. I described it as a psychological phenomenon that is the product of a truly deep bond. In fact, reports of vivid sensory or encounter-like experiences after a death are well documented in bereavement research and are often understood as normative expressions of continuing bonds rather than pathology. Using his memory of this last moment with his daughter as a stabilizing platform for adaptive meaning-making, we began to explore a different kind of ongoing connection with her. I proposed that he could choose to "invite" his daughter's presence back into his life. I said that this was better than being "haunted" by her absence.

Later he told me that this shift in framing gave him a sense of agency and comfort. With his Christian faith as a foundation and his routine practice of praying that God had received his daughter in heaven, it felt natural for him to spend quiet moments in conversation with her image, just as he had seen her that day, sitting in the corner of his room reading a book.

Nine days later, he returned for a second session. He began by telling me that he continued to feel deep sadness over the loss of his daughter and that he missed her very much. Then he added that positive changes were occurring. After his initial visit with me, his wife had surprised him with a party for his 70th birthday. At this party he laughed, engaged with people, and apologized to his adult children for being so self-absorbed after their sister's death. He was genuinely moved by his son's heartfelt words about how much he loved his father and how he considered him the best father in the world.

As we began exploring the idea of relating differently to his grief, he was able to recognize a deeper emotional layer. He admitted to feeling fear, not just sadness. When asked to elaborate, he explained that he was afraid that if he ever let go of the sadness, he might forget his daughter. That possibility was unacceptable to him. This fear had kept his grief frozen, preventing him from fully experiencing or integrating other emotions.

I invited him to recall specific memories of her that brought him joy. We explored those pleasurable moments together and then used those recollections to guide him through a visualization of seeing her in heaven. This allowed him to connect with her presence in a way that honored both his sorrow and his love.

Later in the session, he reflected on a conversation he had once had with a psychologist friend who had suggested that he might have PTSD. At the time, he hadn't fully understood the implication. Now, sitting in session, he began to realize that recovery was not only possible but also already beginning. He told me that something had shifted even as we were speaking. He began to sense, perhaps for the first time, that healing did not mean forgetting. It could mean remembering differently.

The authoritative language used with this client, such as "Only 15% of the population is blessed with…," appears frequently in this case and clearly positions the practitioner in a leading role. At first glance, this posture may seem at odds with the mission of choice architecture, which emphasizes personal empowerment, autonomy, and self-determination. However, Ericksonian Choice Architecture (ECA) requires attention to existing cognitive biases and the thoughtful construction of an *optimal choice environment* suited to the client's current state of mind. In the first two sessions, this client was not yet ready to engage in client-generated insight. His grief and confusion had created a need for external structure and certainty.

This sequencing fits motivational models showing that outside structure can help at first, but durable progress depends on the person taking ownership and feeling capable rather than simply following directions. Accordingly, ECA treats authority as temporary scaffolding that is deliberately faded as agency returns. Thus, as his self-confidence began to recover, the tone of our conversations naturally shifted. I moved from authoritative statements to more collaborative inquiries, using language such as "Would it feel right to imagine…?", "What would it be like if…?", and "Does that idea seem right to you?" These kinds of questions invite self-reflection and support a growing sense of autonomy.

Three years later, I met with the man's wife. Her own mother had just died. The man joined this session as a collateral participant, noting that it was his turn to support her. During our conversation, she shared how relieved she was that her husband was still free of depression. He added that he still missed his daughter but it was no longer overwhelming or debilitating. He had found a way to carry her memory forward, not as a weight, but as a source of enduring connection.

Recognizing Authority Bias in ECA

Authority bias is a cognitive bias characterized by a heightened dependence on authority figures for direction, validation, and decision-making, particularly in unfamiliar, complex, or emotionally overwhelming situations. At its core, this bias reflects a psychological preference for externally conferred certainty, a tendency to defer to the perceived knowledge, power, or legitimacy of others. This stands in contrast to moments when the individual wishes to evaluate claims or options independently. While this mental shortcut can reduce the cognitive burden of constant analysis and support effective coordination in hierarchical contexts, it can also suppress autonomy, obscure critical errors, and create blind spots in judgment. This tension between the stabilizing function of authority and its potential to override independent thinking makes authority bias both a resource and a risk.

Conceptually, authority bias arises from a fundamental human need for confidence, especially in the face of ambiguity. When individuals feel confused, unprepared, or emotionally unsettled, they often look to others in leadership roles for reassurance and clarity. In the vignette above, this dynamic is visible in how the father organized his grief around authoritative forecasts ("five years," then "ten," then "a parent can never recover"), and how a countervailing authority-based nudge ("only one year is needed for daily crying" and that he had "grieved four years longer than was really necessary,") created enough certainty for him to reconsider what was possible. Thus, the authority figure becomes a symbolic anchor, lending structure to what might otherwise feel like chaos. This dynamic is often unconscious. Individuals may not realize they are deferring or imitating; instead, they experience a comforting sense of guidance, as if the mere presence of the authority figure renders the correct path self-evident.

This bias is rooted in both evolutionary and cultural psychology. The English primatologist Jane Goodall (1986) observed that there is a natural tendency among all organized animal societies for the needy to seek support from those in a dominant position. From an evolutionary standpoint, survival often depends on close association with those who have experience or proven competence. Culturally, children are taught from an early age to heed parents, teachers, and experts, messages that reinforce obedience and receptiveness to authority as virtues. Over time, this can create a default cognitive pattern in which instructions from high-status figures are accepted with minimal scrutiny.

In a classic study, Hofling et al. (1966) conducted a field experiment on obedience and found that 21 out of 22 nurses began to comply with a doctor's order to prepare and administer a drug overdose, despite knowing it violated protocol and posed serious risk. While there have been failures to replicate that study, other recent studies reveal how authority figures can override hesitation in uncertain social situations (Antepuesto et al., 2025). Whether this pattern promotes or impairs adaptive functioning depends on the credibility, intention, and context surrounding the authority figure.

Operationally, authority bias can be observed through several distinct behaviors and psychological tendencies. One clear indicator is a preference for external instruction over autonomous decision-making. When given the choice, many people influenced by this bias will opt to be told what to do rather than engage in exploratory problem-solving. In therapeutic or behavioral design settings, this is often revealed by questions such as, "Do you want to figure this out on your own, or would you prefer I tell you what to do?" When the latter option is chosen, it is an indication of authority bias.

Additional signs include emotional hesitation when presented with open-ended choices, excessive apologizing when speaking to or about authority figures, and an observable pattern of speech modification, rewording statements, ideas, or attitudes to align more closely with those offered by someone in a position of power. In extreme cases, individuals may retrospectively alter their recollections to match an authority figure's narrative, a phenomenon that demonstrates not only deference but also an internalized restructuring of personal truth (Loftus & Pickrell, 1995).

The emotional undercurrent of authority bias is often marked by insecurity, fear of error, or a desire to avoid social scrutiny. These feelings are not always conscious, but they fuel the unconscious drive to seek refuge in the stability that authority provides. In a problem-solving context, individuals influenced by this bias may show signs of emotional relief when responsibility is lifted from them and placed into the hands of a respected leader. They may even express appreciation for being "told what to do," mistaking the relief of relinquished agency for clarity and learning.

Research has confirmed the pervasiveness and complexity of authority bias. The classic experiments conducted by Stanley Milgram in the 1960s remain the most striking example: participants, believing they were administering electric shocks to a learner at the instruction of an experimenter, complied with increasingly severe commands, even when those commands conflicted with their personal moral instincts. Milgram's work demonstrated how the perceived legitimacy of the authority figure could override ethical resistance and prompt individuals to behave in ways that were otherwise unthinkable.

Subsequent studies have explored the broader implications of *role-conferred advantage*, the automatic legitimacy attributed to individuals simply by virtue of their role or title. Karakowsky et al. (2012), for instance, examined how subordinates' perceptions of leadership influenced their receptivity to positive or directive messaging. Their findings suggest that when someone is perceived as an authority, regardless of their actual competence, others are more likely to internalize their evaluations, adopt their expectations, and comply with their guidance. In ECA, this principle becomes particularly relevant when designing for individuals who are currently deferring to external sources of judgment.

Authority bias often operates through the mechanism of *extrinsic motivation*. Instead of being driven by internal values or curiosity, individuals may act primarily to meet perceived expectations, avoid disapproval, or earn praise. This can be helpful when navigating complex systems such as medical protocols, legal procedures, or emergency responses where expertise matters and conformity ensures safety. In these contexts, deferring to authority streamlines communication and enhances group coordination. However, when this tendency becomes a default mode of engagement, it can compromise personal agency and stifle growth.

Emotionally, the experience of authority bias is often saturated with self-doubt, confusion, and a latent desire to avoid blame. Individuals may become hyper-attuned to the perceived preferences of authority figures, treating them not just as guides, but as arbiters of truth and morality, so that authority functions as a truth-substitute, not merely a compliance cue. This dynamic is especially likely in cultural domains such as religion and mental health, where causal attribution is inherently interpretive (Beahrs, 2006). The risk is that even well-intentioned authorities may reinforce regressive dependency, maladaptive norms, or what some researchers call *error propagation*. For instance, if a physician confidently recommends an unnecessary treatment with terrible consequences, patients may comply without question. If a therapist oversteps privacy boundaries, the client may acquiesce to preserve the perceived bond. This dynamic is particularly dangerous when the authority figure is charismatic, emotionally persuasive, or socially validated (trusted by friends), as these features further suppress the individual's instinct to question or challenge.

The most common manifestations of authority bias are context-dependent. In educational settings, students may uncritically absorb the views of professors or mentors, repeating them without reflection. In religious or cultural environments, individuals may cite sacred figures such as Buddha or Jesus when asked to explain deeply personal values, effectively outsourcing their moral reasoning to historical authorities. In corporate settings, junior employees may mirror the language and decision style of high-ranking executives, hoping to gain approval or avoid conflict. In each case, the bias results in a form of naïve acceptance, where internal coherence is sacrificed for external alignment.

As with any state of mind, this pattern is not fixed. Research in behavioral psychology suggests that authority bias can be moderated by several factors. Confidence in one's own knowledge, for instance, reduces reliance on external cues. Training in *critical thinking* and exposure to diverse perspectives help build cognitive autonomy. Perhaps most importantly, the presence of psychological safety (a context in which individuals feel safe expressing dissent) can mitigate the suppressive effects of authority bias.

Authority bias functions as a cognitive marker for a state of mind that often overlaps with *social conformity bias*. Both orient the individual toward external guidance, particularly under conditions of uncertainty, emotional overload, or self-perceived incompetence. This bias appears in multiple forms, each with distinct psychological implications. The most pervasive form is *identity alignment*—the reshaping of beliefs, judgments, or memories to match authoritative or culturally endorsed narratives and norms. Within ECA, this pattern is most effectively engaged through the tactic of *watching eyes*. A second form is *passive compliance*, characterized by accepting guidance without scrutiny or evaluation. This manifestation is best addressed through *permission* or *positively calibrated prediction*, which legitimizes action while preserving dignity and momentum. The third form is *outsourced agency*, captured in the felt stance of "please tell me what to do," in which initiative is relinquished to an external figure. This is most effectively engaged through *agentic framing*, which borrows authority to catalyze action.

Each of these tactics is illustrated in the chapter's cases and followed by a detailed explanation. The overarching objective in designing choice environments for authority-biased states is not to eliminate reliance on external guidance, but to use it as temporary scaffolding: providing enough certainty to restore motion, then gradually repositioning authority so that clients internalize agency—shifting from "I act because you said so" to "I act because this fits who I am."

Erickson's Casework and the Application of Tactical Nudges

Having outlined how authority bias operates as an unconscious deference to external figures, the next question is how this tendency can be engaged constructively. This is where Erickson's work provides a powerful blueprint. It shows how to design choice environments that respect the client's psychological need for explicit guidance while gradually reintroducing a sense of personal agency.

Erickson understood that individuals who habitually deferred to authority were not permanently passive but were often overwhelmed, disoriented, or culturally conditioned to outsource decision-making. His genius lay in offering just enough structure so these individuals could begin making meaningful choices within a context that still felt safe and familiar.

By working with authority bias, Erickson demonstrated that the path to autonomy may sometimes run through compliance. It is a moment of legitimized action, an initial step taken "on the expert's authority," that eventually becomes internalized as the client's own. The examples that follow illustrate this nuanced interplay between structure and freedom, obedience and emergence, showing how even deeply entrenched patterns of passivity can become launchpads for adaptive choice.

Case 6.1: Scratching an Itch

A woman in her 30s came to see Erickson for help with two persistent compulsive habits: She sucked her thumb and scratched both her nipple and her navel to the point that they were constantly scabbed. These behaviors had been present since early childhood.

When she asked Erickson for therapy, he told her plainly, "I won't give you therapy for that problem. But I'll cure it in less than 30 seconds."

Naturally surprised, the woman asked how he planned to do that. Erickson replied, "All that you have to do is say 'Yes' and truly mean 'Yes.'"

Intrigued, she agreed. So Erickson continued, "The next time you want to scratch your nipple, I want you to come to my office, expose your breasts, and do it here." [1]

He then looked at her and asked, "Will you do it?"

She said, "Yes," hesitated, and then said, "You know I'll never do it. I never will."

Watching Eyes

In ECA, the watching eyes tactic is any method of creating the feeling of having one's choices subject to observation. This can be achieved by using visual cues (cameras, mirrors, or pictures of eyes) or an expectation that one could be watched (activating imagination). The tactic draws on a well-documented psychological phenomenon: people tend to behave more prosocially, honestly, and cooperatively when they feel they are being observed. The effect still occurs even if that observation is merely implied. This effect has been widely replicated using simple visual cues, such as images of eyes placed in environments where behavioral decisions occur. These cues activate our sensitivity to being seen, often leading to increased generosity, honesty, charitable giving, and rule-following behavior.

Empirical support for the *watching-eyes effect* is robust. Numerous studies, such as those by Bateson et al. (2013), found that images of watching eyes significantly increased prosocial behavior, even in the absence of actual surveillance. Meta-analyses have since shown that antisocial behaviors can drop by as much as 35% when eye imagery is present. Real-world applications mirror these findings as people are less likely to litter, steal, or ignore honesty boxes when eye images are displayed nearby or when a mirror reflects their eyes. These effects are strongest when the eyes look real, stare directly at the viewer, and are placed near where a decision is made (Dear et al., 2019).

More importantly, recent research has extended the effect beyond visual cues, showing that *imagined* observation can evoke similar neural responses. Simply picturing someone watching, such as a respected therapist, coach, parent, or imagined observer, can enhance self-control and reinforce social norms. This intersects with the *coach effect* in behavioral design, where recalling a moment of being observed or evaluated constructively can foster confidence and accountability. Similarly, the *reflective best-self-portrait* exercise invites individuals to reflect on moments when others *watched* them acting as the best version of themselves, reinforcing identity-aligned behavior (Roberts et al., 2005).

Key theoretical underpinnings include *social facilitation theory*, which shows that the perceived presence of others can improve task performance, and the *spotlight effect*, where individuals overestimate how much others notice their actions. Together, these frameworks explain why even subtle cues, like watching eyes, can shape behavior. However, habituation can reduce effectiveness over time, especially if eye cues are constant and lose novelty. Individual disposition also matters. Those high in need for approval (authority bias or social conformity bias) show greater responsiveness, while individuals with high antisocial traits may be unaffected (Lange & Manesi, 2023).

In ECA, *watching-eyes* cues (physical or imagined) function as gentle nudges, guiding behavior by creating a felt sense of being seen.

Case Analysis

In one of Erickson's brief yet striking collaborations, he addressed embarrassing behaviors that had persisted since childhood and were sustained in private. Most likely, her scratching behavior functioned as unconscious rituals of comfort and self-soothing. Rather than offering traditional therapy, Erickson told this woman he would "cure it in less than 30 seconds." When the woman, curious and skeptical, asked how he would accomplish this, Erickson secured a *precommitment* that would lead her to imagine him watching her every time she got the urge to engage in this infant-like behavior.

Ironically, this nudge was so behaviorally precise that it required almost no intrusion into the private areas of the woman's life. She was not asked to recount personal history, disclose feelings of shame or embarrassment, or reveal hidden thoughts. Erickson simply asked for an unconditional "yes" response. This small commitment, made in relation to a hypothetical public act, implicitly linked her deviant behavior to the watching eyes of a respected authority figure. In doing so, it disrupted the emotional patterns that had previously reinforced the behavior.

As studies have shown, subtle cues of surveillance can alter conduct, triggering innate mechanisms of reputation management and self-monitoring. Erickson activated the same effect internally as he installed an imagined observer at the moment of choice. This shifted the act from private self-soothing to a socially anchored decision. Once imagined eyes were present, the urge automatically ended.

General Application

The watching eyes tactic is especially effective for individuals operating under authority bias or social conformity bias, as these individuals are already primed to regulate their behavior in response to perceived social standards or the presence of a respected figure. At its core, watching eyes capitalizes on our innate sensitivity to being observed. This sensitivity heightens prosocial behavior, self-restraint, and alignment with social norms, even when the observation is symbolic or imagined.

Research by Bateson et al. (2006) found that simply placing a pair of stylized eyes above an honesty box in a university cafeteria significantly increased payment rates for coffee. This demonstrates the low-friction power of perceived surveillance in shaping behavior without confrontation or coercion. For individuals with authority bias, invoking the presence, real or imagined, of a respected figure can help bridge the gap between internal motivation and outward action. Similarly, for those with social conformity bias, the sense of being watched enhances alignment with perceived group values and discourages deviance from social norms.

Watching eyes can be strategically adapted for a wide variety of applications. For example, during a lecture, I heard celebrated naval captain Michael Abrashoff describe his primary decision making strategy. Before finalizing an important choice, he imagined seeing it on the front page of *The New York Times*, as though the entire country were watching and judging his actions. In a clinical setting, a therapist might ask, "Who would be the most effective person to have watching you to help ensure that you follow through with your goals?" In cases where symbolic representation is more appropriate, moving a photograph or mirror into the environment can automatically reshape behavior. A Catholic client might respond well to the suggestion, "What if you placed Mother Mary's picture on the kitchen counter where she can 'see' you when you're deciding what food you should eat?"

Watching eyes can also be adapted for clients who are unmotivated following grief or trauma. A grief counselor might say, "Imagine your father watching how you get through this week. What would he hope to see you doing?" This imagined observation brings dormant values or responsibilities back into view and can help re-anchor a sense of purpose. In group-based behavior change settings, facilitators sometimes use video recordings or peer review check-ins as forms of delayed but anticipated observation, which can trigger the same effect.

Ultimately, watching eyes works because it embeds a social mirror into private moments, a mechanism that is especially effective for those whose sense of right action is regulated externally. By structuring observation (real, symbolic, or imagined) into the choice environment, practitioners can increase accountability, decrease impulsivity, and promote alignment with the client's aspirational identity.

Case 6.2: Taking Charge of the Restaurant

A husband and wife had gone into business running a restaurant together. The wife claimed that she wanted her husband to manage the establishment so she could stay home, sew, and prepare home-cooked meals. That was her stated intention. However, as the husband explained,

> Yes, now she tells me that I should run that restaurant. But I'm the busboy and the janitor. I scrub the floors and she nags at me because I don't do the buying. She nags at me because I don't do the bookkeeping. She nags at me because I don't run the business. She runs it.

He went on to describe the cycle that left him stuck in a subordinate role,

> She points out to me that the floor needs scrubbing and that I really ought to get someone to scrub the floor. But I can't wait until somebody comes in and asks for the job, so I wind up doing it myself. Then there's no need of hiring someone to do it.

Erickson observed, "The wife had no insight into the situation at all." Despite her verbal insistence that she wanted her husband to manage the restaurant, her actions contradicted that claim. As the husband put it, "Yes, that's what she says. You can hear it. I can hear it. But she'll be right back in the restaurant tomorrow morning."

The use of questions can be an effective means of creating a new context of understanding. Erickson demonstrated this by turning to the wife and asking, "Who carries the keys to the restaurant? Who locks up?" Then he asked, "Who ought to carry the keys?" Her answer should have aligned with her conscious intentions (self-consistency), which was for her husband to be responsible for the operations of the restaurant. But this is not what happened.

Instead, the wife replied, "We both carry the keys. I always get there first, while he is parking the car."

With the first nudge having failed, Erickson spoke to her as an authority figure, "You ought to see to it that your husband gets there a half hour before you do." She objected, noting that they had only one car. But Erickson pointed out that their home was only a few blocks away and gave her permission to drive her husband to the restaurant or have him walk. This seemingly logistical suggestion was a symbolic shift. By delegating to the husband the exclusive responsibility for opening the restaurant, Erickson put him in the lead.

As he began showing up early, unlocking the doors, and preparing for the day's business on his own, the husband found himself stepping into the leadership role he had longed for but had not felt entitled to claim. With this new role, he naturally assumed more responsibility and authority. He began managing the restaurant. The wife, meanwhile, gradually found fulfillment in the domestic life she had originally claimed to want and her presence at the restaurant became limited to times when her help was truly needed.

Permission

In ECA, the behavioral tactic of permission involves the strategic use of authority, validation, or approval to make a particular choice feel safer, more legitimate, and more attractive. Rather than directing behavior, permission operates indirectly. It lowers perceived risk, neutralizes uncertainty, and increases follow-through by granting individuals psychological clearance to act on preferences they may already hold. This tactic is particularly effective when it taps into latent inclinations, reinforcing an existing desire.

The power of permission has been supported by research on authority bias and motivation. Iyengar and Lepper (1999) found that some individuals feel more satisfied and motivated when a trusted authority validates a choice, especially in complex or high-stakes contexts. Additionally, recent studies on obedience and conformity (Dolinski & Grzyb, 2020) illustrate the functional value of prosocial authority. In ethical helping relationships this influence can be harnessed to dignify and embolden personal agency.

This nudge is most likely to succeed when three key elements are present. First, the permission should come from a credible source, such as a respected coach, therapist, or spiritual guide. Second, it should align with the client's long-term goals. Finally, the *permission* should be delivered with a non-coercive tone, which preserves autonomy and reinforces the individual's sense of agency. As Burger (1989) notes, coercive environments can backfire by increasing stress and diminishing control. In contrast, subtle permission can lead to higher satisfaction and stronger commitment because it allows individuals to feel they arrived at the decision themselves.

In sum, permission in ECA is not about issuing directives. It is about creating psychological clearance for actions the client already wants to take. When done well, it quietly emboldens, reassures, and dignifies the choice, making it feel more natural and less risky to embrace.

Case Analysis

In this case, Erickson's nudge centered on granting the husband permission to carry the keys and open the restaurant each morning. This action may appear minor but it held significant psychological weight. Through the small but strategic act of shifting the timing of their arrival and redefining who held the keys, Erickson reframed their roles and gave the husband clearance to lead. Reflecting on the outcome, Erickson explained,

> His wife arrived a half an hour late. There have been so many things that he had already set in motion. He was managing them, do you see that?...She arrived at the restaurant completely out of step and way behind.

Although the wife claimed she wanted to stay home and return to sewing and cooking, she had remained over involved often arriving before her husband, which reinforced the existing dynamic. By suggesting that the husband arrive earlier, Erickson introduced a behavior that embodied managerial leadership in a practical, observable way. This gentle guidance from Erickson allowed both partners to grow into the roles they had been struggling to define.

General Application

Permission, as a behavioral tactic within ECA, involves offering psychological clearance through a respected source, enabling individuals to take action in a way that aligns with their latent desires. This approach is especially effective for individuals influenced by authority bias, who tend to delay or avoid action unless they sense validation from a credible figure. For such individuals, internal hesitation often stems not from a lack of interest or ability, but from a fear of overstepping, making mistakes, or acting without "official" sanction. By receiving permission, whether explicitly stated or subtly implied, the person gains a sense of legitimacy and reduced risk, which helps unlock behavior that feels otherwise prohibited.

In a variety of helping relationships, permission can take many forms depending on the client's dominant concern. When uncertainty is the issue, a statement like, "You have the right to learn through trial and error, just like everyone else," offers cognitive relief and normalizes exploratory behavior. For clients who are risk-averse, therapists might say, "If it doesn't go well, then you can blame it on me," which uses shared responsibility to lower the emotional cost of action. For self-inhibiting clients who struggle to validate their own desires, offering overt permission, such as, "You have not given yourself *permission* to do it. Would you like for me to give you official permission?" can serve as a powerful source of motivation. These seemingly simple statements reframe the decision environment, providing a socially sanctioned bridge between intention and behavior.

Recent innovations in the use of permission include its integration into digital coaching platforms, where pre-scripted messages from perceived experts can boost user engagement and action. For example, apps designed for mental wellness or habit formation often include prompts like "You're allowed to rest," or "It's okay to start small," mimicking the authoritative reassurance of a supportive guide. In group settings, facilitators have also begun using structured rituals of permission, which help reduce inhibition and build psychological safety. An example of structured rituals of permission might be a group facilitator opening a meeting by saying, "Let's begin by giving ourselves and each other permission to not have the answers, to be curious, and to not worry with perfection."

In all its forms, permission works by helping individuals recognize that the action they wish to take is already acceptable, already possible, and already theirs to claim.

Case 6.3: A Cradle for Children

A medical technician at the hospital, where Erickson worked, had a uniquely large buttocks, which Erickson surmised she disliked. He observed, "I noticed that when she passed somebody, she'd swing her butt[2] angrily toward that person," suggesting both discomfort and defensiveness about her body.

On visiting days at the hospital, she often scheduled the day off to stand near the entrance and offer to babysit visitors' children. Erickson inferred from this that she had a strong affinity for children and likely longed for a family of her own. However, she had learned to protect herself from rejection by keeping others at a distance. Her deep personal longings remained unspoken.

One day, she developed a case of uncontrollable hiccups so severe that she was hospitalized. Every physician on staff attempted to treat her, but none were successful. Eventually, she was referred to Erickson. Initially she refused psychiatric care, but after her boss threatened to discontinue her free hospital care, she reluctantly agreed to see the psychiatrist.

When Erickson entered her room, he used a very dominant approach, saying:

> Keep your mouth shut. Don't say anything. I've got a few things to say to you and I want you to listen because you need understanding.

He then addressed what he suspected to be her core issue, saying:

> I KNOW you have the biggest butt in creation. I know you don't like it, but it IS yours. And you like children, therefore you'd like to get married and have children of your own. And you are afraid that great big butt of yours is a barrier...that's your error.

This introduction seems rude and harsh. However, ironically, the command to keep her mouth shut most likely provided immediate relief from her hiccups and her fear that she would have to talk about embarrassing personal secrets. Erickson already knew what she needed. He was upfront about that fact.

To reinforce his authority, Erickson drew from a literary source that was beyond reproach (in Judeo-Christian culture), saying, "You haven't read the Song of Solomon. You should have read your Bible. There, the pelvis is mentioned as the cradle of children." He continued, "The man who will want to marry you will not see a great big fat butt...he will see a wonderful cradle for children."

Erickson concluded the session by sympathizing with her unstated need not to be viewed by others as a "psychiatric patient" (a stereotype threat), stating:

> You can think it over. After I leave, keep on hiccupping. There is no reason for nobody except you and I to know that you don't need those hiccups. You have something of great value, so let your hiccups disappear around 10:30 tonight. That way, no one will say that a psychiatrist cured you. They will think that my interview was an utter failure.

A few months later, the technician returned to Erickson and proudly showed him her engagement ring. Not long after, she brought in her fiancé. Together, they were making plans to build a house with lots of bedrooms and a large nursery. Erickson's comments had not only resolved her physical symptom but also helped her reframe a perceived personal flaw into a source of pride and meaning, opening the door to a new chapter in her life.

Positively Calibrated Prediction

In ECA, the behavioral tactic of positively calibrated prediction refers to the strategic use of optimistic forecasting that emphasizes strengths and opportunities while allowing room for setbacks. It functions much like a psychological "blessing" or favorable prognosis, reinforcing an individual's motivation to pursue a goal while buffering against discouragement. Positively calibrated prediction works by selectively highlighting positive cues, thereby priming confidence and persistence, and embedding an "emergency reserve," which is a structured margin that normalizes temporary setbacks without undermining the broader pursuit.

This tactic is supported by several strands of research. The *Pygmalion effect* (Rosenthal & Jacobson, 1968) demonstrates how others' positive expectations can directly influence a person's performance. Karakowsky et al. (2012) found that individuals are more receptive to encouragement from leaders they respect. This evidence of the role-conferred advantage enhances the persuasive power of positively framed forecasts. Positively calibrated prediction also draws on goal-setting research. Sharif and Shu (2017) found that goals allowing for "emergency reserves" (e.g., acceptable slip-ups) foster higher persistence than rigid standards. This aligns with studies in resilience psychology showing that realistic optimism (the belief that success is likely but not guaranteed) sustains engagement through obstacles.

Key components that make positively calibrated prediction effective in ECA include selective focus, motivational framing, and structured flexibility. Selective focus involves directing attention toward best-case scenarios or known strengths while softening the impact of potential risks. Motivational framing uses confident, future-oriented language to establish a positive expectancy effect (Kirsch, 1985), and encourage proactive behavior. Structured flexibility builds in allowances for lapses, reducing the fear of failure and increasing adaptive persistence. This approach aligns with insights from superforecasting research by Tetlock and Gardner (2015), who found that cautious optimism combined with open-minded updating improves both prediction accuracy and morale.

As an anecdotal illustration, consider the story of Marva Collins, a pioneering African-American educator known for unlocking the potential of students whom the traditional education system had failed. When her work gained national attention, her disadvantaged yet high-achieving students were interviewed about what Collins had done for them. The most common response was, "She believed in me. She told me that I could do great things with my life." Similar to this, positively calibrated prediction in ECA acts as a strategic amplifier of confidence. It legitimizes hope, normalizes setbacks, and fosters momentum by framing the future not as a fragile gamble, but as a direction worth believing in.

Case Analysis

While seeking to help a young medical technician reframe a deeply held body image concern and discover a more hopeful vision of her future,

Erickson used the tactic of positively calibrated prediction. This nudge fuses optimism with high-value outcomes. The woman was experiencing unrelenting hiccups. Erickson seemed to suspect that her hiccups were somehow a reflection of suppressed anger, perhaps stemming from her isolation and painful expectations for a childless future. Lipowski (1984), a foundational figure in psychosomatic medicine, argued that unconscious emotional conflicts, especially unexpressed anger and grief, may manifest somatically in conditions that are resistant to medical explanation, including gastrointestinal symptoms such as hiccups, nausea, and dyspepsia.

Erickson also suspected that she longed for marriage and children but feared that her body was too unattractive for her to be able to realize those dreams. Her defensive body language and her eager volunteerism with visiting children hinted at this underlying desire coupled with evidence of shame and inhibition.

Erickson chose this tactic because it matched her unique psychological state. She was emotionally guarded, self-conscious, and likely mistrustful of flattery. To establish credibility, Erickson did not avoid the painful truth she carried. Instead, he confronted it head-on, "I know you have the biggest butt in creation. I know you don't like it, but it is yours." By acknowledging the very thing she feared others judged, Erickson gained her trust. As he later explained, "I was unafraid to call her butt a big fat butt, so she knew I was telling the truth, so she could believe what I said." His candor laid the groundwork for her to accept what came next, which was a reframe and a prediction.

This type of nudge aligns with behavioral research on trust, believability, and the power of future-oriented suggestions. People are more likely to believe a positive statement about themselves when it follows a credible acknowledgment of something difficult or unflattering, which is known as a *two-sided message* (O'Keefe, 1999). This is especially true when the prediction aligns with a latent desire. Erickson told her, "The man who will want to marry you will not see a great big fat butt...he will see a wonderful cradle for children." This prediction reframed her perceived flaw into a valued asset and linked it directly to her aspiration for family life. By anchoring the prediction in both cultural narrative (referencing the *Song of Solomon*) and personal truth, Erickson made the future imaginable and desirable.

The positively calibrated prediction helped resolve her unstated emotional conflicts by offering a vision of progress she could believe in. Erickson also resolved any conflicting feelings about psychiatric care by suggesting that her symptom could "spontaneously" resolve ("let your hiccups disappear around 10:30 tonight") following his "failure." In other words, she could heal on her own terms and attribute the result to time, not psychiatry, preserving her pride. This case illustrates how a carefully delivered, realistic prediction can serve as a catalyst for adaptive action, especially when it transforms shame into self-efficacy and offers a credible pathway to long-held personal goals.

General Application

Because positively calibrated prediction creates an optimistic yet believable forecast, it is especially valuable for individuals in a state of mind marked by self-doubt, fear of failure, or an overemphasis on past setbacks. Under these circumstances individuals often struggle to visualize positive outcomes without dismissing them as unrealistic or unearned. Positively calibrated predictions can gently shift this mindset by combining credible feedback with forward-looking encouragement, reinforcing a sense of agency and possibility.

Positively calibrated prediction is supported by Merton's (1948) classic research on expectancy theory and the self-fulfilling prophecy, which demonstrated how perceived likelihood of success enhances motivation and persistence. Similarly, a success-framed prediction like, "There is at least a 90 percent chance that you will reach your goal," helps anchor expectations in a positive direction, especially for clients with perfectionistic or risk-averse tendencies. By reinforcing the plausibility of success, these statements reduce hesitation and increase goal-oriented behavior. A resilience-focused variation, such as, "Even if there are setbacks, you're in a strong position to recover," is particularly well-suited for clients with a history of repeated disappointment. This frame validates past experience while simultaneously redirecting focus toward future potential.

While the advantageous use of positively calibrated prediction dates back to ancient oracles, recent innovations in the use of this nudge include integrating it with real-time behavioral data or micro-goal tracking. For instance, digital health devices now deliver adaptive predictions that change based on daily habits, offering messages like, "Because you walked three times this week, you are well on your way to building a lasting routine." These personalized reinforcements mirror predictive techniques and extend their impact through everyday feedback loops. In all cases, the strength of positively calibrated prediction lies in its ability to honor the individual's current reality while redirecting focus toward a credible and hopeful future, one that supports autonomy, persistence, and a shift toward goal-congruent behavior.

Case 6.4: Harvey

A 29-year-old man was brought to a teaching seminar as a challenge for Erickson by a group of psychoanalytically oriented therapists who doubted the value of hypnotherapy.

This man, whom Erickson nicknamed Harvey, was exceedingly passive and had a variety of somatic aches and pains. Erickson described this person as a "mama's dishrag if ever there was one—colorless, coatless, discouraged." This man was ruthlessly bullied by people at work and did not seem capable of standing up for himself.

For example, one employee would park his car in such a way that Harvey was left blocked inside his parking space. He would sit fuming in his car waiting for the other man to get off work, but was helpless to do anything about the situation.

Harvey also held a job that was far below his capabilities. His lack of self-esteem showed up in his illegible writing and he had a disheveled appearance, with poorly tied shoelaces. He was always making social blunders that interfered with developing romantic relationships. Whatever the task was that Harvey would attempt, his expectation was that he would fail. He had been in treatment with a psychiatrist for two years but this had turned out to be another failure.

Erickson began his demonstration with a trance induction that was authoritarian in style. Erickson used this approach recognizing that Harvey would do anything to please authority figures.

During hypnosis, Erickson taught Harvey to imagine different scenes from the past. After Harvey succeeded with these assignments, Erickson had him write his name on a pad of paper, followed by the phrase, "It's a beautiful day in June." Both his name and this statement were written almost illegibly.

Erickson then had a seminar attendee write his name and the same phrase in beautiful handwriting. Next, Erickson praised this sample excessively as Harvey cowered in his seat, visibly ashamed of his writing.

Erickson then turned to Harvey and asked:

> How do you suppose Dr. Jones feels about what I said about his handwriting? How do you think he feels about that handwriting? How do you think the pencil feels in his hand? How do you think a pen would feel? How do you think his hand would feel against the pad of paper when he writes so beautifully? How do you think he will feel a year from now when he reads that?

Harvey sat for a while, reflecting on these questions. Then Erickson asked him, "How much would you like to do that sort of thing?" Harvey said, "I'd give anything if I could write legibly, but I can't."

Erickson instructed Harvey to go into a trance again and review some of the difficult moments from his life. Harvey saw some tragic scenes, including one in which he got severely punished for writing with his left hand.

Erickson then asked Harvey to write the same phrase again with his naturally dominant hand, which was his left hand. He then suggested that when he awakened Harvey from trance, Harvey would not recall that he had written it. Next, Erickson told him that if anyone in the room tried to tell him that this beautiful writing was his, he was to call them a damn liar, to their face. He also suggested that Harvey would have a strong urge to show the sample to all the different doctors in the room.

When Harvey was reoriented from trance, he followed through with his instructions, calling these authority figures a bunch of damn liars. Erickson then had him write the same phrase one more time, but this time he was to watch himself write it. This exercise convinced Harvey that it was his beautiful handwriting after all. Filled with joy and enthusiasm, Harvey went around the room and made everyone praise his writing. Before leaving the auditorium, Harvey stopped to tie his shoes, and re-tie his neck tie so that he looked sharp.

Harvey then went back to work and started asserting himself. He went to his boss and demanded a raise and a promotion, which he received. He also confronted the man who had been blocking his car and suggested they go have a beer and talk about that situation and how they might resolve it. Soon after, Harvey started dating and eventually got married.

Agentic Framing

In ECA, agentic framing refers to a behavioral tactic in which individuals engage in assertive or bold actions under the perceived authority or endorsement of a respected authority figure. Feelings of duty, obligation, or loyalty can increase the probability of follow-through. Acting from more than personal initiative, the individual's action is legitimized by the implicit or explicit message, "You are doing this on my authority." As illustrated in the example above, a powerful form of agentic framing occurs when an individual is convinced that even after leaving the office, they are still responding automatically to a hypnotist's commands (post-hypnotic suggestion).

This framing is particularly useful in cases where individuals struggle with excessive inhibition, as it leverages their responsiveness to trusted direction while reducing the perceived personal risk of acting outside habitual patterns. The psychological foundation of this tactic lies in *agentic state theory*, first articulated by Stanley Milgram (1974), which describes how individuals shift responsibility for their actions onto an authority figure, thereby experiencing themselves less as autonomous actors and more as agents carrying out an endorsed directive. While originally studied in contexts of obedience, this same mechanism can be a supportive way to release individuals from paralyzing self-consciousness and encourage meaningful behavior aligned with personal goals.

Research by Galinsky et al. (2003) shows that individuals primed with power or structural authority demonstrate greater decisiveness and goal-directed behavior, a finding that aligns closely with how agentic framing promotes action in those who otherwise hesitate. In ECA, the tactic is most effective when several elements align: the perceived authority of the person giving the directive, the legitimacy of the task (especially when framed in terms of the individual's core values and goals), and the release from personal responsibility, which enables the individual to act without the full burden of responsibility. Importantly, although the agentic state can briefly suspend self-reflection, ECA uses this window to increase self-efficacy and engagement. Over time, these sanctioned actions become bridge experiences that lower inhibition and support autonomous behavior. In this way, agentic framing turns passive deference into an adaptive use of social influence, reactivating dormant strengths under trusted permission.

Case Analysis

This case illustrates how the ECA tactic of agentic framing was effectively applied to Harvey's unique psychological state and challenges. Harvey was deeply entrenched in passivity, low self-esteem, and learned helplessness. His life was characterized by a chronic expectation of failure, social awkwardness, and a pervasive inability to assert himself in everyday situations. The behavioral design targeted these issues by leveraging Harvey's strong motivation to please authority figures, a psychological state Erickson recognized and used as an entry point for personal growth. By using an authoritarian trance induction and positioning himself as a credible authority, Erickson created a context in which Harvey's compliance became a vehicle for fostering agency.

In this case, agentic framing involved assigning Harvey an empowered role under Erickson's authoritative guidance. This enabled him first to confidently deny others' claims that the beautiful handwriting was his, and later to reverse that mindset and publicly assert ownership of it. Within the conceptual framework of hypnosis, a "post-hypnotic suggestion" implicitly allows one person to carry out another's directives as their agent. This strategic use of authority created psychological space for Harvey to adopt a more confident self-image and to challenge his own negative expectations.

Behavioral research on authority bias and *self-efficacy* supports this approach. For example, Bandura's (1972) *self-efficacy framework* highlights that mastery experiences are critical to building confidence and initiating behavioral adaptation. Initially resigned to failure, Harvey's newfound ability to produce legible handwriting and publicly claim it symbolized a shift toward embracing success and competence. This behavioral breakthrough catalyzed further adaptive choices, such as demanding a raise, resolving workplace conflicts, and pursuing meaningful romantic relationships.

General Application

Agentic framing is a behavioral tactic that leverages an individual's responsiveness to authority by encouraging assertive or bold actions under the perceived endorsement of a respected figure. This approach is especially useful for people whose state of mind is characterized by authority bias. By framing actions as being carried out "on my authority," agentic framing reduces the individual's sense of personal risk and responsibility, allowing them to act with greater confidence and decisiveness than they might on their own. Across the helping professions, this tactic helps clients overcome inhibition or self-doubt by shifting motivation from internal pressure to trusted external guidance. For example, in couples counseling, I told a man,

> Part of your wife's pain stems from childhood trauma. I need her to put those memories into words. This will likely be destabilizing for her. Ideally, she should have someone's arm around her or be able to rest her head in the lap of a secure attachment figure. I cannot play that role. Would you be willing to act as a therapeutic agent and do those things for me?

He readily stepped into this role, despite the fact that their marital problems centered on his emotional and physical unavailability. As his wife revisited painful childhood experiences, she curled up in his lap while he stroked her arm. Before this nudge, he had always sat at the far end of the sofa with his hands folded in his lap. In follow-up sessions, he sat beside his wife and often held her hand.

Designing an Optimal Choice Environment (OCE) for Authority Bias

Designing an optimal choice environment for individuals dominated by authority bias requires recognizing the importance of distributed cognition and human interdependency. Such an environment supports the individual's best interests, values, and long-term goals while reducing cognitive, social, and emotional barriers to effective decision-making. One key feature of an optimal choice environment tailored to authority bias is transparency. Authority figures need to openly disclose their expertise, intentions, and potential biases to enable individuals to make more informed and reflective choices versus relying on blind obedience. This openness fosters trust and helps individuals understand the rationale behind guidance, which is critical for internalizing recommendations in a meaningful way.

Another essential aspect of an optimal choice environment for those influenced by authority bias is value-based guidance. Authority figures should ensure that their advice aligns closely with the individual's core values and long-term goals, providing clear directives that lead toward personal empowerment. This approach encourages a transition from passive obedience to autonomous responsibility, helping individuals learn to critically evaluate authoritative input and take ownership of their decisions. Research indicates a strong overlap between authority bias and social conformity bias, suggesting that environments designed to support those with authority bias also benefit individuals influenced by social conformity (Kim et al., 2021). Both biases involve a tendency to defer to perceived social cues or norms. A well-designed choice environment can increase autonomy by promoting openness, personal control, and choices that reflect the person's own values.

Thought Exercise

Next, you will have the opportunity to apply your design skills. When creating an optimal choice environment for someone experiencing an authority bias, remember that this environment can include mental landscapes such as identity, beliefs, and social roles, or changes to their physical surroundings. The only requirement is that you respect the individual's need for external structure, desire for role clarity (knowing "who is supposed to do what"), and tendency to respond to power hierarchies (wanting to follow "the doctor's orders").

For this thought exercise, imagine speaking with 52-year-old woman who is suffering from severe existential depression. She lives alone, with no husband or children. She is independently wealthy and she goes to the Episcopalian church on every possible occasion. Unfortunately, she has no friends at the church or elsewhere. She has a house keeper, a maid, and a grounds keeper. These individuals come daily to care for her house and do her cooking as she sits idle. She attends church regularly but then silently slips away as the sermon ends. She has a sister but does not speak with her. You learn that she has become horribly depressed during the past nine months.

Before reading further, consider how you would respond to this person. What would you say or do to design an optimal choice environment that recognizes the unique contextual needs for someone who is in a state of mind characterized by authority bias (we recognize this because of her dependency on the external structure provided by the church)?

***

Erickson described a case (6.5 in the case index) involving these same circumstances. After being approached by a man who was very worried about his aunt and how depressed she had become, Erickson agreed to conduct a home visit the next time he was lecturing in Milwaukee (where she lived).

After completing his lecture, Erickson went to her house to introduce himself and explain why he was there. Upon meeting her he observed that she was passive. So, he demanded a personal tour of her house.

While looking around, he discovered that she was interested in plants. In a sun room he saw three adult African violets of different colors in full bloom and a potting pot where she was sprouting another African violet. Erickson was intrigued by the skill set noting that African violets are very delicate plants and are very easily killed by the slightest amount of neglect.

After seeing those plants, Erickson turned to the woman and said, "I'm going to give you some medical orders, and I want them carried out. Now you understand that. Will you agree that you will carry them out?" She passively agreed.

Then Erickson said, "Tomorrow you send your housekeeper to a nursery or a florist and you get African violets of all different hues." Erickson recalled that at that time there were 13 different hues of African violets. Then Erickson told the woman, "Those will be your African violets and you are going to take good care of them. That's a medical order."

After she agreed to those instructions, Erickson continued:

> Then you will tell your housekeeper also to purchase 200 gift flower pots and 50 potting pots and potting soil. I want you to break off a leaf from each of your African violets and plant it in the potting pots and grow additional mature African violets. And when you have an adequate supply of African violets, I want you to send one to every baby that is born in any family in your church. I want you to send an African violet to the family of every baby christened in your church. I want you to send a gift adult African violet to everyone who is sick in your church. When a girl announces her engagement, I want you to send her an African violet. When they get married, I want you to send African violets. In the case of death, you send a condolence card with an African violet. And at the church bazaar contribute a dozen or a score of African violets for sale.

Erickson later learned that at one point she had 200 adult African violets in her home. The importance of this was explained by Erickson, "Anybody that takes care of 200 African violets is too busy to be depressed." The woman died in her 70s. In her obituary, she was given the title of "the African Violet Queen of Milwaukee."

As a result of her special mission, she developed an endless number of friendships. Explaining his work with this woman, Erickson stated that there was just that one interview. As Erickson put it, "I just pointed her nose in the right direction and said, 'Giddy-up,'" which is another way of saying that he provided a behavioral nudge. Erickson emphasized the importance of autonomous stability and self-determination, stating that she did all the rest of the therapy.

With closer examination, we see that Erickson's nudge was simply to activate social momentum through what would now be recognized as agentic framing. This behavioral tactic leveraged her authority bias by assigning a meaningful action. By prescribing her plant care as a "medical order," Erickson allowed her to act with purpose without the emotional risk of self-initiation. The tasks were structured, prosocial, and anchored in her existing competence, creating a low-friction path toward social reengagement. In doing so, Erickson transformed passive deference into adaptive action. While discussing this case, Erickson emphasized that the important thing about therapy is finding the personal potential that is readily accessible for your clients and then providing strong encouragement to move forward on a specific task.

Conclusion

This chapter explored authority bias through the lens of ECA, revealing how the tendency to defer to authority can be both a limiting habit and a useful gateway to growth. When unexamined, authority bias can suppress independent thought, prolong distress, and reinforce passivity. However, as shown through the cases presented, this same bias can become a valuable tool when approached with empathy, clarity, and thoughtful design. Erickson did not try to eliminate his clients' reliance on authority. Instead, he used it as scaffolding, providing structure and validation during times when clients felt overwhelmed or directionless. By speaking with credibility rooted in research, cultural resonance, and personal honesty, he earned the trust necessary to support clients in accessing agency they had not yet reclaimed for themselves.

Behavioral tactics such as watching eyes, permission, positively calibrated prediction, and agentic framing demonstrate how specific nudges, when offered by someone perceived as credible, can help individuals move from dependency to engagement and from passivity to adaptive action (Table 6.1).

Research in interpersonal theory further supports this approach. Complementarity, or the sense of mutual fit between practitioner and client, is key to therapeutic alliance and continuity (Lichtenberg & Tracey, 2003). Studies have shown that satisfaction with the intake interview is the strongest predictor of whether clients return for further sessions (Kokotovic & Tracey, 1990). When a client's state of mind reflects authority bias, the formal or obvious provision of expert guidance can serve as a complementary gesture. As the client's confidence grows, this guidance should naturally evolve. The practitioner gradually reduces their directive stance to make space for the client's initiative and personal reasoning. Research on motivation and learning has shown that clients who attribute progress to their own actions, rather than to external agents such as the therapist, experience greater resilience and lower relapse rates over time (Harackiewicz et al., 1987; Weinberger, 1995).

Across all the cases described in this chapter, the initial appeal to authority was not the solution itself but a way to activate abilities already latent within the client. Once clients experienced success in a structure that felt both safe and credible, they began to internalize new possibilities. Their choices were no longer governed by what others allowed, but by what made sense within their personal value system. What followed was not mere compliance, but genuine adaptation.

True empowerment in ECA does not occur when clients follow instructions, no matter how well-intended. It occurs when clients reclaim authorship over their own decisions and learn to trust their evolving sense of what is meaningful and right. The ECA practitioner's role is not to chart the course, but to build a choice environment that honors the individual's readiness, reveals overlooked options, and allows the client to step forward with confidence when the path becomes clear.

Quick-Reference Tactic Map

Table 6.1 Tactics Suited for *Authority Bias* and the Broader Architecture of Strategic Influence

If Client...	*Then Use...*	*Because*
Needs accountability or moral consistency	*Watching* eyes: Creating the feeling of having one's choices subject to observation by using visual cues or an expectation that one could be watched.	*Primes* prosocial values through observation or symbolic oversight.

(*Continued*)

Table 6.1 (Continued)

If Client...	*Then Use...*	*Because*
Self-inhibition or hesitation stands in the way of progress	*Permission*: Sanctioning a new choice as an authority figure.	*Utilizes* the need for external validation by legitimizing self-efficacy and autonomy.
Lacks confidence or motivation to persist	*Positively calibrated prediction*: Providing an optimistic yet realistic forecast about an outcome, behavior, or future event.	*Primes* expectancy, increasing motivation and persistence by making success feel credible rather than merely desirable.
Feels uncertain, powerless, or unqualified to act independently	*Agentic framing*: Leading an individual to act as an agent of a respected authority figure, out of duty, obligation, or loyalty.	*Frames* action as duty to a respected authority, transferring confidence and legitimacy to the behavior.

Notes

1 This intervention reflects an earlier clinical era and would not be considered ethically appropriate today. Contemporary standards require clear professional boundaries, especially in matters involving a client's body or possible exposure. Erickson's apparent aim was to make the behavior incompatible with the client's own social limits, not to invite literal compliance.

2 Erickson used the colloquial term *fanny* rather than *butt*. At the time, it functioned as a polite euphemism, though in some English-speaking cultures this term has more vulgar connotations.

References

Antepuesto, J. J. B., Catandijan, N., Gecain, K., & Culajara, C. L. (2025). How the presence of an authority figure influences students' choices and stress levels: A one-time experimental study. *Asian Research Journal of Arts & Social Sciences*, *23*(2), 25–37. https://doi.org/10.9734/arjass/2025/v23i2638

Bandura, A. (1972). *Self-efficacy: The Exercise of Control*. W.H. Freeman.

Bateson, M., Callow, L., Holmes, J. R., Roche, M. L. R., & Nettle, D. (2013). Do images of 'watching eyes' induce behaviour that is more pro-social or more normative? A field experiment on littering. *PLoS One*, *8*(12), e82055. https://doi.org/10.1371/journal.pone.0082055

Bateson, M., Nettle, D., & Roberts, G. (2006). Cues of being watched enhance cooperation in a real-world setting. *Biology Letters*, 2(3), 412–414. https://doi.org/10.1098/rsbl.2006.0509

Beahrs, J. O. (2006). Assessing attributive causation in psychiatry: Psychotherapeutic results correlate with self-therapeutic activity. *Clinical Neuropsychiatry*, *3*, 154–161.

Burger, J. M. (1989). Negative reactions to increases in perceived personal control. *Journal of Personality and Social Psychology*, *56*(2), 246–256. https://doi.org/10.1037/0022-3514.56.2.246

Dear, K., Dutton, K., & Fox, E. (2019). Do 'watching eyes' influence antisocial behavior? A systematic review & meta-analysis. *Evolution and Human Behavior*, *40*(3), 269–280. https://doi.org/10.1016/j.evolhumbehav.2019.01.006

Dolinski, D., & Grzyb, T. (2020). *The Social Psychology of Obedience Towards Authority: An Empirical Tribute to Stanley Milgram*. Routledge. https://doi.org/10.4324/9781003049470

Galinsky, A. D., Gruenfeld, D. H., & Magee, J. C. (2003). From power to action. *Journal of Personality and Social Psychology*, *85*(3), 453–466. https://doi.org/10.1037/0022-3514.85.3.453

Goodall, J. (1986). *The Chimpanzees of Gombe: Patterns of Behavior*. Belknap Press of Harvard University Press.

Harackiewicz, J. M., Sansone, C., Blair, L. W., Epstein, J. A., & Manderlink, G. (1987). Attributional processes in behavior change and maintenance: Smoking cessation and continued abstinence. *Journal of Consulting and Clinical Psychology*, *55*(3), 372–378. https://doi.org/10.1037/0022-006X.55.3.372

Hofling, C. K., Brotzman, E., Dalrymple, S., Graves, N., & Pierce, C. M. (1966). An experimental study in nurse-physician relationships. *The Journal of Nervous and Mental Disease*, *143*(2), 171.

Iyengar, S. S., & Lepper, M. R. (1999). Rethinking the value of choice: A cultural perspective on intrinsic motivation. *Journal of Personality and Social Psychology*, *76*(3), 349–366. https://doi.org/10.1037/0022-3514.76.3.349

Karakowsky, L., DeGama, N., & McBey, K. (2012). Facilitating the Pygmalion effect: The overlooked role of subordinate perceptions of the leader. *Journal of Occupational and Organizational Psychology*, *85*(4), 579–599. https://doi.org/10.1111/j.2044-8325.2012.02056.x

Kim, D., Kim, J., & Kim, H. (2021). Increased conformity to social hierarchy under public eyes. *Frontiers in Psychology*, *12*. https://doi.org/10.3389/fpsyg.2021.636801

Kirsch, I. (1985). Response expectancy as a determinant of experience and behavior. *American Psychologist*, *40*(11), 1189.

Kokotovic, A. M., & Tracey, T. J. (1990). Working alliance in the early phase of counseling. *Journal of Counseling Psychology*, *37*(1), 16–21. https://doi.org/10.1037/0022-0167.37.1.16

Lange, P. A. M. V., & Manesi, Z. (2023). Reputation reminders: When do eye cues promote prosocial behavior? *The Spanish Journal of Psychology*, *26*, e8. https://doi.org/10.1017/SJP.2023.4

Lichtenberg, J. W., & Tracey, T. J. G. (2003). Interaction rules and strategies in psychotherapy. *Journal of Counseling Psychology*, *50*(3), 267–275. https://doi.org/10.1037/0022-0167.50.3.267

Lipowski, Z. J. (1984). What does the word "psychosomatic" really mean? A historical and semantic inquiry. *Psychosomatic Medicine*, *46*(2), 153–171. https://doi.org/10.1097/00006842-198403000-00007

Loftus, E. F., & Pickrell, J. E. (1995). The formation of false memories. *Psychiatric Annals*, *25*(12), 720–725. https://doi.org/10.3928/0048-5713-19951201-07

Merton, R. K. (1948). The self-fulfilling prophecy. *The Antioch Review*, *8*(2), 193–210. https://doi.org/10.2307/4609267

Milgram, S. (1974). *Obedience to Authority: An Experimental View*. Harper & Row.

O'Keefe, D. J. (1999). How to handle opposing arguments in persuasive messages: A meta-analytic review of the effects of one-sided and two-sided messages. *Annals of the International Communication Association*, *22*(1), 209–249. https://doi.org/10.1080/23808985.1999.11678963

Roberts, L. M., Dutton, J. E., Spreitzer, G. M., Heaphy, E. D., & Quinn, R. E. (2005). Composing the reflected best-self portrait: Building pathways for becoming extraordinary in work organizations. *Academy of Management Review*, *30*(4), 712–736. https://doi.org/10.5465/amr.2005.18378874

Rosenthal, R., & Jacobson, L. (1968). Pygmalion in the classroom. *The Urban Review*, *3*(1), 16–20. https://doi.org/10.1007/BF02322211

Sharif, M. A., & Shu, S. B. (2017). The benefits of emergency reserves: Greater preference and persistence for goals that have slack with a cost. *Journal of Marketing Research*, *54*(3), 495–509. https://doi.org/10.1509/jmr.15.0231

Tetlock, P. E., & Gardner, D. (2015). *Superforecasting: The Art and Science of Prediction*. Crown.

Weinberger, J. (1995). Common factors aren't so common: The common factors dilemma. *Clinical Psychology: Science and Practice*, *2*(1), 45–69. https://doi.org/10.1111/j.1468-2850.1995.tb00024.x

Chapter 7

Two Voices, One Choice

Ambivalence

Two Voices, One Choice: *Ambivalence*

A 25-year-old woman attending college at ASU came to therapy reporting chronic depression, confusion, difficulty concentrating, and disconcerting emotional shifts. She described her emotional struggles as chronic, dating back to seventh grade when she first began seeing therapists for depression. However, during her second session we speculated that her recent emotional volatility and weight gain might be due to pregnancy, which was confirmed by a doctor the following day.

By the third session, she was overwhelmed: "I can't possibly think of going through with it...every part of me tells me that I can't handle this!" The doctor had told her she had one week to decide and assured her that an abortion would be simple. When I asked whether she had been encouraged to explore other options, such as adoption or talk to anyone, she said, "No...She just directed me to a website about abortions."

Her history revealed a deep desire for connection and a history of suicidal ideation. She had been traumatized in high school from the public shaming that followed a sexual assault at a high school party by a man ten years older than her. My guess was that she longed to be restored to her family but low self-esteem stood in the way. Although I worried that abortion might deepen her depression and trigger suicidal ideation, I avoided trying to manage her decision. Instead, I focused on helping her explore her ambivalence.

Before making such a big decision, I told her she owed herself at least one honest debate about it. I then placed two chairs in front of her. I explained that one chair represented the part of her that wanted to become a mother, and the other, the part that wants to have the abortion. When asked which chair she wished to sit in first, she chose to begin with the "abortion chair." Expressing fear, anger, and hopelessness, she pleaded with her other self not to let this "thing" derail her education and future. As I listened, I was impressed by the sensibleness of her argument. After about 12 minutes, she moved to the other chair.

DOI: 10.4324/9781003797876-8

There, tears came almost instantly. She admitted how badly she wanted to give and receive love. She rebuked the voice from the other chair, stating, "All of your life you have longed to be loved. And, now when you are about to have a little being that will love you unconditionally—you want to kill it? That makes no sense!" Eventually, signs of self-compassion emerged and she said quietly, "I know in my heart I could be a good mother, even if no one else believes in me."

After exploring both sides, I affirmed her courage and let her know that I could see how thoughtful she was being. I then offered to let her listen to an audio recording of the dialogue. She sat silently, jaw clenching and unclenching as she absorbed her inner turmoil from an outside perspective. By the end of this review, it was time to end the session.

Before she left my office, I learned that she was not planning to tell her family about her dilemma, fearing judgment due to her parents' religious beliefs and her sister's ongoing struggle to conceive: "The last thing I feel like dealing with is the judgment from my family." I shared my view that in moments like these, when so much is at stake, it's usually helpful to turn toward family, not away from them. I added that the only exception is when parents do not genuinely love their children. She rejected this possibility expressing confidence that her parents and her sister loved her. Without applying pressure, I casually remarked, "You know, sometimes people can really surprise you with their reactions."

By the following week, she appeared much less emotionally distraught. After taking a seat, her first comment was, "I told my parents about the pregnancy. Their response REALLY surprised me!" Her parents had been supportive in a way that she was not expecting. Her father was excited to become a grandfather, enthusiastically declaring, "You have made me the happiest man on the planet!" But it was her mother's response that surprised her most.

Her father had been talking about shopping for baby cribs when her mother asked him to get off the call so that they could have a private discussion as mother and daughter. Her mother then offered,

> Your father is excited. But I want you to know that you have options. This is your body. You need to make the choice that is right for you. And you should know that we will love you just as much no matter what decision you make.

She had assumed her mother was staunchly opposed to abortion.

Given both the loving support and the freedom that she needed to make her own choice, she confidently came to a decision. She was no longer ambivalent in her desire to keep "her" baby. At the next visit, we discussed the practical challenges of raising a child as a single-mother. The father was in a drug rehabilitation center in Florida and had decided that he did not want to be involved in the child's life. Months later, after the birth, she reflected: "For the first time in years I feel like I trusted myself and made a really good decision." Until then, she had seen her life as a string of missteps. This choice design supported her in recognizing her emotional needs and reconnecting with an internal wisdom.

Recognizing Ambivalence in Ericksonian Choice Architecture

Ambivalence, as conceptualized in this chapter, is not a flaw in reasoning or a failure of will, but an adaptive mental state that arises when there is a *simultaneous activation of competing internal systems* (*goals*, *beliefs*, *attitudes*, *emotions*, or *relational needs*). In the vignette above, this simultaneous activation was made explicit when she moved between the "abortion chair" (protecting education, stability, and future safety) and the "mother chair" (longing for love, connection, and a repaired sense of self). The two-chair dialogue served as a tactic for engaging *critical thinking* on both sides of the issue, so that eventually a self-endorsed choice could emerge.

Many different psychological theories agree that ambivalence is a common state of mind. For example, *cognitive dissonance theory* (Festinger, 1954) highlights the discomfort of holding incompatible thoughts or values. Discomfort is one possible outcome of ambivalence. This tension also compels deliberation (e.g., reviewing pros and cons) or assimilation (e.g., automatically changing beliefs to align with behaviors). Ambivalence is not merely a sign of psychological conflict. Rather, it reflects a core feature of human cognition and motivation—the capacity to hold contradiction without collapsing into chaos.

Other theories, like *dual-process models* (Kahneman, 2011) and *goal systems theory* (Kruglanski et al., 2023) show that our behavior is often shaped by two mental systems. One is fast and automatic, based on impulses or habits (system 1—unconscious mind). The other is slower and more reasoned, based on goals and planning (system 2—conscious mind). Sometimes these systems pull us in opposite directions. For example, when we intentionally buy healthy food at the grocery store and on the way home thoughtlessly pull into a fast-food drive-through.

Ambivalence can be viewed as a signal of developmental complexity, value pluralism, or transitional identity (Luescher & Pillemer, 1998). In this light, ambivalence can serve as a portal to growth when approached with reflective awareness rather than prematurely collapsed into certainty. However, when disavowed or ignored, these inner contradictions often spill over into behavior manifesting as inconsistency, rationalization, hesitation, or projection. Interpersonal theories (Rossberg et al., 2007; Wiggins &

Trobst, 1997) further point to the complexity of ambivalence by showing that many interpersonal conflicts are actually expressions of emotional contradictions that are projected outward and enacted as *dynamic opposition* between people.

Interpersonally, unresolved ambivalence may lead to approach-avoidance conflicts in relationships and complementary behavior cycles with mutually reinforcing roles. For example, one romantic partner might pursue closeness while the other pulls away. This pattern is known as the pursuer-distancer dynamic (Gottman & Silver, 1999). Yet, like a teeter-totter, these roles can reverse if the pursuer begins to withdraw or the distancer starts to seek closeness. This back-and-forth is what is meant by dynamic opposition and tends to happen when both people feel ambivalent about staying in the relationship. Accordingly, research on attachment (Mikulincer, 1995) and approach-avoidance conflicts (N. E. Miller, 1944) demonstrates how people can simultaneously feel the desire to connect and the urge to pull away.

Using a common clinical scenario, Erickson (1957) illustrated the effects of dynamic opposition. He described how a client might feel they should talk about a problem but also feel overwhelmingly nervous about becoming so vulnerable. Instead of coaxing the person to self-disclose, Erickson would recommend they withhold anything they are not yet ready to discuss. Ironically, this often made the choice to fully self-disclose much easier. The opposite is also true. If someone feels pressured to talk, they may experience a strong need to withhold. Putting pressure on one side of a person's ambivalence tends to amplify the opposing side.

A closely related concept, *empathy-induced dissonance* (Batson et al., 1997), emphasizes how moral discomfort can arise when our care for others clashes with our own self-interest. This kind of inner conflict is not limited to thoughts or feelings. It is also fueled by emotional connection. Being attuned to someone else's experience can make it harder to ignore or dismiss our own conflicting motives. Neuroimaging studies (Decety & Lamm, 2006) support this idea, showing that such dissonance activates both emotional and cognitive systems in the brain. These findings reveal the depth and complexity of ambivalence, not as something to avoid or correct, but as a meaningful signal guiding the alignment of our actions with our values.

Social and cultural systems also play a significant role in shaping ambivalence. Not only do they reflect our mixed feelings, but they also often make them stronger or harder to sort out. For example, *ambivalent sexism* (Glick & Fiske, 2001) is a theory that explains how someone can express both kindness and control toward women at the same time. A person might say they want to protect women by ensuring that they stay in traditional roles. These attitudes may seem caring on the surface, but they also limit women's freedom, thus showing both positive and negative attitudes at once.

Another example is *moral licensing* (Merritt et al., 2010), which describes how people sometimes give themselves permission to do something wrong after doing something good. For instance, after donating to charity, someone might feel it is okay to act selfishly later as if their good deed nullifies subsequent bad deeds (mental accounting). In both cases, people are not necessarily being hypocritical. Instead, they are navigating between personal desires, social pressures, and the need to feel like a good person (ego protection). Ambivalence can manifest as a balancing act between competing values and expectations.

It is important to recognize the difference between ambivalence and a related, but separate, bias called *psychological reactance*. Ambivalence happens when a person feels torn between two or more meaningful desires or goals that conflict with each other. In contrast, *reactance* arises when someone feels that their freedom to choose is being threatened by outside pressure. In these situations, inner conflict is absent. Instead, the conflict is social and shows up as a reaction to feeling trapped or controlled.

Even though reactance can *look* like ambivalence (such as showing hesitation, defiance, or ironic reversals) it represents a different agenda. Reactance defends autonomy when choice feels threatened, while ambivalence opens space to reflect on competing values. This matters in relationships, especially when collaboration is the goal. A person may genuinely want to cooperate but still be uncooperative if a nudge feels like persuasion or if responsiveness is rushed. From an Ericksonian point of view, this shows why it is so important to create low-pressure environments where people can align with choices willingly.

For these reasons, ambivalence should not be framed as "resistance." Rather, it should be appreciated as evidence of complexity. In this state of mind, we hesitate not because we do not wish to move forward but because both paths matter. The psychologist and philosopher William James (1916) recognized ambivalence as a central feature of human psychology, noting that choice does not exist except where there is deliberation. Indeed, people can feel paralyzed not because they lack direction, but because their needs and desires point to meaningful, yet incompatible, outcomes. Erickson intuitively worked within the same conceptual framework as James (Short, 2020). Instead of seeking to resolve ambivalence through insight or pressure to commit, he created environments where both sides of a conflict could be expressed safely—using paradox, double binds, and permission to explore without judgment.

Within Ericksonian Choice Architecture (ECA), ambivalence is not something to overcome but something to engage. As illustrated in the opening vignette, hearing both voices gives individuals the psychological and relational space to arrive at choices that reflect a complex array of needs. Research on collaborative relationships supports this view. In motivational interviewing, Miller and Rollnick (2012) found that people are more likely to modify habitual behavior not when pressured, but when both sides of their ambivalence are heard, allowing "change talk" to strengthen as "sustain talk" is respectfully reflected. In this sense, ambivalence is not weakness but a form of dynamic tension, reflecting values that deserve careful weighing. When that tension is honored, the self becomes more fully engaged, and clarity can emerge from allowing all parts of the person to speak.

Erickson's Casework and the Application of Tactical Nudges

Now that we have examined how to recognize ambivalence (not as resistance or reactance but as an internal signal of conflicting values), we can begin to see its deeper significance. Erickson did not merely acknowledge these tensions, he designed around them. His communication strategies reveal a subtle mastery of micro-level choice architecture, crafting environments in which those facing an impasse could begin to move without force through carefully structured opportunities to *choose differently*.

Erickson understood that people do not experience greater quality of life simply because they are told what to do. Rather, they engage more fully in life's challenges when their options are framed in ways that feel safe, meaningful, and self-authored. To accomplish this, he used a range of tactics that anticipated modern behavioral science, including *momentary allurements*, *reverse positioning*, *future contrasting*, and *tandem anchoring*. In the pages that follow, we will explore how these tactics function not as tools of persuasion, but as invitations to rediscover choice. For those who feel powerless, stuck, or fragmented, these tactics offer a way back to coherence.

Case 7.1: The Dominant Husband

A woman came to Erickson for help with what she described as a serious problem in her marriage. She had been with her husband for several years and together they had worked hard to save money for a house, a milestone that held great personal meaning for both. But now that they were finally ready to buy, her husband insisted she have no voice in the decision. He declared that choosing the house and selecting the furnishings was entirely *his* responsibility as the head of the household. She told Erickson that while he had always been somewhat controlling, this issue felt different, more personal, and she was determined to have some say in the kind of home they would build together.

Erickson managed to convince the husband to come to his office for a session without his wife. Rather than challenge the man's entrenched beliefs about male authority, Erickson aligned with them, agreeing that the husband should be the boss and that the final decision on the house and furnishings should rest with him. However, despite his bravado, the man had not yet chosen a house or a furniture plan. These unknowns introduced a subtle but useful state of ambivalence.

Using his own authority as a psychiatrist, Erickson focused the conversation on a more reflective question: *What kind of man is really the boss of his family?* Erickson shared his honest opinion, which was that true authority is expressed through skill, flexibility, and strategic generosity. These ideals had strong ego appeal and were simultaneously modeled in Erickson's immediate behavior.

Erickson suggested that, "A man who's really the boss is powerful enough to allow his underlings to have a say in minor matters." This reframe created a new choice structure. It shifted conceptualization from dichotomous reasoning to a continuum. Instead of debating whether the wife should have the final say or no say, Erickson illuminated a point midway between these two extremes, in which the man would *permit* his wife to exercise choice within a range of opportunity (*bounded choice*).

To make the compromise actionable, Erickson helped the man develop a clear set of *implementation intentions*: The husband would select 20 possible floor plans and 20 furnishing schemes and his wife would then choose from the options he had pre-approved. This structure satisfied both partners. The wife, perhaps ambivalent about asserting too much control, felt acknowledged and included. The husband, who had no doubt about his role as the decision-maker, felt respected and maintained his sense of authority. In the end, Erickson did not challenge their values (neither the husband's need for dominance nor the wife's need for self-assertion). Instead, he restructured their choices so that both could act in alignment with their cultural identities without conflict.

Tandem Anchoring

Tandem anchoring is a behavioral tactic within ECA that uses continuum-based thinking to find a workable position between opposing options. Rather than accepting a binary choice, such as "no change" or "complete change," it identifies value in both sides and introduces a broader range of possibilities. For example, some things may need to change while others should remain the same. Treating both anchors as reasonable can reveal new options that were hidden by all-or-nothing thinking.

The following case illustrates how tandem anchoring can preserve the value in opposing positions while opening a workable path beyond all-or-nothing thinking. Recently, I met with a couple teetering on the edge of a final breakup. He had spent all his savings to buy land for a house he planned to build. She was not included in the decision and learned about the purchase only after speaking with one of his sons. Although the plan was for them to move into the house together, he refused to show her the blueprints or include her in contract negotiations. He insisted he had everything under control, that every design choice reflected her needs, and that she should simply trust him. He cleaned swimming pools for a living. She worked at the corporate offices of a large organization, handling complex contracts and coordinating logistics across multiple branches—work she did exceptionally well.

For much of the session, I openly challenged their chances of success and asked, with frank skepticism, what had originally drawn them together. Despite the conflict, each remained convinced of the other's positive character. With only a few minutes left, I offered a narrow path forward. It required strict, explicit concessions from both sides. To both I said, "You're going to have to commit to some difficult compromises." Turning to her, I said, "His family tradition is patriarchal. He expects the man to make the major family decisions. Can you accept that?" She agreed without complaint. Turning to him, I said,

> You've told me you're attracted to her intelligence, and you've said more than once today that she's a smart woman—yet you're not letting her use any of those strengths. If this relationship is going to work, you must bring her into the decision-making process, even if that means spreadsheets and detailed planning. Are you willing to do that?

He agreed.

The tactic was not to split the difference or ask either partner to surrender a valued identity. Tandem anchoring preserved the value in both positions: her need for partnership and his wish to lead. This made compromise feel less like defeat and more like a shared path toward preserving the relationship.[1]

Tandem anchoring is especially effective because it moves decision-making beyond all-or-nothing choices without forcing a particular outcome. By identifying value in each opposing position, it creates a continuum of workable options between them. This broader choice landscape supports autonomy, encourages reflection, and helps the person discover a course of action that feels both reasonable and self-directed.

Case Analysis

In the case above, a woman sought Erickson's help with a conflict between an overly domineering husband and her own need for creative self-expression. This type of ambivalence was social (see Table 7.1). Erickson recognized that confronting the man's personal beliefs directly would likely trigger defensiveness and further entrench his position (*backfire effect*). Instead, Erickson employed tandem anchoring—treating each person's beliefs and aspirations as important. Rather than framing the situation as a binary conflict between domination and equality, Erickson proposed a structure that preserved the husband's sense of identity while expanding the space in which the wife could act on her creative talents.

Notably, Erickson did not challenge the husband's position outright. He verbally affirmed the husband's right to be "the boss," echoing the idea that a man should have the final say in major household decisions. This approach is supported by recent research on receptiveness to opposing views, which shows that acknowledging the other person's perspective (even when disagreeing) makes people feel more understood, less defensive, and more likely to engage productively (Minson & Chen, 2022). In effect, Erickson's verbal agreement modeled what this research describes as *receptive disagreement*, using empathy and alignment to open a more flexible dialogue.

This nudge created conditions in which both partners could act in ways that felt self-directed and personally congruent. For the husband, who felt no ambivalence about being in charge, Erickson's recommendation that he select 20 possible floor plans and 20 furnishing schemes (allowing his wife to choose among them) reinforced his sense of authority. For the wife, the opportunity to choose among meaningful options gave her a voice in shaping their shared future, satisfying her need to be seen and valued. This approach also aligns with research on *bounded choice*, which suggests that people feel more empowered and less overwhelmed when given a structured range of options that affirm their agency. By using tandem anchoring to create a middle ground, Erickson helped both partners move toward a future that neither had previously imagined, but both could support.

Table 7.1 Psychological Domains in which Ambivalence Commonly Manifests

Types of Conflict	
Cognitive Holding conflicting beliefs, attitudes, or values	**Motivational** Competing impulses or goals
Emotional Opposing feelings toward a person or situation	**Social** Dissonant intentions or behavior

General Application

Tandem anchoring is especially useful for clients experiencing ambivalence because it reframes a binary dilemma into a continuum of nuanced, viable options. It is particularly effective when a client feels trapped between two unacceptable choices. Rather than asking them to choose one extreme or simply split the difference, the tactic identifies the valid concern within each position and uses continuum-based thinking to reveal a workable option between them. For example, an employee who feels unfairly pressured by a boss may value both self-protection (staying silent) and communication (speaking out). A choice architect might ask, "How could you make your needs known while still protecting your role as a valued employee?" Ultimately, tandem anchoring works because it transforms the discomfort of ambivalence into a guided exploration of personal agency. It invites clients to see decision-making as a creative process in which acceptable choices can be discovered rather than forced concessions between rigid extremes.

Case 7.2: Dancing Nude before Bed

A woman came to Erickson overwhelmed by recurring episodes of choking, gasping, and chest pressure that left her fearing for her life. Her reaction seemed unpredictable to her, though Erickson noticed these episodes clustered around bedtime and social situations involving sexual innuendo. This suggested a misalignment between her immediate emotional needs and marital expectations.

Rather than humiliating her by labeling her experience as a symptom of panic disorder and fear of sex, Erickson gently redirected her inhibitions. He discouraged her from sharing the details of those risqué stories, stating, "let's not discuss such things," thereby meeting her emotional need for withholding. What had been expressed physiologically as restricted breathing was now addressed dialectally, allowing her to remain engaged without becoming overwhelmed.

Erickson gradually linked her physical distress to her bedtime routine. He asked whether the steam from the shower might aggravate her choking and gasping. Gradually, the conversation became more explicit. When Erickson inquired about her stepping out of the shower onto her bathmat, he had her consider the feeling of the cooler bathroom air on her skin. He asked whether drying herself with a towel and rubbing her body might improve it or lessen it. These questions served as veiled references to nudity, helping her link imagery of her nude body to feelings of curiosity versus feelings of panic and fear.

As her trust and confidence grew, Erickson introduced a *choice preview* by inviting her to fantasize about "the most horrible thing" she could imagine doing in relation to preparing for bed. She was also instructed to consider "the most amazing thing she could do." This created two contrasting sets of motivation. Erickson continued, "Don't tell me, just speculate on it." She flushed, paled, then burst into laughter, eventually admitting: "Joe would drop dead if I came into the bedroom in the nude, dancing." Erickson replied playfully, "We ought not to give him heart failure," indirectly implying that she had something else to offer him. Erickson then suggested a safer alternative: Instead of performing for Joe (something she was still too inhibited to do), why not dance nude alone at home, with the lights off, while her daughter was at nursery school? This made it easier for her to explore physical freedom, in private, without scrutiny.

Erickson continued to guide her toward sexual disinhibition using very subtle nudges. For example, he linked provocative undressing to her creative interest in sewing, eventually encouraging her to "run up" a nightgown herself, a double entendre for making a dress or undressing. In a later session, Erickson's seeding became more explicit as he spoke of letting her nightie "run up to her neck" and later of letting it "run up to the head of the bed."

At home, when she felt ready, she danced nude into her darkened bedroom, telling Erickson afterward that it was "the first time in her life" she enjoyed entering that space. Instead of choking, she went to sleep giggling, secretly pleased and now enjoying her husband's curiosity. Erickson built on her momentum with more contrasting: "What's the most utterly horrifying, amazing thing you could pull on your husband?" Again, he told her not to share, just to imagine. She engaged in her private *choice preview*, then decided that she wished to share her joyful experience with Erickson. She had pictured undressing in front of Joe with the lights on, revealing red ribbon bows tied around her nipples.

Erickson responded not with shock but with pragmatic considerations, asking, "What size ribbons?" This normalized the fantasy and encouraged her to treat it as an important task to be completed (implementation intentions). At home, when she implemented *her* plan, her husband expressed his own ambivalence toward sex relations, stating, "I think you're beginning to get some sense" just before rolling over and going to sleep. It is likely that he both wanted to have sex and was not yet ready to risk disappointment or sexual rejection. Fortunately, his hesitation allowed Ann more time to continue developing her fantasies around sex.

Throughout their marriage, sex had been rare, extremely brief, and done under protest. Following the optimization of her choice environment, this woman was able to enter the bedroom on her own terms, her laughter replacing her gasping and her fantasies displacing her fears. The contrast between a life of silent suffocation and one of private pleasure and playful daring gave her access to the experience of choice, and with it progress toward a new developmental milestone.

Future Contrasting

Future contrasting is a behavioral tactic in ECA that involves vividly imagining two divergent future outcomes. The first possibility represents a maladaptive, value-inconsistent response and the other a value-affirming, adaptive alternative. Each scenario is mentally extended to include its longer-term consequences, creating a contrast that sharpens motivational focus and reveals internal preferences. Rather than eliminate contradiction, future contrasting, like many of Erickson's strategies, embraces it as a source of insight. While describing his willingness to enable clients to simultaneously express contradictory behaviors, Erickson (1959) emphasized that "this need to fully meet the demands of the patients, however manifested, ought never to be minimized." For instances of ambivalence, these demands are self-contradictory.

This tactic is particularly effective in situations involving approach/avoidance conflicts, especially those in which emotion-driven impulses (System 1) are at odds with rational intentions (System 2). By inviting the client to inhabit both extremes (the worst-case, short-sighted choice and the best-case, values-based alternative) future contrasting gives emotional and physiological shape to internal conflict. Research on a similar technique, *mental contrasting*, shows that vividly contrasting a desired future with a counter-reality (whether an obstacle or an undesired alternative) strengthens commitment and improves self-regulation (Oettingen et al., 2005). Interestingly, these effects hold for both positive fantasies and negative ones. When either is contrasted with a meaningful counterpoint, motivation and clarity increase.

The power of future contrasting lies in its ability to activate and compare possible selves (visions of the self in different future states). According to Oyserman and James (2009), possible selves serve as guideposts that orient decision-making in the present. When placed in contrast with one another, these imagined identities create psychological tension that can dramatically increase goal salience and self-consistency. In other words, when a client sees who they might become depending on their choices, the present moment becomes more meaningful and actionable. Research shows that this way of thinking does not remain in the realm of imagination. It tends to affect how people behave afterward in real-life situations (Galinsky & Moskowitz, 2000).

During choice design, future contrasting can be delivered formally or informally. A formal version might sound like: "Close your eyes and picture yourself handling this situation poorly, see what consequences occur... Next, imagine the best version of yourself responding. What does that look like? How does it feel afterward?" Informally, it might sound like: "What's the most horrible thing you can imagine doing at that meeting?

Now, what would it look like if you were at your best?" These exercises simulate choice in a safe virtual space, allowing emotional rehearsal without real-world consequences.

Three key elements make future contrasting particularly effective within the ECA framework. First, it relies on contrasting outcomes: The client must explore both best- and worst-case futures related to a specific decision. Second, it promotes embodied awareness as the client is guided to notice what each version feels like emotionally and physically. This brings unconscious associations into conscious awareness. Third, it cultivates motivational clarity by comparing the emotional impact of each imagined outcome. This enables the client to more clearly align with the version that reflects their values, goals, and identity. In this way, future contrasting is not just about visualizing outcomes. It is about *embodying the wisdom of choice* so the preferred future feels more compelling and achievable.

Case Analysis

This woman came to Erickson overwhelmed by episodes of choking and chest tightness, unconscious choices linked to her sexual inhibitions. This problem was something she needed to address but was too inhibited to discuss. The same motivational ambivalence extended to the bedroom, where she also struggled with a desire to share and an impulse to conceal (see Table 7.1). Instead of confronting her ambivalence, Erickson offered her options she could comfortably accept, such as withholding the details of risqué stories. Paradoxically, this resulted in her sharing explicit details about her own nudity before bed. Remember, like a teeter-totter, applying pressure to influence one side of a person's ambivalence tends to amplify their need to move in the opposite direction.

The deeper work began when Erickson invited her to imagine, but not reveal, "the most horrible thing" she could possibly do while preparing for bed. He paired this with a second prompt: "the most amazing thing" she might do. This setup created the core dynamic of future contrasting: two vivid, emotionally charged outcomes, one feared, one longed for. Her initial reaction was visceral. She flushed, paled, then burst out laughing and eventually confessed her worst-case fantasy: "Joe would drop dead if I came into the bedroom in the nude, dancing." Erickson playfully responded, "We ought not to give him a heart failure," acknowledging her fantasy while again acting to inhibit her behavior, thus creating the space she needed to further explore her readiness to become uninhibited. He then delayed the option of enacting her fantasy by prescribing a prerequisite, which was dancing nude alone at home with the lights off. This would be a private exploration of embodied freedom in a safer context. It served both as needed practice and as a subtle form of *escalating commitment*.

This case eloquently illustrates all three elements of future contrasting. First, *contrasting outcomes* were clearly established through guided fantasy (one horrible; the other amazing). Second, Erickson cultivated *embodied awareness* by inviting her to scan her physical and emotional state as she imagined experiences occurring in her shower, bedroom, and in her bed. After evoking creativity and play, her habit of choking was replaced with giggling and devious pleasure. Finally, *motivational clarity* emerged as she began to act in alignment with her deeper values and identity; she wanted to be a gift to her husband. The fantasy of red ribbon bows on her nipples, once unthinkable, was symbolic of her deepest wishes and implemented with joyful pride. Erickson's matter-of-fact response, "What size ribbons?" signaled that the fantasy was not only permitted but also actionable.

Importantly, these contrasts were not just thought experiments. They were embodied learning derived from the actions of a possible self. This liberated her from the tyranny of the established associational chain of events. As explained almost a century ago by child psychologist Lev Vygotsky (1933),

> "Since a situation is always, psychologically, accessed through perception, and perception is not separated from affective and motor activity, it is understandable that...the [person] cannot act otherwise than as constrained by the situation, or the field, in which he finds himself."

This means that all our actions, emotions, and thoughts are deterministically shaped by the environment, until creative play is introduced. Vygotsky recognized that when children play, they change their environment to fit their future needs. He observed how a bundle of rags can become a baby and the child can become a mother. As Vygotsky puts it, "In play, external things lose their motivating force." Through play and fantasy, children and adults practice making new choices, thereby establishing new emotional associations. In this way, creative play and self-determination are closely related.

When she entered her bedroom dancing nude, she said it was "the first time in her life" she had enjoyed doing so. Her laughter replaced her gasping; her sense of choice displaced her fear. Like the children Vygotsky described, she used playful action to disrupt old emotional patterns shaped by her environment. Instead of remaining trapped by situational cues that triggered anxiety, she reshaped her experience through embodied imagination. Erickson not only addressed her immediate fear, but he also helped her rehearse a future grounded in autonomy and self-determination.

General Application

Future contrasting is especially helpful for individuals experiencing ambivalence because it externalizes internal conflict and gives it narrative structure. By vividly imagining both a maladaptive, impulsive response and a value-aligned alternative (then extending each into its longer-term consequences) clients can more clearly sense the emotional and identity-based implications of their choices. Rather than resolving ambivalence by argument or advice, this technique lets clients *feel* the difference between their options.

In a problem-solving context this might sound like:

> Picture what it would look like if you avoided that uncomfortable conversation. What happens because of that? How do you feel a month later?...Now picture yourself having the conversation. What's different? How do you feel a month later?

The ECA practitioner guides the client to embody both versions, making the tension between possible futures visceral. This helps bypass abstract deliberation and activates what Oyserman and James (2009) call "possible selves." Importantly, the power of future contrasting lies not in fantasizing (though fantasy can be useful for rehearsing actions) but in the juxtaposition itself, as the contrast between potential futures becomes the source of motivation.

Practically, future contrasting works because it honors ambivalence versus seeking to suppress various parts of it. It allows clients to fully express their conflicting impulses without judgment, and in doing so, reveals which version of themselves feels most authentic, most meaningful, and most worth becoming.

Case 7.3: The Pianist with Stage Fright

A man who had trained as a concert pianist came to Erickson for help with severe stage fright. The first time he attempted to perform in public he became so paralyzed with fear that he could not walk onto the stage. Ten years passed and although he continued to practice diligently, he could never perform for more than one person at a time in an otherwise empty auditorium.

Erickson told him, "Well, your problem is very simple. I want you to buy a stack of colored towels...red, green, blue, purple, flowered, and so on." He instructed the pianist to return to the concert hall and carefully spread the towels out across the stage floor. "Save the last two," Erickson added, "one for the piano bench, and the very last towel to place on top of the piano."

Next, Erickson told him to send out invitations and fill the auditorium. This was a public commitment he could not easily back out of. "When it comes time to go out on stage," Erickson said, "you stop and look at the first towel...ask yourself if you want to faint on that one, or would you prefer to faint on the second one?"

Following these instructions, the man walked from towel to towel, silently debating: *Should I faint on this one? Or the next?* When he reached the piano bench, he realized fainting there would be awkward and fainting on top of the piano would be even worse. So instead, he sat down and played.

That night marked the beginning of a successful performing career. From that moment on, he was able to approach performance with greater confidence and self-direction.

Momentary Allurements

Momentary allurements is a behavioral tactic in ECA that involves the activation of high-priority goals using low-priority temptations. For example, a person struggling to endure a challenge might be reminded that they can give up. As a result, the person becomes even more committed to achieving their goal. Building on the foundations of identity-based motivation and implementation intentions, this tactic has empirical support from research by Fishbach et al. (2003). Their study demonstrated that exposure to temptations can paradoxically increase commitment to long-term goals if those temptations serve as reminders of the goal itself.

In this model, temptations are not always detrimental. When interpreted through a goal-focused lens, they act as motivational cues. Momentary allurements leverage this principle by deliberately introducing low-priority, ego-discordant temptations as *reverse primes*. These are cues that typically represent failure or indulgence but, when exaggerated or reframed, end up reinforcing the very goals they seem to threaten.

The behavioral tactic of momentary allurements most directly addresses value versus impulse ambivalence, a subtype of conflict described in dual-process theories of decision-making (Kahneman, 2011) and moral licensing frameworks. This form of ambivalence arises when automatic, emotion-driven behaviors (System 1) are at odds with conscious, reflective intentions (System 2). Instead of suppressing the temptation (which often intensifies its appeal) momentary allurements use its presence to trigger thoughtful self-correction, often by appealing to a person's sense of identity. By making the temptation feel silly, exaggerated, or out of character, the tactic invites the client to re-identify with their higher-order goals, creating a moment of internal coherence.

Defined simply, momentary allurements involve using fleeting, seemingly low-stakes temptations to activate a person's deeper priorities. These temptations are most effective when they are brief and emotionally charged (evocative), not part of an existing habit (novel), and feel absurd or uncharacteristic (ego-discordant). For example, telling a dieter "If you're going to break your diet, do it all the way with a slice of pie and some cake" plays on the mismatch between the temptation and the person's identity ("I am a careful eater"). This not only evokes self-awareness, but also activates a countervailing goal response. This tactic is in line with Fishbach et al.'s (2003) finding that "temptation cues may serve as reminders of the goal and thus enhance the motivation to pursue it" (p. 129).

When people see a temptation not as a serious threat to self-control, but as a sign that their goal really matters and might be at risk, it can trigger self-control processes that strengthen their commitment (Fishbach et al., 2003). Furthermore, research led by Angela Duckworth on self-control and grit supports the premise that self-control processes protect long-term, personally meaningful goals (Duckworth et al., 2016). These beneficial results are more likely when three conditions are met. First, the temptations should be easy to reject, those that feel a little ridiculous, a little off-brand, or out of sync with personal values. This allows the client to instinctively distance from them. Second, this *reverse prime* should be embedded in moments when the temptation would naturally arise, making the behavioral cue both timely and relevant. Third, it is important to amplify self-relevance by linking the moment to personally meaningful narratives, stories that invoke prior accomplishments, future aspirations, or core values to shift attention toward the self that one wants to become. By amplifying the contrast between who the client could be and who they momentarily feel like being, the tactic resolves ambivalence by tipping the balance toward long-term, value-consistent choices. In doing so, it transforms impulse into insight and unhelpful urges into surprisingly effective motivators.

Case Analysis

The man was a skilled concert pianist who had not performed publicly due to paralyzing stage fright. Despite continued private practice, he avoided audiences entirely. The type of ambivalence he was experiencing is categorized as opposing feelings (see Table 7.1), which in this case was a desire to perform in conflict with a fear of judgment or failure.

Instead of addressing the emotional conflict directly, Erickson assigned an unusual task involving a stack of towels spread across the stage. While the instruction seemed odd, it served a strategic purpose: to use momentary allurements (seemingly irrelevant, low-priority temptations) to activate or reinforce a higher-priority goal.

Each towel served as a *reverse prime*, an invitation to faint, that paradoxically weakened the urge. Erickson instructed, "When it's time to go on stage, stop and look at the first towel...ask yourself if you want to faint on that one, or maybe the second?" Even small choices can reignite a sense of agency. Better than fighting the urge to faint, the towels offered safe, deliberate points of surrender. Ironically, giving himself permission to faint gave him control. With each delay ("just one more towel") he built momentum. The weakness of the temptation transformed the towels into stepping stones.

Erickson also *escalated the experience of commitment* by having the man send out invitations and fill the auditorium. This public declaration likely heightened his desire to perform. For his ambivalence to be resolved, a tipping point needed to be reached. There needed to be a moment in which his desire clearly surpassed his fear. The question of how badly he wanted to perform was resolved through movement across a stage. Each forward step increased the salience of his true goal: to reach the piano and play. When he finally reached the bench, the idea of fainting there became "awkward" and fainting on top of the piano seemed "even worse." In this way, the act of moving forward past the tipping point transformed his ambivalence into conviction. After that concert, he never stopped performing.

General Application

Momentary allurements are especially effective for individuals experiencing ambivalence, particularly when impulsive urges clash with long-term values. Instead of suppressing temptations, this tactic *frames* them in exaggerated or humorous ways, prompting clients to instinctively reject the impulse and re-align with their deeper goals. The approach works by making the temptation feel absurd or off-brand, which activates identity-based motivation and self-signaling processes. Clients aren't talked out of the behavior. They are nudged into rediscovering what feels consistent with their values and identity.

For example, while working with a woman who struggled with binge eating, I asked her, "What's your greatest food temptation, the one thing you find impossible to resist?" Without hesitation, she said Krispy Kreme donuts, especially while on vacation as it was a time when she felt justified in indulging. She happened to be leaving for vacation the next day so I gave her an unexpected homework assignment. After leaving my office she was to go directly to a Krispy Kreme store, buy a dozen donuts, and place each one in its own individual plastic bag. I explained, "The best time to face temptation is right before bed. Each night, in your bathroom, eat at least one donut. Keep doing this until you cannot continue." She was confident that she could happily eat her way through the assignment.

Three weeks later, with a look of chagrin she declared, "I will never eat another Krispy Kreme donut for the rest of my life." The stale, slimy donuts were too gross to ingest. When I asked about other unhealthy foods, she replied that she no longer had any desire for them either. Absurdity invites self-awareness, breaks the automaticity of the urge, and helps clients reconnect with their long-term ambitions.

Recent innovations include digital delivery through *just-in-time adaptive interventions*, where behavior-change apps use momentary allurements to counter urges in real time. For instance, a fitness app might be programed to say, "Tired of running? Look for a lovely patch of grass to nap on." Augmented reality is also being explored, using surreal or ego-discordant visual prompts (like a floating donut suspended in front of a treadmill) to provoke value-driven responses.

Ultimately, momentary allurements transform impulse into insight by leveraging the very presence of temptation as a motivational cue. Their power lies in playful disruption and in helping clients re-identify with their preferred selves when it matters most.

Case 7.4: The Less Intelligent Fiancé

A young woman came to Erickson for help preparing herself emotionally for marriage. She began by describing her opinion of her fiancé:

> He is stubborn and he is much more confident of his intelligence than he has any right to be. He doesn't know I'm a lot more intelligent than he is and he's not the kind of person who would ever find it out.

She continued,

> Whereas I am excitable and quick-tempered, he is always calm and unruffled. He is exactly the kind of man who will make up for, and correct, the deficiencies in my own personality. We are very much in love. I have tried to fight against it because I'm afraid I will make him unhappy, but it is no use.

At her request, Erickson induced a trance and suggested that she meditate quietly on how to make the marriage work. After two and a half hours of deep, silent reflection, she opened her eyes and calmly explained the role she wanted Erickson to play.

"If there is to be any negative attitude toward our marriage," she said,

> it is better for you to have it and not me. I want you to be pessimistic and doubtful and not encourage [the marriage]. Don't say anything openly; just take a general negative attitude. I want you to keep that attitude for at least two years, when it won't make any difference, because then I will be able to show you.

She asked Erickson to keep in touch during that time, stating, "I will write you newsy letters which you will answer politely, and in some subtle way, such as hoping all is going well with George's work. Express your negative attitude."

Over the next two years, Erickson received occasional letters from her. He always replied promptly, inserting a mild, ambiguous skepticism into each one, just as she had requested. After the two years had passed, she wrote again, this time with pride. She was pregnant and George had been promoted to a more personally gratifying position.

Five years later, she wrote once more. She was still married and content.

Reverse Positioning

Reverse positioning (sometimes referred to as *strategic self-anticonformity*) is a paradoxical approach in which the choice architect temporarily aligns with the problematic side of an internal debate. By deliberately applying persuasive pressure on one side of an argument it increases the client's emotional investment in the opposing position. Though the dynamics of momentary allurements and reverse positioning are similar, reverse positioning is distinct in its focus. While momentary allurements address instrumentality (what to do) reverse positioning focuses on interpretation (what to think). In ECA, the core aim of reverse positioning is to facilitate deeper cognitive exploration of the neglected side of one's ambivalence.

For instance, if someone describes their relationship as "abusive" but does not feel ready to leave, a brief comment like, "Maybe the abuse isn't serious enough to warrant ending things," can provoke lengthy reflection on the reality of the situation and its consequences. The client's rejection of the professional's statement does not weaken the professional's credibility; instead, it fosters clarity. By adopting a devil's advocate stance, the professional invites the client to articulate and defend their deeper needs. This is done on their terms and with later validation from the choice architect. When used skillfully, this method resolves ambivalence, restores self-agency, and enables the client to commit authentically.

Erickson (1959) described this phenomenon with striking precision, noting its usefulness "particularly with defiant, resistive patients, and especially 'incorrigible' juvenile delinquents." He emphasized that the significance of the method lay in helping patients "successfully achieve contradictory goals" while maintaining the sense that the choice arose from their own behavior. As early as 1939, Erickson recognized ambivalence as an unconscious conflict that must be "discharged through behavioral means," often by offering patients the chance to act out one side of the conflict in a safe and circumscribed way. In his 1959 work on utilization techniques, Erickson argued that the therapist's task is to give patients the opportunity to express their ambivalence in a form that allows for resolution.

Reverse positioning is especially effective when clients experience *projected ambivalence*, which is a form of internal conflict about identity, values, or relational needs that gets displaced onto others, often without the client realizing the shift has occurred. As described by Robert Beavers (1985), this dynamic turns intrapsychic tension into interpersonal disagreement, frequently triggering power struggles or push-pull dynamics. In these cases, the client is not merely indecisive; they are caught between two deeply held but conflicting desires with the discomfort externalized and expressed by others. For example, a woman in an abusive relationship may have her mother, sister, best friend, and counselor all urging her to leave, allowing her to avoid directly confronting the conflict herself. Using a non-critical posture, the ECA practitioner aligns with the over-represented side of the internal conflict—not to persuade, but to prompt deeper exploration of the neglected half, allowing novel insights to emerge.

This approach is particularly effective in attachment-related ambivalence (e.g., "I want help, but I don't trust you to help me") or identity dilemmas (e.g., "Should I play it safe or take a bold leap?"). The tactic can be implemented across a spectrum of intensities. Subtle reverse positioning may involve a neutral, cautionary remark like, "Maybe you should stick with the status quo. Change can be risky." Assertive reverse positioning heightens the provocation: "You're probably not ready for that challenge, or maybe it's just not that important to you." Satirical reverse positioning uses humor or exaggeration to provoke pushback: "Maybe what seems unwise now will make good sense later." Across all forms, the effectiveness lies not in coercion, but in catalyzing the client's ability to reposition their argument.

Remember, reverse positioning is distinct from the tactic of momentary allurements. While both use seemingly counterintuitive stimuli (*reverse prime*), momentary allurements work through behavioral *redirection.* This is achieved by introducing a low-priority, ego-discordant temptation (something silly, novel, or impulsive) that paradoxically activates a person's higher-priority goal. In contrast, reverse positioning involves engaging the client's need to off-load part of their ambivalence so that they can focus on the other half. When temptation is not an issue, reverse positioning is more appropriate.

In collaborative relationships, reverse positioning affirms the principle that people are more likely to invest in ideas they feel they have discovered or defended themselves (*counter-attitudinal advocacy*). Instead of confronting a client's ability to disagree, ECA practitioners welcome it. In doing so, choice architects transform internal chaos into clarity and hesitation into conviction.

Case Analysis

The young woman who came to Erickson for help was not conflicted about whether she loved her fiancé (she stated plainly, "We are very much in love") but about whether she could sustain the relationship without causing harm. Her deeper fear was not about George's shortcomings but about her own. "I'm afraid I will make George unhappy," she confessed, revealing a conflict between her value for commitment and a belief that she was somehow flawed. Her description of their personalities (her quick temper versus his calm demeanor) suggested she viewed the relationship as corrective, yet also fragile. This ambivalence was not cognitive alone; it was also attitudinal (see Table 7.1). It was tied to her sense of identity and self-worth.

This woman showed remarkable insight into the dynamics of *projected ambivalence*, which Erickson skillfully utilized by taking the role of pessimist. Rather than reassuring her, he gave her a place to project doubt, which naturally evoked a defense of the relationship. By making himself the skeptic, he allowed her to become an advocate, strengthening her sense of agency. This fits with motivational interviewing research (W. R. Miller & Rollnick, 2012), which suggests that people are more likely to commit to new choices when they voice their own reasons. Erickson's subtly doubtful letters ("I hope George's work is going well") gave her something to push against, reinforcing her identity as a devoted partner. By taking on the emotional weight of pessimism, Erickson gave her more freedom to explore her reasons for hope.

General Application

Reverse positioning is especially useful for individuals in ambivalent states where they feel torn between conflicting desires and are thus reluctant to commit. Instead of persuading the client directly, the therapist deliberately takes the most salient side of the internal debate, thereby creating space for the client to more carefully consider the neglected side of the ambivalence. This tactic transforms self-contradiction into self-persuasion and interpersonal conflict into productive debate.

When speaking with a client who is unsure about quitting smoking, a choice architect might say, "Maybe you're just not ready yet. There is no real rush." The likely rebuttal, "No, I am ready," signals a shift from indecision to personal commitment. Similarly, when someone hesitates to pursue a challenging goal, a choice architect might say, "You're probably not ready for something that bold." This statement can elicit a strong counter-response grounded in agency and desire. Even subtle versions, such as saying, "Maybe it's safer not to change your career path," allow clients to clarify the values they find most compelling. By gently siding with the impulse the client has fixated on, the ECA practitioner creates space for expressing the other side of the conflict. This facilitates resolution through contrast, not confrontation. Reverse positioning works because it honors the ambivalence rather than trying to resolve it prematurely.

Designing an Optimal Choice Environment (OCE) for Ambivalence

Designing an *optimal choice environment* for someone dominated by ambivalence requires recognizing that indecision is not simply a lack of clarity, but often a result of conflicting internal values, competing goals, or fear of regret. An optimal choice environment is not about eliminating conflict; it's about creating the psychological conditions in which conflict can be resolved productively. In this context, the optimal choice environment must serve as a mental foundation that supports the individual's long-term interests and values while minimizing cognitive overload, social pressure, and emotional friction. Instead of forcing a premature resolution, an effective optimal choice environment allows the person to *dwell meaningfully* in their ambivalence until a more self-consistent direction emerges.

Key features of such a mental environment include a big-picture focus, which shifts attention away from immediate anxieties, and short-term trade-offs toward deeper values and broader life aspirations. Research on goal systems theory and identity-based motivation suggests that when people are guided by long-term identity and values, they are more likely to resolve ambivalence in a direction that supports personal coherence. Additionally, an effective optimal choice environment reduces decision pressure by creating space for reflection, removing the expectation of immediate action and emphasizing the value of learning over finality.

Another essential component is the use of decision-making frameworks that provide structured, yet flexible ways to evaluate choices. These frameworks (such as pros/cons mapping, value sorting, or future contrasting) can help the ambivalent person view their choices through a clearer lens. For individuals prone to ambivalence, the goal is not to push them to decide, but to offer objectives that promote productive deliberation. For example, inviting them to explore how each option aligns with different aspects of their identity increases both clarity and commitment. In this way, the optimal choice environment does not feel like a pressure cooker for decisions, but a thoughtfully designed greenhouse for value-driven growth.

Thought Exercise

Next, you will have the opportunity to apply your design skills. When creating an optimal choice environment for someone experiencing ambivalence, remember that this environment can include mental landscapes such as imagery, beliefs, and goals, or modifications to their physical surroundings. The only requirement is that you respect their right to set their own priorities and to discuss those things they wish to discuss while avoiding those topics that they wish to avoid.

For this thought exercise, imagine speaking with a woman who discloses that there are several things that she does not want to tell you.

Furthermore, she really does not want you trying to pry into her private affairs. What she does let you know is that her current husband does not know that she has had 13 other marriages prior to him. She also confesses that they are currently having arguments because she has forged some checks, had affairs with other men, and wrecked her husband's car in a fit of rage.

Before reading further, consider how you would respond to this woman. What would you say or do to design an optimal choice environment that recognizes her need for privacy, defiance, and accountability, while still creating opportunities for engagement, reflection, and developmental progress?

***

Erickson described a case (7.5 in the case index) with these same details. This woman had sought him out for consultation and then warned him not to pry, which was an apparent attempt to off-load her internal conflict by externalizing the struggle. Erickson responded with acceptance, saying, "All right, I won't, but if you tell me spontaneously, don't accuse me of prying."

For much of the hour, Erickson spent the time listening and watching her with a kind, sympathetic look. Eventually, she relaxed and shared that she felt like she could tell him anything. This was when Erickson found out about all the checks she had forged, the multiple affairs, and the wrecked car.

Erickson did not tell her what to do. Instead, he asked a question that deserved attention, asking her, "Are you going to tell your husband about the other 13 marriages?" She said no. Erickson ended the discussion by saying, "Well, that is your answer. Stick to it!"

The woman left his office, went home to her husband, and told him about all her previous marriages. The husband asked with how many of her former husbands had she forged checks and committed adultery. She answered his question honestly. Then he told her that he would stay married to her if she shaped up because he really did love her. According to Erickson, after having made herself uncharacteristically vulnerable, she complied with her husband's terms.

In this case, Erickson's brief but evocative comment seems to encapsulate at least two tactics simultaneously. The first is the tactic of *injunctive reversal,* which is described in the chapter on reactance. Erickson's statement "stick with it" is an authoritative command (restricting her liberties). Based on her history of subversion, it was likely that she would defy any authority exercised by Erickson.

There is also reason to suspect strong ambivalence. She sought out Erickson to confess something but then told him not to pry. Similarly, she expressed a desire to be more accountable to others but then insisted she would not tell her husband the truth. When Erickson argued for one side of her ambivalence by saying, "Well that's your answer" (you don't want to tell him), she likely began to explore the other side of the issue (maybe I do want to tell him). This made it an ideal nudge for someone experiencing strong ambivalence. Because Erickson was responding to a decision instead of a temptation, this nudge is best described as an implicit form of reverse positioning.

When designing an optimal choice environment for individuals with ambivalence, it is essential to prioritize self-exploration over persuasion. The goal is to create an environment that allows both sides of their ambivalence to emerge and be examined, enabling them to discover and commit to their own resolution. By working within the individual's existing framework of understanding, ECA facilitates natural, self-directed adaptation.

Conclusion

At the heart of ECA is a subtle innovation in how we relate to human conflict, not by eliminating tension, but by designing with it. This chapter has explored ambivalence not as a flaw, but as a form of psychological depth. It is a structured, often necessary expression of the self in transition. Instead of reducing it to indecision or dysfunction, ambivalence is framed as a developmental signal and motivational asset. It reflects the mind's profound capacity to hold contradiction without collapsing into chaos, a balancing act that allows for plural values, layered intentions, and emotionally honest decision-making. The goal then is not to resolve ambivalence prematurely but to cultivate environments in which its value can be expressed and integrated.

These principles are put into practice through four tactics that allow ambivalence to reorganize without forcing an immediate resolution. Tandem anchoring opens a workable middle path; future contrasting clarifies values by comparing possible futures; momentary allurements use minor temptations to renew stronger commitments; and reverse positioning gives the neglected side of an internal debate more room to emerge (Table 7.2). Together, these tactics preserve tension long enough for a more integrated choice to develop.

This perspective has implications not just for clients but for practitioners as well. Professionals often carry their own ambivalence about methods, outcomes, or even how much influence they should exert. Research by Minson and Chen (2022) shows that intellectual humility, while cognitively virtuous, is often socially penalized. Those who express uncertainty may be perceived as less competent or less committed, especially in environments that prize confident certainty over reflective doubt. Rather than concluding that practitioners must always disguise ambivalence, ECA encourages practitioners to be contextually oriented and thus more nuanced in one's understandings.

For clients struggling with ambivalence, a practitioner's willingness to reflect, hesitate, and question out loud models a crucial thought process. It also clarifies that within this relationship it is safe not to know, safe to weigh options, and safe to move at a pace that respects complexity. Of course, those in a different state of mind, such as *authority bias* or *risk aversion*, may think less of an authority figure who does not display absolute self-confidence. In this light, the practitioner's ambivalence is not a problem, if it is expressed in a fitting social context.

This is a paradox that Erickson mastered. His nudges often looked light or even whimsical on the surface, but underneath they carried a profound respect for complexity. Whether through indirect suggestion (affordances), reframed choices, or permissive silence, he treated every hesitation as data and every contradiction as an opening. In doing so, he shifted the aim of practice from eliminating resistance to cultivating coherence. This occurs when the full spectrum of their inner life is welcomed and when their choices feel both personally relevant and deeply aligned.

Quick-Reference Tactic Map

Table 7.2 Tactics Suited for Ambivalence and the Broader Architecture of Strategic Influence

If Client...	*Then Use...*	*Because*
Is stuck between all-or-nothing choices or competing values	*Tandem anchoring*: Treating opposing positions as containing valid concerns while using continuum-based thinking to reveal a workable option between them	*Reframes* polarized options by making a workable middle path easier to perceive and justify
Is torn between two futures or unable to decide	*Future contrasting*: Mentally picturing both a choice that goes against one's values and an alternative that aligns with them, while imagining the long-term consequences of each path in vivid detail to highlight the contrast between them	Makes long-term consequences emotionally salient, *priming* value-oriented motivation
Is tempted by self-defeating impulses or compulsion	*Momentary allurements*: The activation of high-priority goals using low-priority temptations as a prime.	*Primes* goal activation and value-oriented behavior
Defends unhelpful behavior with strong emotion or debate	*Reverse positioning*: Deliberately applying persuasive pressure on one side of an argument to increase emotional investment in the opposing position	*Primes* internal re-alignment through the need to win (arguments)

Note

1 After nine months of reflection, the couple concluded that their differences were too far apart and they ended the relationship amicably.

References

Batson, C. D., Early, S., & Salvarani, G. (1997). Perspective taking: Imagining how another feels versus imaging how you would feel. *Personality and Social Psychology Bulletin*, *23*(7), 751–758. https://doi.org/10.1177/0146167297237008

Beavers, R. W. (1985). *Successful Marriage: A Family Systems Approach to Couples Therapy*. Norton.

Decety, J., & Lamm, C. (2006). Human empathy through the lens of social neuroscience. *The Scientific World Journal*, *6*(1), 280363. https://doi.org/10.1100/tsw.2006.221

Duckworth, A. L., Gendler, T. S., & Gross, J. J. (2016). Situational strategies for self-control. *Perspectives on Psychological Science*, *11*(1), 35–55. https://doi.org/10.1177/1745691615623247

Erickson, M. H. (1939). Experimental Demonstrations of the Psychopathology of Everyday Life. In E. Rossi, R. Erickson-Klein, & K. Rossi (Eds.), *Collected Works of Milton H Erickson: Advanced Approaches to Therapeutic Hypnosis* (Vol. 5, pp. 177–190). Milton H. Erickson Foundation Press.

Erickson, M. H. (1957). *A Lecture by Milton H. Erickson: Ocean Monarch Staff Lectures, January 1957. (Audio Recording No. CD/EMH.57.1)* [CD]. CD/EMH.57.1. The Milton H. Erickson Foundation Archives.

Erickson, M. H. (1959). Further clinical techniques of hypnosis: Utilization techniques. *American Journal of Clinical Hypnosis*, *2*(1), 3–21. https://doi.org/10.1080/00029157.1959.10401792

Festinger, L. (1954). A theory of social comparison processes. *Human Relations*, *7*(2), 117–140. https://doi.org/10.1177/001872675400700202

Fishbach, A., Friedman, R. S., & Kruglanski, A. W. (2003). Leading us not into temptation: Momentary allurements elicit overriding goal activation. *Journal of Personality and Social Psychology*, *84*(2), 296–309. https://doi.org/10.1037/0022-3514.84.2.296

Galinsky, A. D., & Moskowitz, G. B. (2000). Counterfactuals as behavioral primes: Priming the simulation heuristic and consideration of alternatives. *Journal of Experimental Social Psychology*, *36*(4), 384–409. https://doi.org/10.1006/jesp.1999.1409

Glick, P., & Fiske, S. T. (2001). An ambivalent alliance: Hostile and benevolent sexism as complementary justifications for gender inequality. *American Psychologist*, *56*(2), 109–118. https://doi.org/10.1037/0003-066X.56.2.109

Gottman, J., & Silver, N. (1999). *The Seven Principles for Making Marriage Work: A Practical Guide from the Country's Foremost Relationship Expert*. Harmony/Rodale/Convergent.

James, W. (1916). *Talks to Teachers on Psychology; And to Students on Some of Life's Ideals*. Project Gutenberg. https://www.gutenberg.org/ebooks/16287

Kahneman, D. (2011). *Thinking, Fast and Slow*. Farrar, Straus and Giroux.

Kruglanski, A. W., Fishbach, A., Kopetz, C., & Kopetz, C. E. (2023). *Goal Systems Theory: Psychological Processes and Applications*. Oxford University Press.

Luescher, K., & Pillemer, K. (1998). Intergenerational ambivalence: A new approach to the study of parent-child relations in later life. *Journal of Marriage and Family*, *60*(2), 413–425. https://doi.org/10.2307/353858

Merritt, A. C., Effron, D. A., & Monin, B. (2010). Moral self-licensing: When being good frees us to be bad. *Social and Personality Psychology Compass*, *4*(5), 344–357. https://doi.org/10.1111/j.1751-9004.2010.00263.x

Mikulincer, M. (1995). Attachment style and the mental representation of the self. *Journal of Personality and Social Psychology*, *69*(6), 1203–1215. https://doi.org/10.1037/0022-3514.69.6.1203

Miller, N. E. (1944). Experimental Studies of Conflict. In J. M. Hunt (Ed.), *Personality and the Behavior Disorders* (pp. 431–465). Ronald Press.

Miller, W. R., & Rollnick, S. (2012). *Motivational Interviewing, Third Edition: Helping People Change* (3rd ed.). The Guilford Press.

Minson, J. A., & Chen, F. S. (2022). Receptiveness to opposing views: Conceptualization and integrative review. *Personality and Social Psychology Review*, *26*(2), 93–111. https://doi.org/10.1177/10888683211061037

Oettingen, G., Mayer, D., Thorpe, J. S., Janetzke, H., & Lorenz, S. (2005). Turning fantasies about positive and negative futures into self-improvement goals. *Motivation and Emotion*, *29*(4), 236–266. https://doi.org/10.1007/s11031-006-9016-y

Oyserman, D., & James, L. (2009). Possible Selves: From Content to Process. In K. D. Markman, W. M. P. Klein, & J. A. Suhr (Eds.), *Handbook of Imagination and Mental Simulation* (pp. 373–394). Psychology Press.

Rossberg, J. I., Karterud, S., Pedersen, G., & Friis, S. (2007). An empirical study of countertransference reactions toward patients with personality disorders. *Comprehensive Psychiatry*, *48*(3), 225–230. https://doi.org/10.1016/j.comppsych.2007.02.002

Short, D. (2020). *From William James to Milton Erickson: The Care of Human Consciousness*. Archway Publishing from Simon & Schuster. https://www.bokus.com/bok/9781480891623/from-william-james-to-milton-erickson/

Vygotskiĭ, L. S. (1933). Igra i ee rol v umstvennom razvitii rebenka. *Voprosy Psihologii* [Problems of Psychology], *12*(6), 62–76.

Wiggins, J. S., & Trobst, K. K. (1997). When is a Circumplex an "Interpersonal Circumplex"? The Case of Supportive Actions. In *Circumplex Models of Personality and Emotions* (pp. 57–80). American Psychological Association. https://doi.org/10.1037/10261-003

Chapter 8

I'll See It When I Believe It

Confirmation Bias

I'll See It When I Believe It: *Confirmation Bias*

On July 19, 2024, my client decided that his life was no longer worth living. For over a year he had been tormented by grief after unexpectedly losing his beloved spouse. Now, he was also enduring relentless chronic pain. With a look of profound exhaustion, he limped into my office, his knees, shoulders, and hands inflamed with arthritis. But the worst pain radiated from his back, the aftermath of neck surgery, multiple vertebrae fusions, and bone removal. His misery was palpable.

Previously, I had encouraged him to engage with his neighbors to ease the feeling of loneliness. He had volunteered on his HOA board, but tensions arose when the board president lashed out at him with unfair and unkind remarks. His isolation was intense. Both parents were gone, his sister had died of cancer just before his partner's passing, and now his body was failing him. With all this weighing on his mind, he meant what he said when he told me that he no longer wished to be in this world.

Previously I had tried talking to him about his interests, things he could still do to find joy in life. However, every day he only saw accumulating evidence that his need for companionship would never again be fulfilled. His mind was fixated on a single hypothesis: *Life without my husband is too painful to endure,* and every day, he found validation for that belief. Though I tried, I could not get him to consider an alternative hypothesis: that there might still be reasons to live beyond his prior relationship.

But on this day, I stopped trying to convince him to *want* to be alive. Instead, I shifted my tone. I told him, "Very few people are lucky enough to decide when they die. And only the most fortunate among us get to die exactly the way we choose." Then I asked, "Would you rather die during the day or in your sleep at night?"

With a look of uncertainty and hesitation, he answered that he would prefer to die in his sleep. I followed up, "And what would you like to be the cause of death?" He replied that he wanted his heart to simply stop beating.

DOI: 10.4324/9781003797876-9

I told him that fortunately hypnosis could help not only with pain control but also with end-of-life decisions. I explained how hypnosis influences blood flow, heart rate, and even respiration. I pointed out that it is our unconscious mind that keeps us breathing throughout the night and that this is a choice. Then, I described the power of self-hypnosis, telling him, "I don't think it would take much for you to get your heart to stop beating tonight as you sleep." I offered the possibility of him laying on his pillow and repeating to himself, "Tonight is the night I want to die. Heart, you can stop beating as I sleep." I added, "I don't think you'll need to say it more than a hundred times for the result you are seeking."

He sat in complete silence as I spoke. I ended the session enthusiastically describing the unconscious mind's ability to achieve unexpected outcomes. After scheduling another appointment for three weeks out, he left my office silent but no longer limping.

At his next appointment, he walked into my office laughing, showing no signs of physical or emotional distress. For the first 20 minutes, he excitedly shared details about a recent trip, multiple outings with friends, breakthroughs with others on the board, and, most importantly, a deepening relationship with his young nephew and the nephew's wife.

Listening to all this, I remarked, "I've never seen you so happy and engaged in life." Then, with curiosity, I asked, "What brought about this change?"

In a booming voice, he declared, "You did! That last session scared the shit out of me!"

He explained, "After all that talk about dying in my sleep, all I could think about on the way home was, I'm not ready to die." He continued, "That night, I could hardly sleep. I lay there, wide awake for hours, repeating to myself, I want to live! I want to live! I've got so much more to do with my life!" He said he was making sure his heart and body knew to keep functioning through the night. I told him it was clearly the right choice. I felt confident that he *does* have so much more to live for. I also congratulated him on figuring out how to reduce the painful inflammation, which was no longer a concern. He attributed his somatic improvement to movement exercises conducted during routine visits to physical therapy and a Pilates program.

At the time of this writing, it has been a year since that discussion and his optimism has held. I've seen him several times since and he has never again mentioned wanting to die nor has he had as much trouble with isolation and loneliness. He was reelected to serve on the board for his HOA, is considered a valued contributing member to his community, and has referred a close friend to me who was struggling with intense depression. He set favorable expectations for therapy by telling her, "You can trust this psychologist. He knows what he is doing."

For a critical analysis of this case, it is fair to say that my approach caused some discomfort. After our session he had an uneasy drive home and that night he lay awake for several hours. Additionally, we need to recognize that this method is not appropriate for someone in an acutely suicidal state with a concrete plan. That is an entirely different state of mind, which requires different tactics. In this case, my client's strong confirmation bias made it necessary to stop trying to change his mind. Up until that point, I had been carrying the burden of finding a reason for him to live. Furthermore, he was not experiencing any consequences for entertaining thoughts of suicide. This all changed when I shifted to a stance of absolute acceptance and non-interference with his agenda (*permissive destabilization*).

Recognizing Confirmation Bias in Ericksonian Choice Architecture

Confirmation bias is a tendency to automatically seek out, interpret, and remember information in ways that reinforce existing beliefs. This bias creates a closed style of processing in which people give greater weight to evidence that supports what they already think while discounting information that challenges it. In practice, this means that a person's beliefs can become self-sealing, especially when those beliefs organize how they interpret emotionally important experiences. For example, in the vignette above, the man's thinking was organized around a single self-sealing hypothesis ("Life without my husband is too painful to endure"). To have meaning, my communication needed to accept his stated conclusion while adding value by making the consequences of turning away from life more salient.

Confirmation bias is sustained by both motivational needs and cognitive habits. On the motivational side, people often want consistency, coherence, and protection from doubt. Existing beliefs may also serve self-affirming functions, especially when intelligence, competence, identity, or control feel threatened. On the cognitive side, people tend to rely on belief to search memory selectively, interpret new information through prior expectations (Lord et al., 1979), and test only one favored hypothesis at a time (Kunda, 1990). Together, these tendencies make belief revision less likely.

Once activated, confirmation bias narrows inquiry and reduces genuine openness to alternative interpretations. Instead of asking, "What else might be true?" people ask, often implicitly, "How does this confirm what I already know?" This closed style of processing strengthens certainty while weakening curiosity. In many cases, the issue is not a lack of intelligence, but a reduced willingness to examine competing interpretations with equal care. As expected, self-affirming confirmation effects are more likely to occur when dealing with low self-esteem individuals (Nail et al., 2004).

Confirmation bias is mediated by reasoning ability, personal investment, and emotional state. Greater analytical ability can reduce the bias when a person is motivated to be accurate (Stanovich & West, 2008). However, *motivated reasoning* can override intelligence when beliefs are tied to identity or self-interest, leading even highly analytical individuals to rationalize their existing beliefs when they are personally invested in an issue (Kahan, 2013). Emotional states can further intensify this process. Fear heightens vigilance for confirming signs of danger (Remmerswaal et al., 2014), anger narrows attention and supports adversarial reasoning, and pride shifts the goal from understanding to winning. Anxiety and stress also increase defensiveness, making people less willing to engage disconfirming evidence flexibly (Westen et al., 2006). In conflict, these forces often operate on both sides, leaving each person more convinced of their own position and more likely to see the other as unreasonable (Nickerson, 1998).

Subjective validation occurs when information feels true because it resonates emotionally, regardless of whether it is objectively accurate. This bias helps explain why people may perceive meaningful connections between unrelated events. Emotionally compelling interpretations can harden into self-sealing beliefs, particularly when they are rarely tested against evidence. Common examples can be found in religious ideology and superstition. For example, "God is punishing me" or "anytime I allow myself to feel confident, something bad happens." In this way, subjective validation reinforces confirmation bias by allowing personal meaning to substitute for careful evaluation.

The *Forer effect*[1] strengthens subjective validation by making vague or general statements feel uniquely personal. People often project specific meaning onto ambiguous descriptions and then experience them as highly accurate. This helps explain the appeal of astrology, psychic readings, and similar systems built on generalized claims. Here, ambiguity is not resisted but embraced, because it allows the person's own beliefs and emotions to complete the meaning.

Need for closure reinforces confirmation bias by favoring certainty and familiar explanations over ambiguity. Where subjective validation makes use of ambiguity, need for closure resists it. When people feel uncertain, overwhelmed, or destabilized, they may cling to established beliefs simply because those beliefs reduce discomfort. This can produce cognitive rigidity, diminish *perspective taking*, and reduce openness to new evidence.

Although they operate differently, subjective validation and need for closure both strengthen confirmation bias. One bias accepts ambiguity when it supports personal meaning; the other rejects ambiguity to preserve certainty. Despite moving in opposite directions, both protect prior beliefs from revision.

Confirmation bias can be recognized cognitively, emotionally, and behaviorally. Cognitively, people spend little time considering opposing views. Emotionally, they operate defensively. The discovery of supporting evidence brings a sense of pride and reassurance, while opposing evidence may trigger discomfort, fear, or even anger (Taber & Lodge, 2006). Behaviorally, this bias may lead individuals to distort new information so it fits prior assumptions. A client may misremember prior conversations, reinterpret feedback selectively, or claim support for beliefs that were never actually endorsed. Because confirmation bias can distort memory and perception, a simple indicator is speed: When invited to consider both sides of an issue, a person influenced by confirmation bias often moves quickly back to the side already favored.

More specifically, confirmation bias often appears in two common forms: *biased assimilation* and *polarization*. In *biased assimilation*, people interpret mixed evidence as support for their existing view. In *polarization*, people increasingly consume belief-consistent information while avoiding dissenting perspectives, causing attitudes to grow more extreme. Social media can accelerate this process by repeatedly exposing users to emotionally charged, belief-confirming content. The addictive nature of emotionally charged content further deepens polarization as heightened arousal strengthens memory encoding and reinforces cognitive biases, making individuals more resistant to opposing viewpoints. Over time, either form can weaken curiosity and intellectual humility, paving the way for *epistemic arrogance*, which is excessive confidence in one's own conclusions and resistance to alternative viewpoints.

In Ericksonian Choice Architecture (ECA), confirmation bias is best addressed not by direct argument, but by designing conditions that make alternative interpretations safer to consider. Different forms of confirmation bias call for different responses. Subjective validation can be met with the tactic of *selective validation*, which lowers defensiveness by affirming a constructive part of the person's experience. Biased assimilation can be addressed through the *steelman argument*, which builds on existing views by articulating the strongest version of the person's argument. Polarization may be reduced through *counter-attitudinal advocacy*, which enhances cognitive flexibility. *Epistemic arrogance* can be engaged through *reality testing*, which shifts belief evaluation toward direct experience and systematic observation. In all cases, effective choice architecture does not confront confirmation bias head-on with force. Instead, it creates conditions in which new interpretations become safe, interesting, and experientially grounded.

Erickson's Casework and the Application of Tactical Nudges

Having explored the mechanisms and various manifestations of confirmation bias, we can now shift our focus to how certain nudges can help individuals glimpse new options that better fit their values. Recognizing an unstated bias is only the first step; creating an environment where individuals feel empowered to consider alternative perspectives requires skill as a choice architect.

Erickson, a master of experiential design, demonstrated how *micro-level choice architecture* can be used to reshape perceptions and guide individuals toward more adaptive decisions. The following examples illustrate how his methods aligned with principles of choice architecture, allowing people to move past their cognitive blind spots and embrace more optimal outcomes. These cases illustrate how research on confirmation bias can be translated into tactical design methods that expand openness to alternative interpretations.

Case 8.1: Nude Dancing Men

Erickson described a patient who was both "plagued and pleased, annoyed and delighted" by the hallucinations she experienced (nude young men who floated above her as she walked down the street). These figures spoke to her, sometimes engaging in discussions about art, literature, and music, while at other times horrifying her with crude remarks about sex.

After arriving at Erickson's office, the woman became highly concerned about a hallucinated bear trap. She demanded an explanation from Erickson about his reasons for having a bear trap in his office. Erickson did not argue with the woman or dismiss her concerns. Instead, he took it as an opportunity to suggest her need for extended therapy. As Erickson put it, "I told her that it was a rather involved matter that couldn't be explained in just one session."

When the telephone rang, Erickson recalled, "I stupidly, thoughtlessly, started walking into that bear trap." The woman reacted urgently, leaping to her feet and putting out her hand to stop him. Though it was just a hallucination, Erickson explained, "Thereafter, I walked around the bear trap."

Initially, Erickson refrained from explaining the purpose of the bear trap. "I told her eventually that I would remove it." In this way, Erickson established boundaries for each of them. She had every right to act on her subjective realities and he had the right to make his own decisions and choices. As Erickson put it, I told her that "my purposes were mine, and I didn't feel accountable to her on how I ran my psychiatric office."

However, the woman's greatest concern was not the bear trap, but the half-dozen nude dancing girls she believed Erickson kept in his office. She objected strenuously, particularly to the way her young men were looking at the girls. Erickson responded in a way that symbolically suggested equal rights for her and him by stating, "If you can have young men, then I can have dancing girls."

With Erickson's guidance, the woman gradually discovered new ways to engage with her reality. He gently introduced questions that encouraged self-determination, asking when she wanted those young men floating around her. Did she want them present all the time? He suggested they probably should not accompany her to the bathroom and she agreed. After mentioning his nude dancing girls, which he kept out of sight for patients who might not appreciate them, Erickson asked whether she really wanted her nude dancing men to follow her into job interviews. She concluded it would be best to leave them behind in Erickson's office.

After she secured a job, Erickson let her know that she was at liberty to come to his office every day and enjoy her young men. Thus, Erickson's office became a safe harbor, a place where she could converse without inhibition.

Eventually, the woman gained enough stability to work as a high school teacher, later becoming a successful counselor. After that, she worked as a secretary to the president of a large corporation. When she got a job that took her out of state, they worked out a system in which she could place her psychotic episodes in a large manila envelope and mail them to Erickson's office. Erickson's expectation was that she would be able to live independently until age 45.

Selective Validation

Selective validation is the practice of affirming some aspect of a person's thoughts, emotions, or experience without endorsing the overall meaning they assign to it. To reduce defensiveness, this tactic makes use of subjective validation by guiding attention toward a valid, experience-based point of affirmation. This approach is particularly vital when individuals are faced with life-altering experiences that must be acknowledged and integrated into their personal reality framework. By recognizing a useful aspect of the person's experience, selective validation helps maintain rapport, reduce defensiveness, and create a psychologically safe environment for meaningful progress. It also helps people feel understood and less alone.

This tactic is deeply rooted in the concept of consensus reality, which suggests that our shared understanding of reality is a social construct much like language. The classic conformity experiments by Solomon Asch (1955) demonstrated that individuals are highly influenced by social validation, often adjusting their perceptions to align with group consensus. Selective validation leverages this principle by strategically reinforcing aspects of a person's narrative in ways that facilitate adaptive growth versus confronting problematic tendencies.

The effectiveness of selective validation hinges on several core components. First, it redirects attention toward constructive areas of focus without directly invalidating a person's belief system. Effective validation is not about fixing, but about *meeting someone where they are* and ensuring they feel heard and accepted. For example, I once had a client who was experiencing a severe form of mania state, "I can levitate objects with my mind. I can also turn the sky purple." My question to her was, "What thoughts are you having about me and my office? I HOPE they are good thoughts." I did not question the validity of her thoughts. Instead, I validated the importance of her opinion and our collaborative endeavor.

Second, selective validation maintains engagement by recognizing and affirming an individual's need for acknowledgment and self-consistency. This means different things for different people. For a person with high self-esteem, validation occurs when you acknowledge their gains. For a person with low self-esteem, validation occurs when you acknowledge their faults or shortcomings. When someone with low self-esteem assumes they are being a burden, a useful response selectively validates their concern while reframing the situation in a way that fosters collaborative problem-solving. For example:

Client: I can tell that I am boring you. I am sorry that you must listen to all my troubles.

Dan: As strange as it sounds, I like listening to people's problems. Some of the details that you are sharing are boring, but I probably need to hear them. Eventually, we will discern the essence of your troubles.

Though it seems counter-intuitive, people with very low self-esteem or a dysphoric self-conceptualization are more likely to feel at ease with unfavorable feedback than with praise or affirmation. For example, in one study when dysphoric subjects were given a choice between a roommate who likes them and one who does not, those with negative self-views chose the one who evaluated them unfavorably. They also preferred friends or dating partners who evaluated them unfavorably (Swann et al., 1992). This level of precision is what differentiates selective validation from more ordinary forms of validation.

Finally, selective validation encourages self-efficacy and progress by affirming personal growth when individuals express uncertainty about their own development. This reinforcement, even in the absence of full progress, strengthens motivation. For example:

Client: I think I am making progress...what do you think?
Dan: Definitely! I do see progress. Tell me some more about the progress you are most pleased with.

Selective validation aligns with theoretical perspectives from motivational interviewing (Miller & Rollnick, 2012) and self-determination theory (Deci & Ryan, 2008), both of which emphasize the importance of autonomy-supportive environments for enhancing *intrinsic motivation* and psychological growth. By affirming the subjective reality of an individual while subtly guiding them toward more adaptive perspectives, selective validation serves as a powerful tool for fostering resilience, self-awareness, and behavioral adaptation.

Case Analysis

As we see demonstrated in this case, Erickson's response was tailored to the woman's unique psychological state, which involved vivid hallucinations that were both distressing and gratifying. Instead of directly challenging the hallucinations, Erickson validated her experience by mirroring it. He discussed the hallucinations as if they were an indisputable reality (the dancing girls and the bear trap) to create a shared frame of reference. This approach allowed her to engage with her perceptions more flexibly rather than becoming entrenched in defensiveness or feelings of social isolation. Using a medical analogy, Erickson explained, "Why should I dispute that patient's delusions and hallucinations? They were hers. I had better respect them in the same way I respect a broken leg or a broken jaw."

Selective validation helped the woman feel acknowledged. By accepting the premise of her hallucinations in a way that introduced a playful contradiction, Erickson encouraged her to question the rigidity of her experiences without feeling invalidated. As Erickson explained,

> My rights are to be respected and her rights are to be respected. I validated her hallucinations; and she could view her hallucinations in the same way I could view mine. And if I could take a good view of my hallucinations, then she could take a good view of her hallucinations.

This method aligns with research on cognitive restructuring, which suggests that individuals are more likely to alter their perceptions when they feel psychologically safe as opposed to feeling confronted (Edmondson, 1999; Ezawa & Hollon, 2023).

A closer look at Erickson's use of selective validation reveals three key elements. First, he framed their interactions as collaborative problem-solving, treating her hallucinations not as obstacles but as shared experiences to navigate together. For instance, when she hallucinated a bear trap, she pointed it out, and Erickson walked around it, transforming even her psychosis into a joint endeavor. Over time, she entrusted her episodes to him and he found a symbolic "safe place" to store them. This cooperation was possible because Erickson validated both the reality of her distress and her wish to overcome it. Second, he fostered a co-creative dialogue, treating even her hallucinations as negotiable experiences versus fixed or uncontrollable phenomena. Finally, rather than trying to strip away the only reality available to her, Erickson empowered her by working within her experience and gently opening new paths for choice and growth.

General Application

Selective validation acknowledges aspects of a person's thoughts or experiences without necessarily agreeing with them, creating a dialogue characterized by open engagement. This approach is especially useful for individuals experiencing confirmation bias as it allows them to explore alternative perspectives without feeling invalidated. Research on consensus reality (Asch, 1955) suggests that people adjust their perceptions based on social validation, making selective validation a powerful tool for integrating life-altering perceptions into a functional reality framework.

Across a wide range of contexts, selective validation functions as a form of micro-level choice architecture by shaping an environment that supports openness, momentum, and collaboration. A useful metaphor comes from comedian Tina Fey whose first rule of improvised comedy is "Say yes," meaning, accept your scene partner's offer and work within the reality they have created. In this spirit, selective validation creates a frame where clients feel their perspective is acknowledged, reducing defensiveness and increasing their willingness to explore new directions. By affirming a person's narrative, practitioners help structure a space where more adaptive choices become visible and accessible.

Case 8.2: Imposing Academic Perfection

Erickson recounted a case in which a physician attempted to use hypnosis to improve his son's academic performance. The doctor was proud of his 12-year-old son, Jonny, who was highly responsive to hypnosis. So, when Jonny brought home a report card with one D, several Cs, and a single B, his father conducted a trance induction and insisted that he earn more As and Bs. "Whenever you try to use hypnosis for a purely selfish purpose, you lose," Erickson explained.

The unintended consequence was that Jonny refused to enter into a trance for his father again. His need for autonomy and self-determination had been violated. Realizing his mistake, the father brought Jonny to Erickson for help. Meeting privately with the boy, Erickson summed up the situation saying, "Jonny, your father tried to tell you that you had to have all A's and B's." He then added, "Let's be honest about this; let's be fair and decent."

Next, Erickson argued on Jonny's behalf, saying, "You didn't feel too badly about the D, did you? You didn't think it was important. You didn't feel too badly about the C's. They are perfectly good grades. They are average grades." Finally, he reinforced Jonny's positive experience, saying, "And you REALLY did enjoy the B grade, didn't you?" Following this brief conversation, Jonny's grades naturally improved, rising to mostly Bs, without coercion or pressure.

Steelman Argument

The *steelman argument* is a behavioral tactic that involves identifying and articulating the strongest, most compelling part of another person's argument to engage with it. Unlike the *straw man fallacy*, which weakens an argument for easy refutation, *steelmanning* involves reconstructing an argument in its best possible form before engaging with it. Accurately representing another viewpoint weakens confirmation bias by reducing the defensive need to protect one's original position. This tactic serves as both an act of advocacy and an opportunity to strengthen one's own reasoning. By focusing on the strongest part of a client's viewpoint, steelmanning functions as a trust-building tactic that fosters deeper intellectual engagement and reduces defensiveness in interpersonal interactions.

The theoretical foundations of this tactic can be traced back to John Stuart Mill (1859), who argued that genuine understanding requires engaging with the strongest opposing arguments: "He who knows only his own side of the case, knows little of that." Mill believed that in order to learn something new, one must test the weakest part of their own argument against the strongest part of their opponent's.

Modern research on motivated reasoning (Kunda, 1990) and intellectual humility (Leary et al., 2017) supports this view, showing that individuals are more receptive to dialogue when they feel their perspective has been genuinely understood and validated. Additionally, in a study of *cognitive dissonance* Cancino-Montecinos et al. (2018) found that when people feel heard and are free to make their own choices, they become more open to re-evaluating their established position.

My first use of steelmanning was during a talk at a women's domestic violence shelter. At age 26, this was my first public presentation. I was presenting data on men showing behavioral change after domestic violence intervention work. Midway through the lecture, an audience member stood up and aggressively accused me of putting women at risk by overstating the probability of change. I was caught off guard. It was strong data systematically collected from the men's partners under conditions of absolute privacy and anonymity. Instead of explaining this, I responded,

> Thank you! You're raising a critical point I almost missed. Most abusive relationships, especially those that lead to shelter stays, will not be fixed with a little therapy. What my chart should highlight is how many men never commit to therapy or drop out after one session. I do not know how large that number is. But I do know that only a small percentage complete the full three-month program, and just 32% of those receive the positive ratings I mentioned.

As I spoke, she sat down calmly and listened to the rest of the talk, seemingly satisfied.

As illustrated above, steelmanning transforms potential conflict into collaboration by redirecting a contentious situation into a problem-solving effort. This involves accurate and nuanced re-expression of the client's position, ideally in a way so articulate that they enthusiastically endorse your version of their argument.

Steelmanning is easy to recognize because it commonly begins with the phrase, "You make a good point." For example, when a client expresses distress over what they perceive to be a professional misstep, perhaps arguing that you are rushing to judgment, it is possible to construct a response that validates their experience while also shifting the focus toward constructive engagement. For example,

> You make a good point. It takes time to truly understand someone and I probably haven't heard as much from you as I should. I want to really listen to whatever you think I need to know to better understand your needs.

This response affirms the client's right to be heard while also prompting them to engage in a cooperative process, reducing antagonism and reinforcing their agency in collaborative problem-solving.

Another essential component of steelmanning is empathetic framing, which acknowledges the values, concerns, or emotional significance attached to a viewpoint. By listing points of agreement, this approach fosters goodwill and minimizes emotional turmoil. Finally, steelmanning incorporates an additive perspective (it does not replace or negate the other person's viewpoint but adds to it). While strengthening the opposing argument, steelmanning subtly opens the door for thoughtful reconsideration and the introduction of new ideas.

Research on negotiation highlights the power of seeing things from another person's perspective. While studying perspective taking in the context of formal negotiation, Galinsky et al. (2008) found that when individuals attempt to articulate an opposing viewpoint in its strongest form, they develop greater empathy and a more nuanced understanding of complex issues, thereby increasing individuals' ability to discover hidden agreements. This not only benefits the person employing the tactic but also encourages intellectual humility in their conversational partner making it easier for both to create and claim resources at the bargaining table. Across a variety of contexts, this tactic fosters mutual respect, encourages *critical thinking*, and ultimately leads to more productive and insightful discussions.

Case Analysis

Jonny's sudden non-responsiveness to hypnosis stemmed from his father's coercive attempt to dictate his academic performance. Erickson recognized that Jonny's psychological state required an approach that preserved his autonomy while still fostering motivation. Instead of reinforcing the father's directive, Erickson validated Jonny's own feelings about his personal rights. By strengthening Jonny's agency in the discussion, Erickson ensured that any change in academic performance came from Jonny's own internal motivation.

Erickson's approach aligns with psychological research on self-determination, which suggests that intrinsic motivation flourishes when individuals feel a sense of control over their choices. By approving of Jonny's grades, including the C's and even the D, he diffused any defensiveness and allowed Jonny to reflect on what he personally valued. Erickson explained this saying, "So he raised his grades because he didn't want any more sympathy about his D's," Erickson concluded, saying, "But he did want the emotional satisfaction of more B's. But that was his want." Erickson's nudge facilitated ownership of his academic progress by reinforcing the intrinsic satisfaction Jonny felt from earning better grades, as opposed to framing success as a matter of obligation or emphasizing external standards.

A closer look at Erickson's use of the steelman argument reveals three key elements. First, he employed perspective taking by supporting Jonny's viewpoint and created space for Jonny to explore his own values. Second, he redirected Jonny's understanding of academic success, helping him shift from seeing it as a product of parental control to recognizing it as a personal, meaningful choice. Third, Erickson offered a charitable interpretation by subtly affirming Jonny's growing preference for achieving more B's. This approach reflects core principles of choice architecture: affirm existing preferences, lower the emotional cost of engagement, and make adaptive choices more appealing and accessible. In the end, Jonny's improved performance was not the result of manipulation. It was the product of a well-designed choice environment that helped him connect with what he genuinely wanted.

General Application

The steelman argument involves presenting the strongest and most compelling version of a client's perspective, thus demonstrating genuine understanding and respect for their viewpoint. This tactic is particularly useful for individuals experiencing confirmation bias as it reduces defensiveness and opens the door for constructive dialogue. By validating a client's reasoning, the choice architect can help the individual critically engage with their own beliefs while feeling heard and respected.

In collaborative partnerships, steelman arguments serve as both an act of advocacy and a means of guiding self-reflection. For example, when a new client accused me of shutting her down in the first session, and scolded me for not recognizing the power imbalance between myself and a minority-class female, I responded, "This cannot be easy for you. But let's not fail to recognize that not only did you have the courage to return, now you are confronting me to my face, and with good self-assertion skills." She blushed, motioning with her hand as if to wave away the compliment, and then replied, "Dr. Short, with you, it's easy. I don't have to worry about how you will treat me." After a pause, she added, "Now that I think about it, I'm not entirely sure it was you shutting me down. That was something my mother always used to do to me." By acknowledging the client's concerns, the choice architect builds trust and creates space for further discussion.

Steelman arguments encourage clients to see alternative perspectives without feeling coerced, ultimately promoting deeper self-awareness and personal responsibility. As John Stuart Mill (1859) argued,

> The only freedom which deserves the name is that of pursuing our own good in our own way, so long as we do not attempt to deprive others of theirs, or impede their efforts to obtain it. Each is the proper guardian of his own health, whether bodily, or mental or spiritual.

Case 8.3: The Pimple on the Forehead

A young boy developed a compulsive habit of picking at a pimple on his forehead until it turned into a persistent ulcer. His father attempted to stop the behavior through punishment, even going so far as to break the boy's prized bow and arrow set. However, no amount of punishment curbed the compulsion. As a result, the boy became angry at his entire family.

During a session with both the father and son, Erickson asked, "What is the proper treatment for an ulcerated forehead?" Both agreed that bandages and salves were the appropriate remedies. Erickson then inquired, "And how does breaking a bow and arrow help heal a sore?" This question prompted the father to acknowledge the inappropriateness of his actions. Erickson then encouraged the boy to recognize his father's good intentions despite his "stupid behavior." This framing helped the boy experience other emotions besides anger.

Further discussion revealed that the boy struggled with handwriting at school. Leveraging this concern, Erickson suggested a writing exercise. The boy agreed to practice his handwriting by repeatedly writing the sentence: "I fully agree with Dr. Erickson and I understand that it is neither wise nor good, nor desirable, to keep picking at that sore on my forehead."

To reinforce this commitment, Erickson used a tactic now known as *temptation bundling*, which involves pairing a highly desired activity (temptation) with a less enjoyable but important task (target behavior). In this case, the boy was to complete the writing exercise on weekends (target behavior), while his father took over his weekend chores (temptation). In other words, the boy was given something constructive to do with his fingers, which automatically reduced the amount of idle time for picking.

Additionally, Erickson used selective validation by encouraging the boy to bring in handwriting samples so he could study his progress. During these reviews, Erickson selectively pointed out the most impressive aspects of his handwriting. As the boy's self-esteem increased so did his desire to treat his body well. Within a month the boy's ulcer had healed and his grades improved significantly.

Counter-Attitudinal Advocacy

One persistent challenge within confirmation bias is *belief perseverance*, which is the tendency to hold onto original beliefs even when strong evidence shows they are wrong. In the example above, this shows up in the father's belief that punishment is the best way to teach new behavior. Instead of updating their thinking, people often stick with their initial conclusions. This happens partly because people do not just remember the belief, they also remember and rely on the *explanation* that first made it seem true (Johnson & Seifert, 1994). Therefore, even if we later find out the belief was false, the story behind it still influences how we think and act. This is similar to the *continued influence effect* where corrected misinformation remains active in implicit memory. From there, these memories automatically shape how people understand events.

Because belief perseverance is one mechanism through which confirmation bias persists, tactics that disrupt it directly weaken confirmation bias. To address this kind of cognitive rigidity, one effective tactic is counter-attitudinal advocacy. This tactic disrupts entrenched thinking by encouraging individuals to argue in favor of a position they initially disagree with. The process can create the kind of cognitive dissonance needed to weaken belief perseverance and open the door to meaningful attitude change.

Cognitive dissonance refers to the discomfort people feel when their actions don't align with their beliefs or values. In a well-designed choice environment, this tension can serve as a lever for self-reflection and personal alignment. To reduce dissonance, individuals typically adjust whichever element (belief or behavior) they feel less committed to. Often, this leads to a shift in perspective, especially when the behavior has already occurred. From a choice architecture standpoint, presenting people with low-pressure opportunities to support or consider alternative views can encourage them to reconcile internal conflicts in ways that expand their thinking and promote openness to new insights.

The effectiveness of counter-attitudinal advocacy relies on three key elements. First, voluntary participation is crucial as individuals who feel they are freely engaging in this exercise are more likely to internally justify their advocacy and undergo genuine attitude change (Cooper, 2019). Public commitment further reinforces this effect as making a verbal or written argument in favor of an opposing view increases social accountability. This makes it harder to dismiss the argument later (Cialdini et al., 1999). Second, active engagement plays a pivotal role. When individuals must think critically and articulate reasoning in favor of a contradictory stance, the process deepens cognitive processing and fosters internalization (Tormala & Rucker, 2022). Finally, perspective taking enhances the effect because considering alternative viewpoints often leads to a more balanced and nuanced understanding.

One practical example of counter-attitudinal advocacy can be seen in behavior modification, such as smoking cessation. If an individual enjoys smoking but recognizes its health risks, a choice architect might employ this tactic by prompting them to adopt the perspective of someone trying to dissuade a loved one from smoking: "What if your child was being pressured to smoke? What would be your advice? And what if she argued that smoking has brought you a lot of pleasure in life?" By sustaining this simulated debate, the individual is compelled to engage in reasoning that supports quitting and is led to reassess their own behavior: "Are you willing to keep up this simulated debate, with your daughter, each and every time you take a puff?"

This approach capitalizes on the power of indirect self-persuasion. When dealing with important attitudes, behavior, or lifestyle changes, self-persuasion strategies (such as counter-attitudinal advocacy) produce more powerful and long-lasting effects than do direct techniques of persuasion (Aronson, 1999). Research has shown that engaging individuals in counter-attitudinal advocacy can lead to long-term effects particularly when the advocacy is self-generated and socially reinforced (Leippe & Eisenstadt, 1994).

By guiding individuals to argue for an opposing viewpoint, counter-attitudinal advocacy leverages the principles of cognitive dissonance and social accountability to foster attitude recalibration. This tactic not only encourages more open-minded reasoning, but also serves as a powerful tool for shifting entrenched perspectives in a way that feels self-directed versus imposed.

Case Analysis

The boy's problematic behavior (picking at his forehead sore) was deeply ingrained and previous interventions, such as punishment, had only reinforced his anger, increasing the need to express his autonomy. Instead of directly confronting the habit, Erickson leveraged the boy's personal concern about his handwriting to introduce a counter-attitudinal task: writing a sentence that explicitly opposed his habitual behavior. By engaging in an activity that required him to advocate against his own actions, the boy was able to internalize a new emotional perspective. This method (written self-suggestion) helped the boy shift from an emotionally reactive state, marked by anger toward his family, to one marked by cognitive engagement with the problem. The writing task created a structured way for him to reaffirm his ability to modify his behavior while also improving his handwriting skills, which provided an additional source of motivation (self-pride).

A closer look at Erickson's use of counter-attitudinal advocacy reveals the key elements. First, the boy's participation was voluntary. He was encouraged to engage in a structured writing exercise, but the setup was designed so it would not feel forced. He likely enjoyed seeing his father take on weekend chores. It was a consequence that helped the father make amends for his destruction of the boy's favorite bow and arrow set (*moral cleansing*). Second, the writing task was framed not as a punishment, but as a constructive activity tied to personal improvement. Erickson reinforced his active engagement using selective validation to support the boy's efforts without criticism, ensuring that this affordance fostered a sense of achievement. Third, it leveraged cognitive dissonance by having him write statements that ran counter to his habitual behavior, thereby creating intrinsic motivation for growth. The combined focus on handwriting and skin healing also encouraged a new perspective on self-improvement, which then carried over to other areas of the boy's life. The key takeaway is that when individuals feel ownership over the process, even subtle nudges, like a writing task tied to self-improvement, can open the door to lasting progress.

General Application

Counter-attitudinal advocacy is especially effective for individuals struggling with confirmation bias because it guides them to engage with alternative perspectives in a personally meaningful way. In situations involving conflict (such as a strained marriage, business partnership, or workplace dynamic) counter-attitudinal advocacy can be introduced through *role-reversal* exercises (Cruz et al., 2018). For instance, when co-parents disagree on whether to be more strict or nurturing, having them debate the issue while role-playing each other allows both to inhabit the other's reasoning. If only one party is present, such as a manager dealing with employee dissatisfaction, you can invite them to step into the role of their most outspoken employee. In doing so, they articulate concerns they may have previously dismissed.

These role-reversals function as *choice prompts*. They create structured opportunities for reflection that challenge entrenched narratives without provoking defensiveness. The shifts in attitude and mood are often immediate and visible, with clients frequently surprising themselves by the clarity and empathy they gain through the exercise. Research supports the use of this tactic in a variety of contexts, showing that counter-attitudinal advocacy can lead to lasting behavioral shifts by encouraging individuals to see their actions from a new, self-reflective perspective (Kim et al., 2014).

Case 8.4: Listening for Danger

A construction worker came to see Erickson for help with a fear of heights (after his wife had successfully consulted Erickson for her fear of dental procedures). At his current job site there were deep holes in the ground that he experienced as terrifying. The fear was so intense that he worried he might have to quit. To avoid interfering with the man's work schedule, Erickson arranged to see him on a weekend.

During the session, Erickson told him several metaphorical stories. One was about a tribe of Native Americans who were completely unafraid of heights. Another recounted how Erickson's son became fearful of getting off the couch, after breaking his leg. Erickson helped his son overcome the fear by gradually inching his feet closer and closer to the floor. Yet another story described Erickson's experiments observing psychological and physical changes in people during hypnosis, particularly when he altered the location of his voice.

Erickson explained to the man that fear of heights is a natural response and one of its least recognized components is how the unconscious mind detects subtle differences in the way sounds echo at heights and around holes. He suggested that the man test his ability to "hear holes" while at the construction site.

Although the man initially felt that the stories Erickson had told him were unhelpful, he found himself curious about the idea of sound differences. He began experimenting by making noises at various distances from the holes and noticing how the echoes changed. To his surprise, he discovered Erickson's observation was correct. Through this process of investigation, he overcame his fear of heights and was able to keep his job.

Reality Testing

Direct, first-hand experimentation is one way to "open" a closed processing system. Commonly known as *reality testing*, this behavioral tactic involves actively comparing one's expectations or interpretations with actual outcomes through personal experience. Research in cognitive and behavioral science shows that direct experiential feedback is one of the most reliable ways to correct biased expectations. Instead of relying solely on expert opinions or abstract reasoning, individuals engage higher cognitive functions to interact with concrete evidence from the real world. Evoking mental processes of attention, perception, memory, and judgment helps guide individuals toward forming logical conclusions about how their internal experiences relate to external reality. As Erickson et al. (1959) put it, "Now when you want to prove something to a subject, and really prove it to them, try to let the proof come from within them. And let it come from within them in a most unexpected way" (p. 80). The appeal of this approach is captured in the adage: "I'll believe it when I see it."

This approach is uniquely suited to addressing confirmation bias because it creates a structured opportunity to disconfirm inaccurate beliefs. When individuals test their assumptions and see outcomes that contradict their expectations, they are more likely to revise their beliefs in light of this new evidence. In doing so, reality testing promotes psychological flexibility, encourages *critical thinking*, and supports *autonomous problem-solving*. Reality testing serves as a corrective mechanism by introducing first-hand experience into decision-making, reducing reliance on outdated beliefs.

The implementation of reality testing involves creating small, manageable experiments to test hypotheses about behaviors, events, or outcomes. These structured tests provide concrete feedback that allows individuals to reassess their beliefs or adjust future behavior based on observed evidence. For example, a mother brought me her 12-year-old son, who had become depressed following an acrimonious divorce. The central problem appeared to be his relationship with his father. The boy described how his father often became angry and impatient with him, frequently accusing him of disobedience. His mother confirmed that the father was overly harsh, yelling like a drill sergeant, but because the court had ordered shared custody, the boy had no choice but to stay with him every other week.

I told the boy that we needed to conduct an experiment to determine how much influence he could have over his father. I instructed him that, whenever his father yelled at him, he should respond with a loud, clear, "Yes sir!" I told him to say nothing else, and added, "The first time you do this, your father will probably stop talking and leave the room. I do not think he will say nice things to you, but I do think it will stop the criticism."

At our next meeting, the boy looked eager rather than depressed. He excitedly reported that he had tried the experiment and that his father had stopped yelling and left the room as I predicted. I then told him, "I know from your mother that your father is a big, two-hundred-and-thirty-pound man. If you can exercise this much influence over him, imagine what else you are capable of." This single act of reality testing significantly improved his mood and sense of self-efficacy.

Reality testing in ECA involves several key features that help individuals replace problematic beliefs with evidence-based understanding. Empirical verification means checking things out in the real world instead of relying on untested assumptions. Manageable experimentation involves trying small, low-risk tests to see whether certain beliefs or fears are true. Guided reflection helps people think about what happened in these tests so they can make sense of the results based on facts. Together, these strategies empower individuals to make more informed choices and engage with their experiences in a way that supports greater self-understanding and autonomy.

By incorporating reality testing into collaborative problem-solving, practitioners empower individuals to engage with evidence-based reasoning, fostering resilience, adaptability, and cognitive flexibility. This tactic is particularly effective for individuals struggling with anxiety, paranoia, or rigid belief systems as it provides a structured pathway toward greater psychological insight and personal growth.

Case Analysis

In this case, Erickson employed the ECA tactic of reality testing to help a construction worker overcome his fear of falling into a pit. The task (testing the way sound echoes near holes) was deceptively simple yet strategic. Instead of interpreting the man's fear as a pathological reaction, Erickson framed it as a natural perceptual phenomenon. He suggested that the man's unconscious mind was reacting to subtle differences in auditory cues, such as changes in echo, that occur at heights or near open spaces. This subtle shift transformed the fear from something internal and fixed into something external and investigable.

This affordance was particularly well-suited to the man's occupational and psychological context. As a construction worker, he would have seen or heard what happens when a worker is careless and falls. There are numerous stories of men being impaled by rebar or buried alive in sand. Any effort to assure him that he did not need to worry about falling into the holes would have been instantly dismissed as sheer nonsense. Theories from evolutional psychology suggest that survival-oriented fear often results in confirmation bias or *negativity bias*. Those most likely to survive automatically search for evidence that the threat is real and possibly immanent.

By assigning a task that could be carried out on the job site (where the fear was occurring) and that aligned with the man's need to pay attention to the threatening stimuli, Erickson ensured the task felt both feasible and highly relevant. More importantly, by emphasizing curiosity and experimentation Erickson activated a different motivational system that was rooted in exploration rather than avoidance.

Research in cognitive-behavioral and motivational psychology supports this approach. Studies show that curiosity can displace fear by shifting attentional focus and activating approach behaviors (Schutte & Malouff, 2023; White et al., 2009). Exposure-based interventions are most effective when the individual has some sense of agency and control and when the feared stimulus is approached gradually. In this case, the man engaged in a form of exposure therapy by approaching the holes repeatedly but he did so on his own terms and with a spirit of inquiry. His discovery, that the echo differences were real, possibly created a moment of mastery and reorientation.

The task Erickson offered provided more than a distraction or coping mechanism. Kinesthetic or auditory sensations that we cannot explicitly account for are more terrifying than those we understand and can accurately anticipate. I call this *the haunted house effect* and it aligns with studies on infrasound (a type of sound wave that humans generally cannot perceive as audible) and the outsized fear it produces (Dagnall et al., 2020). As a result of systematic experimentation, the man likely improved his perceptive abilities. Through this lens, we see that the role of the practitioner is *not* to overcome resistance to change but to illuminate and scaffold the pathways that support adaptive growth.

General Application

Reality testing is a cognitive process that helps individuals evaluate their thoughts and perceptions against objective evidence, allowing them to distinguish between assumptions and reality. It is especially effective as a response to confirmation bias. A related issue, *selective exposure*, leads people to seek out supporting information and avoid contradictory information. This negative spiral (looking only for evidence of X and therefore becoming increasingly convinced of X) can be reversed with surprising simplicity, even without a single office visit.

For example, here is a text message exchange between me and a young woman who was willing to pay any amount for help, despite needing all her income for basic living expenses. As you'll see, my approach was to support her progress as much as possible without making her dependent on costly office visits:

Woman typed: Is it possible to have PTSD even after working through trauma therapy? I feel like I have two hurdles left that I just cannot seem to overcome, even after all that therapy [with the previous therapist]. It could be I need additional therapy for: (1) eating "disorder," (2) fear of driving, and (3) task paralysis (not sure if that's accurate).

Dan typed: Which of those three are you most likely to overcome first?

Woman typed: The most likely would the driving. But the one I would like to overcome the most would be the eating (it's not really eating, it's resistance and paralysis about making food). Would your hypnosis be appropriate?

Dan typed: The driving sounds like a great place to start. Think of this like dominos knocking over—the progress and momentum tends to carry forward.

Is there someone who will ride beside you and give you affirming messages? I don't think you will need hypnosis for the first accomplishment. After you get that success under your belt, you can text me and we will set up a hypnosis session to work on the eating.

Woman typed: The driving is a mix of things. It's similar to the eating; I struggle to get OUT of the house and INTO the car. The years of psychosomatic seizures, years of getting lost and driving because I had to and not because I wanted to and then the caregiving of my parents killed it.

I won't even get in the car to go do something I want to do. I'm fine as a passenger. It's isolating. Once I'm out of the house and driving, as long as I'm not exhausted, in pain, or stressed, I don't mind the driving. If the stars line up, I've enjoyed it a few times.

Dan typed: That is probably why you picked driving as your first breakthrough...because you have already learned that you can enjoy it.

Make certain not to pressure yourself. This should be an enjoyable activity, something that makes you feel free and strong.

As you make progress, send me updates so I can see how you are doing it.

Here we see the woman being gently nudged to explore her fears (particularly around driving) by engaging with real-life experience instead of avoiding it. Rather than relying on assumptions or past negative associations (e.g., seizures, caregiving stress, getting lost), she is invited to test what happens now under safer and more supportive conditions. The false assumption being tested is that she lacks the autonomy or resilience to reclaim driving as an enjoyable, empowering activity. The woman appreciated this affordance. Three weeks later, she drove herself to my office and proudly described how much progress she had been making in overcoming her self-limiting inhibitions. This illustrates how reality testing can help individuals critically examine their beliefs, consider alternative viewpoints, and reduce counter-productive thinking.

Designing an Optimal Choice Environment (OCE) for Confirmation Bias

An *optimal choice environment* for someone influenced by confirmation bias should reduce defensiveness, protect self-image, and gently increase engagement with alternative viewpoints. Because this bias leads people to discount contradictory evidence, belief revision is more likely when disconfirming information is introduced in a non-threatening way and linked to the person's long-term goals (Nickerson, 1998).

One useful design principle is to build on self-pride. When people feel effective and recognize their own progress, they are more willing to engage information that might otherwise feel threatening. Tools such as self-reflection exercises and personalized feedback can strengthen self-efficacy by highlighting prior successes.

Consistency bias can also be used strategically by linking present choices to a person's historical view of who they have been at their best. For example, when working with a man who doubted his current abilities, but recalled feeling successful in college, I said, "You described a great deal of growth during college. Are you ready to build on that again?" This resulted in immediate progress.

The goal is not to confront confirmation bias directly, but to design conditions in which new evidence feels compatible with identity, agency, and forward movement.

Thought Exercise

Next, you will have the opportunity to apply your design skills. When creating an optimal choice environment for someone with a confirmation bias, remember that this environment can include mental landscapes such as imagery, beliefs, and goals, or modifications to their physical surroundings. The only requirement is that you respect their right to confirm their personal reality.

For this thought exercise, imagine speaking with a young female client who is considered attractive by others but is extremely self-conscious and complains of "awful inferiority feelings." She is so bothered by a small, star-shaped scar, near the corner of her mouth, that she refuses to let anyone including you see it. She has behaved this way since a car accident in adolescence when she was thrown from the vehicle, with the small cut near her mouth as her only injury.

As you talk to her about her concerns, she continues to cover the scar with her right hand. Despite being a sophomore in college, she refuses to drive a car, swim, play sports, or any other activity that would force her to reveal the scar. She is willing to date and enjoys kissing, but only in complete darkness.

Before reading further, consider how you would respond to this extremely rigid belief that has been reinforced by years of deeply ingrained avoidance behavior. What would you say or do to design an optimal choice environment that recognizes this woman's need for autonomous decision-making and respects her own judgment while also satisfying her desire to feel beautiful?

***

Erickson described a case (8.5 in the case index) involving these same circumstances. The young woman was a sophomore in college majoring in economics. While recounting the automobile accident, she described the minor cut as "a gash on the right side of my face." Her belief was that this accident left her with awful scarring. That was why she insisted on always covering that side of her mouth with her hand or turning her head so others would not see it.

While speaking with Dr. Erickson, she refused to show her scar, stating that it would "disgust" him. It was only at home that she would briefly stop hiding it. Even then, she tolerated no mention of it. In public or at school she always kept the right side of her mouth hidden. She only agreed to romantic outings that involved walking outdoors, provided her date stayed on her left side and it was dark. She allowed kissing only in darkness so her face could not be seen.

Her parents had offered to help her conceal the scar using specialized cosmetics, but she refused this solution without being able to explain why. She had independently visited three plastic surgeons for opinions on the scar. Like her parents, all three concluded that the scar was barely noticeable. She described the surgeons as having "the same unreasonable and unsympathetic attitude my parents took," which led her to develop intense hostility toward the medical profession.

Her goal in seeking therapy was not to change her behavior but to learn how to better "adjust" to what she saw as her handicap. She showed no interest in altering her view of the scar and it wasn't until the third session that she allowed Erickson to see it. He examined the scar at length without comment. Finally, he told her she could resume covering it, which brought her visible relief.

In learning more about her, Erickson discovered that she had considerable talent in sketching and took great pride in this ability. Tapping into this associational anchor, he gave her an assignment: to go home and in the privacy of her room make a life-size, scientifically accurate sketch of her face that showed the exact position, shape, and size of the scar. She was to bring the drawing to him only when she felt confident it was a true and faithful representation. To reduce anxiety, he offered the option of submitting the sketch in a sealed envelope, which would not be opened without her permission.

She spent the rest of that day and much of the night perfecting the drawing and returned with it in an unsealed manila envelope. Erickson glanced at it briefly, then placed it in her file. Though she still covered her scar, Erickson noticed she seemed less tense and anxious.

Her next assignment was to research the historical use of beauty patches, which are small, decorative pieces once used to highlight attractive facial features. She was to explore this through the college library, by consulting her mother, and by speaking with fashion experts. She was also to make a series of self-portrait-like sketches of women's faces, each displaying a different type of beauty patch in various locations on the face. While this was being done, she was encouraged to wonder why she felt so compelled to complete the task. Erickson also gave her a post-hypnotic suggestion of temporary amnesia regarding the purpose of the assignment.

Two weeks later, she returned with a collection of detailed sketches. She expressed curiosity and confusion over the emotionality of the assignment.

All the sketches were on paper the same size as her initial self-portrait and all the female faces resembled her own.

While reviewing the drawings with her, Erickson covertly slipped her original self-portrait into the pile. He then asked her to lay the sketches out and explain each beauty patch: its shape (crescent, star, diamond, its placement) and its intended effect. She unwittingly described the scar in her self-portrait as a six-pointed star-shaped beauty patch meant to draw attention to an attractive mouth. However, she was puzzled by its six points, remarking that she had only drawn five-pointed stars. Suddenly, she recognized the sketch as her self-portrait and that realization caused shock.

For several minutes, she struggled to reconcile two conflicting perceptions: the scar as a disfiguring flaw and the scar as a beauty-enhancing feature. Erickson then gently offered his interpretation:

> Your parents, your brother, your friends were all so unreasonable as to think that your scar was just a beauty patch. The plastic surgeons thought so too and brushed you off as a silly girl who refused to recognize the scar for what it was. I too am sufficiently unreasonable as to see that scar as a little white, star-shaped beauty patch at the corner of a very pretty mouth. And you yourself—in fear, distress, abhorrence—drew your portrait, accurately and well. And without knowing it, you portrayed that scar for what it was: a beauty patch, which you unguardedly recognized correctly.

Erickson explained the scientific value of continued experimentation and reality testing. He added:

> Beauty patches are meant to draw attention to the most attractive features. You have pretty eyes, a charming dimple in your left cheek, and a beautiful mouth. You enjoy being kissed, and several boys have kissed you. Go out with them again. Let them kiss you goodnight under the porch light. Take mental note of where they kiss you—on the left side of your mouth, full face, or on the right. I think they'll kiss the side with the beauty patch. You'll find out.
>
> Now go home. Take these sketches with you. You did them carefully and well. You've learned a tremendous amount from them. Keep them, give them away. It doesn't matter. But what you've learned from them, you will always keep.

At a follow-up session she confirmed that she was consistently kissed on the right side of her mouth. This served as concrete proof of her beauty.

Having come to her own conclusions (using reality testing), she stopped covering her mouth and no longer felt the painful inferiority that once governed her behavior. Two years later, she married and eventually became the mother of four children, which was an ideal outcome for the culture of her time.

Conclusion

Throughout this chapter, we have examined confirmation bias as a dynamic state of mind. It is shaped by underlying needs for certainty, identity preservation, and emotional regulation. While commonly understood as the tendency to seek evidence that supports our existing beliefs, confirmation bias can also influence how we perceive, remember, and interpret information across domains as diverse as politics, religion, education, and mental health. Whether driven by ideological commitments, self-esteem maintenance, or the ease of post-hoc rationalization, confirmation bias reflects a psychological state that prioritizes coherence over complexity.

Importantly, confirmation bias is not merely a cognitive flaw. It often arises from adaptive mechanisms meant to reduce uncertainty, conserve mental energy, or sustain social belonging. However, the very functions that make it adaptive can also limit openness, distort feedback, and suppress learning. When left unexamined, this bias encourages us to confuse certainty with accuracy and to continue to defend familiar narratives even in the face of disconfirming evidence.

The central insight is this: While confirmation bias is common, it is not immutable. As a fluid mental state, it can be reshaped through strategic micro-level choice architecture. The four tactics presented in this chapter create different pathways toward greater openness. Selective validation reduces defensiveness by affirming a meaningful part of the person's belief. The steelman argument strengthens the alliance by presenting the strongest version of that position. Counter-attitudinal advocacy loosens rigid thinking by inviting the person to argue for an opposing view, while reality testing promotes belief revision through direct experience (Table 8.1).

Together, these tactics create environments that support reflection, curiosity, and intellectual humility without requiring people to abandon their beliefs on command. By fostering psychological safety, inviting dissent, and prompting people to actively consider alternative viewpoints, we can shift the decision-making environment in ways that support more flexible and productive thinking. In this way, the goal is not to eliminate confirmation bias entirely, but to create the conditions in which openness becomes a viable and rewarding choice.

Quick-Reference Tactic Map

Table 8.1 Tactics Suited for *Confirmation Bias* and the Broader Architecture of Strategic Influence

If Client...	*Then Use...*	*Because*
Feels invalidated or fears judgment	*Selective validation*: Selectively acknowledging useful aspects of a person's experience versus challenging problematic aspects	*Utilizes* a credible part of the person's experience to reduce defensiveness and keep revision psychologically possible
Is emotionally attached to a given belief	*Steelman argument*: Presenting the strongest version of another person's argument to engage with it	Leverages the need to feel understood by using the best parts of an argument to examine competing ideas *critically* in a cooperative manner
Clings to ideological certainty or habitual self-justification	*Counter-attitudinal advocacy*: Encouraging individuals to argue in favor of a position they initially disagree with	*Framing* an opposing position as one's own creates dissonance through voluntary reversal, encouraging re-alignment with the stated evidence and values
Has expectations, fears, or assumptions that diverge from observable reality	*Reality testing*: Actively comparing one's expectations or interpretations with actual outcomes through personal experience	Activates *critical thinking* by confronting expectation with direct evidence

Note

1 Also known as the Barnum effect.

References

Aronson, E. (1999). The power of self-persuasion. *American Psychologist*, *54*(11), 875–884. https://doi.org/10.1037/h0088188

Asch, S. E. (1955). Opinions and social pressure. *Scientific American*, *193*(5), 31–35.

Cancino-Montecinos, S., Björklund, F., & Lindholm, T. (2018). Dissonance reduction as emotion regulation: Attitude change is related to positive emotions in the induced compliance paradigm. *PLoS One*, *13*(12), e0209012. https://doi.org/10.1371/journal.pone.0209012

Cialdini, R. B., Wosinska, W., Barrett, D. W., Butner, J., & Gornik-Durose, M. (1999). Compliance with a request in two cultures: The differential influence of social proof and commitment/consistency on collectivists and individualists. *Personality and Social Psychology Bulletin*, *25*(10), 1242–1253. https://doi.org/10.1177/0146167299258006

Cooper, J. (2019). Cognitive dissonance: Where we've been and where we're going. *International Review of Social Psychology*, *32*(1). https://doi.org/10.5334/irsp.277

Cruz, A., Sales, C. M. D., Alves, P., & Moita, G. (2018). The core techniques of morenian psychodrama: A systematic review of literature. *Frontiers in Psychology*, *9*. https://doi.org/10.3389/fpsyg.2018.01263

Dagnall, N., Drinkwater, K. G., O'Keeffe, C., Ventola, A., Laythe, B., Jawer, M. A., Massullo, B., Caputo, G. B., & Houran, J. (2020). Things that go bump in the literature: An environmental appraisal of "haunted houses." *Frontiers in Psychology*, *11*. https://doi.org/10.3389/fpsyg.2020.01328

Deci, E. L., & Ryan, R. M. (2008). Self-determination theory: A macrotheory of human motivation, development, and health. *Canadian Psychology / Psychologie Canadienne*, *49*(3), 182–185. https://doi.org/10.1037/a0012801

Edmondson, A. (1999). Psychological safety and learning behavior in work teams. *Administrative Science Quarterly*, *44*(2), 350–383. https://doi.org/10.2307/2666999

Erickson, M. H., Haley, J., & Weakland, J. H. (1959). A transcript of a trance induction with commentary. *American Journal of Clinical Hypnosis*, *2*(2), 49–84.

Ezawa, I. D., & Hollon, S. D. (2023). Cognitive restructuring and psychotherapy outcome: A meta-analytic review. *Psychotherapy (Chicago, Ill)*, *60*(3), 396–406. https://doi.org/10.1037/pst0000474

Galinsky, A. D., Maddux, W. W., Gilin, D., & White, J. B. (2008). Why it pays to get inside the head of your opponent: The differential effects of perspective taking and empathy in negotiations. *Psychological Science*, *19*(4), 378–384. https://doi.org/10.1111/j.1467-9280.2008.02096.x

Johnson, H. M., & Seifert, C. M. (1994). Sources of the continued influence effect: When misinformation in memory affects later inferences. *Journal of Experimental Psychology: Learning, Memory, and Cognition*, *20*(6), 1420–1436. https://doi.org/10.1037/0278-7393.20.6.1420

Kahan, D. M. (2013). Ideology, motivated reasoning, and cognitive reflection. *Judgment and Decision Making*, *8*(4), 407–424. https://doi.org/10.1017/S1930297500005271

Kim, S.-Y., Allen, M., Preiss, R. W., & Peterson, B. (2014). Meta-analysis of counterattitudinal advocacy data: Evidence for an additive cues model. *Communication Quarterly* (World). https://www.tandfonline.com/doi/abs/10.1080/01463373.2014.949385

Kunda, Z. (1990). The case for motivated reasoning. *Psychological Bulletin*, *108*(3), 480–498. https://doi.org/10.1037/0033-2909.108.3.480

Leary, M. R., Diebels, K. J., Davisson, E. K., Jongman-Sereno, K. P., Isherwood, J. C., Raimi, K. T., Deffler, S. A., & Hoyle, R. H. (2017). Cognitive and interpersonal features of intellectual humility. *Personality and Social Psychology Bulletin*, *43*(6), 793–813. https://doi.org/10.1177/0146167217697695

Leippe, M. R., & Eisenstadt, D. (1994). Generalization of dissonance reduction: Decreasing prejudice through induced compliance. *Journal of Personality and Social Psychology*, *67*(3), 395–413. https://doi.org/10.1037/0022-3514.67.3.395

Lord, C. G., Ross, L., & Lepper, M. R. (1979). Biased assimilation and attitude polarization: The effects of prior theories on subsequently considered evidence. *Journal of Personality and Social Psychology*, *37*(11), 2098–2109. https://doi.org/10.1037/0022-3514.37.11.2098

Mill, J. S. (1859). *On Liberty*. J. W. Parker and Son.

Miller, W. R., & Rollnick, S. (2012). *Motivational Interviewing, Third Edition: Helping People Change* (3rd ed.). The Guilford Press.

Nail, P. R., Misak, J. E., & Davis, R. M. (2004). Self-affirmation versus self-consistency: A comparison of two competing self-theories of dissonance phenomena. *Personality and Individual Differences*, *36*(8), 1893–1905. https://doi.org/10.1016/j.paid.2003.08.019

Nickerson, R. S. (1998). Confirmation bias: A ubiquitous phenomenon in many guises. *Review of General Psychology*, *2*(2), 175–220. https://doi.org/10.1037/1089-2680.2.2.175

Remmerswaal, D., Huijding, J., Bouwmeester, S., Brouwer, M., & Muris, P. (2014). Cognitive bias in action: Evidence for a reciprocal relation between confirmation bias and fear in children. *Journal of Behavior Therapy and Experimental Psychiatry*, *45*(1), 26–32. https://doi.org/10.1016/j.jbtep.2013.07.005

Schutte, N. S., & Malouff, J. M. (2023). A meta-analytic investigation of the impact of curiosity-enhancing interventions. *Current Psychology*, *42*(24), 20374–20384. https://doi.org/10.1007/s12144-022-03107-w

Stanovich, K. E., & West, R. F. (2008). On the relative independence of thinking biases and cognitive ability. *Journal of Personality and Social Psychology*, *94*(4), 672–695. https://doi.org/10.1037/0022-3514.94.4.672

Swann, W. B., Wenzlaff, R. M., Krull, D. S., & Pelham, B. W. (1992). Allure of negative feedback: Self-verification strivings among depressed persons. *Journal of Abnormal Psychology*, *101*(2), 293–306. https://doi.org/10.1037/0021-843X.101.2.293

Taber, C. S., & Lodge, M. (2006). Motivated skepticism in the evaluation of political beliefs. *American Journal of Political Science*, *50*(3), 755–769. https://doi.org/10.1111/j.1540-5907.2006.00214.x

Tormala, Z. L., & Rucker, D. D. (2022). Attitude Change and Persuasion: Classic, Metacognitive, and Advocacy Perspectives. In *APA Handbook of Consumer Psychology* (pp. 323–350). American Psychological Association. https://doi.org/10.1037/0000262-013

Westen, D., Blagov, P. S., Harenski, K., Kilts, C., & Hamann, S. (2006). Neural bases of motivated reasoning: An fMRI study of emotional constraints on partisan political judgment in the 2004 U.S. presidential election. *Journal of Cognitive Neuroscience*, *18*(11), 1947–1958. https://doi.org/10.1162/jocn.2006.18.11.1947

White, L. K., Helfinstein, S. M., Reeb-Sutherland, B. C., Degnan, K. A., & Fox, N. A. (2009). Role of attention in the regulation of fear and anxiety. *Developmental Neuroscience*, *31*(4), 309–317. https://doi.org/10.1159/000216542

Chapter 9

Conclusion

The Freedom to Thrive

Conclusion: The Freedom to Thrive

This text explores a central paradox of self-determination: Although choosing one's own path is often viewed as an individual pursuit, the more choices we face the more guidance we tend to need. At every stage of life, people form their identities, shape their values, and make decisions within a social context defined by mutual influence and interdependence. As a group species adapted for autonomous problem-solving, humans rely on stratified levels of leadership across a variety of contexts. When the complexity of a challenge exceeds an individual's capacity to resolve it alone, attention naturally shifts toward those higher in the social hierarchy, such as doctors, lawyers, priests, or consultants. We hope that there is someone in a position of power who is willing to offer help, while also respecting our right to self-manifest solution-oriented behavior.

Another layer of complexity arises from the nature of human awareness. Although we rely on conscious awareness to evaluate the quality of our experiences, many of our most powerful needs operate beneath the surface, beyond the margin of conscious thought. Research in cognitive psychology increasingly shows that the reasons we give for our choices are often constructed after the fact. These rationalizations are not necessarily false, but they are often shaped to align with deeper, unconscious needs. In the light of emerging research, rationalization and justification appear to be the norm rather than the exception. As a result, genuine self-governance must include the ability to recognize and work with unconscious biases and the logic of heuristics. This raises a critical question: How do those in need of help discern how to meet personal and social needs that have not yet come into conscious awareness? And, how do care providers guide behavior that arises from automatic processes, which are not subject to deliberate intention?

Ericksonian Choice Architecture (ECA) is one possible solution. At the heart of this approach lies a profound respect for human autonomy

DOI: 10.4324/9781003797876-10

and our innate capacity for adaptive growth. This approach does not ask people to change, nor does it attempt to impose solutions from outside. Instead, it reframes challenges as opportunities for self-directed discovery and shifts the focus from externally imposed goals to internally driven alignment. Because emotional experience and worth are inherently relative (we feel good only in contrast to having felt bad) and because the brain tends to habituate to pleasure, it is existentially impossible to eliminate distress. Thriving, therefore, is not about achieving a permanent state of ease but about cultivating the flexibility to navigate ongoing emotional fluctuations through value-congruent choices that restore meaning, direction, and personal agency.

Milton Erickson's enduring contribution was not simply the ingenuity of his methods but the reverence he showed for each person's capacity to grow through the exercise of free will. His legacy teaches us that meaningful progress emerges not from coercive strategies but from collaborative relationships that honor an individual's unique adaptive abilities. This is in keeping with Charles Darwin's (1868) conclusion that individual variation is the basis of adaptation, making growth and survival possible in changing environments.

ECA extends this philosophy by designing choice environments where individuals perceive personally and socially rewarding options as extensions of their values and natural inclinations. For example, when a person facing an end-of-life scenario is *not* overwhelmed by fear or depression, but is instead able to act as a self-determining agent who confidently constructs their remaining time, then the experience of living regains its depth and dignity. This occurs not because suffering has been avoided, but because each choice affirms a sense of authorship, purpose, and connection to what matters most. In this same way, ECA transforms any perceived limitation into purposeful action.

Rather than focusing on behavioral change as the measure of success, ECA emphasizes the creation of a psychological landscape in which choice becomes more visible, accessible, and aligned with personal meaning. When individuals are supported in clarifying their values and recognizing relevant options, they adapt not because they are told to but because they discover a way forward that makes sense to them. This is the defining feature of choice-centric care: *transformation is not pursued; it is allowed to emerge naturally as a byproduct of increased clarity, autonomy, and alignment between one's actions and one's evolving sense of purpose.*

Central to ECA is the understanding that behavioral adaptation flourishes when guidance feels organic and not prescriptive. Practitioners act as facilitators, using subtle nudges to amplify existing strengths or highlight overlooked possibilities. By avoiding change-centric language, ECA sidesteps the trap of implying inadequacy. Instead, it fosters self-determination by *meeting the client where they are* and then asking, "What choices align with who you aspire to be?" This simple redirection shifts the narrative from fixing problems to expanding agency, allowing individuals to naturally reach new conclusions through self-discovery.

ECA does not treat distress or dysfunction as flaws to be corrected but as a source of motivation to optimize the alignment between values, perception, and action. The practitioner's role is not to "fix" broken people but to create the conditions in which high value options can be seen and chosen. In this paradigm, even limitations can become assets. When a perceived flaw is reframed as a sign of resilience or uniqueness, the client is not being deceived. Rather, they are being reconnected with the time-tested logic of a growth mindset. This mindset then produces internal guidance toward more adaptive and authentic choices.

In direct contrast to Freudian notions of insight and rational control, this book invites us to trust the capacities of unconscious intelligence. Doing so requires relinquishing the impulse to manage every aspect of life through conscious oversight. This does not mean abandoning ideas grounded in experimentation and skeptical analysis. Rather, to fully thrive, we must often allow ourselves the freedom of spontaneity. Even the most complex choices are often better informed by creating time and space for intuitive insight (Dijksterhuis, 2004). To promote these capabilities, it becomes essential to surround ourselves with influential individuals who not only respect our autonomy but also actively strengthen our ability to choose freely and grow authentically.

The ethical foundation of ECA ensures that autonomy remains paramount. Unlike manipulative tactics that prioritize compliance, ECA's nudges are transparent, grounded in mutual trust, and responsive to the person's own sense of timing. Research in behavioral science confirms that any form of guidance will gain credibility and influence when it resonates with personal truths and cultural narratives. Rather than attempting to steer another person's choices, practitioners of ECA offer cues that fit the client's worldview, thereby illuminating new opportunities.

Ultimately, ECA's strength lies in recognizing that life is in constant motion and that thriving depends on adaptive growth rather than conformity to a fixed doctrine of well-being. Because no state of mind is final, and no preference is unchanging, individuals must continually realign with their evolving priorities. ECA provides a structure that supports this realignment through self-realization versus explicit persuasion or coercion. At its core, ECA is a communication model, and its primary unit of action is the present moment of discourse. It examines how concrete words and actions shape meaning, perception, and regulation as events unfold in real time. Experienced practitioners know that a single statement, delivered in the right way at the right moment, can permanently alter the trajectory of a person's life. In this sense, ECA does not promise enduring "change" through the installation of insight or behavioral programming. Instead, its long-term influence emerges indirectly, through resonant experiences of authored choice within the context of a supportive relationship.

What endures is not some isolated behavior but the strengthened capacity for self-directed realignment. Whether someone is facing a career transition, a strained relationship, or existential uncertainty, collaborative engagement begins by asking: *Which choices feel most aligned with who you are becoming, and what support is needed to implicitly recognize and access them?* In this way, ECA is more than a methodology; it is a philosophy of engagement with implications for social relationships and for humanity's rapidly evolving relationship with artificial intelligence.

It affirms that autonomy and value identification are not optional for mental coherence; they are essential. Growth within this framework is not something to be engineered but something to be nurtured. Like a plant that grows when given the right balance of water and sunlight, human thriving occurs in environments where meaningful challenges are met with an exploration of choice and agency.

It is understandable, and wise, to feel cautious whenever we talk about subtle yet powerful means of guiding human choices. In such situations, concerns about manipulation or corruption naturally arise. How can individuals ensure their personal interests will be protected? Some may conclude that tools like choice architecture are inherently risky and should be avoided altogether. This conclusion often rests on an implicit belief that remaining uninfluenced, or even unaware, offers the best protection from exploitation. But is that truly the most ethical or effective response?

Consider this analogy. Language is one of the most powerful tools humans possess. It can be used to facilitate wars or justify genocide, but it can also be used to teach, to comfort, and to inspire. Should we respond to its potential for harm by refusing to study or teach it? Similarly, as the challenges facing humanity grow increasingly complex (climate change, social polarization, inequality) should those most committed to ethical leadership and transparency refrain from using these powerful tools of influence, leaving them to be exploited by those less concerned with fairness, inclusion, or long-term well-being?

When elevated to macro-level choice architecture, ECA offers an evaluative framework not only for individual growth, but also for shaping systems that foster autonomy, dignity, and cooperation at scale. Economically, it offers an antidote to manipulative marketing and coercive design by prioritizing informed, intrinsically motivated choice over short-term compliance or consumption (exploitive commerce). Socially, ECA values diversity in how people engage with options, encouraging environments that respond to individual differences. Politically, it stands for the ethical use of influence, guiding without controlling, activating without polarizing (fear mongering), and building capacity without dependency.

ECA is grounded in the understanding that adaptation is ongoing and that healthy decision-making involves both conscious reflection and unconscious responsiveness. It fosters the kind of *critical thinking* and psychological flexibility needed not only for personal agency but also for democratic participation and collective resilience. The responsible use of ECA is not about exercising unilateral power. It is about the shared benefits of working collaboratively to expand meaningful choice, especially in contexts where complexity or pressure might otherwise narrow it.

Ultimately, the issue at hand is not whether power and influence should be used. They always are, whether we acknowledge it or not. The practical need is to better understand how power and influence can be structured and applied in ways that promote both individual flourishing and the greater good. Non-conscious influence is ubiquitous to parenting, leadership, education, media, and everyday exchanges. When used irresponsibly, it can distort choices, undermine autonomy, and reinforce inequity. But when guided by ethical principles, self-awareness, and a commitment to transparency, influence becomes a tool for empowerment—one that helps people access their own values, clarify their direction, and take meaningful action.

In a world facing increasingly complex social, economic, and ecological challenges, we cannot afford to leave the most powerful tools of engagement and decision-shaping in the hands of those who disregard accountability or act solely in self-interest. The question is no longer whether we should use non-conscious influence (negotiations with an unconscious intelligence), but whether we are prepared to use it wisely, with humility and integrity. In carrying Erickson's work forward, we see that thriving is not a destination but a process of continual adaptation. When individuals perceive their choices as authentic expressions of their values, they cultivate a form of resilience that transcends circumstance.

The future of ECA lies not in perfecting techniques but in deepening our commitment to collaborative exploration. ECA's mission is to strategically construct interactions that honor the dignity of self-determination and the transformative power of choice. For you, the reader, there is one last question: *Are you willing to be the one who is trusted to carry that responsibility with dedication and care?*

References

Darwin, C. (1868). *The Variation of Plants and Animals under Domestication Vol. 1 and 2* (Combined edition). CreateSpace Independent Publishing Platform.

Dijksterhuis, A. (2004). Think Different: The Merits of Unconscious Thought in Preference Development and Decision Making. *Journal of Personality and Social Psychology, 87*(5), 586–598. https://doi.org/10.1037/0022-3514.87.5.586

Case Index

The sourcing for Erickson's casework draws on multiple sources: my interviews with his wife and children; review of more than 1,000 hours of archival recordings; interviews with several former clients; and the published record. Because Erickson sometimes recounted the same case with varying details, these narratives cannot be reconstructed with absolute precision. The details I include reflect my best judgment about what he most likely said and did with a given individual. Below is a case index that lists published versions of each report.

Case Descriptor	*Source Material*
1.1 Work without Pay	O'Hanlon & Hexum, 1990, p. 330; Zeig, 1980, pp. 249–250
1.2 Fear of Sex	Haley, 1985a, p. 124
1.3 Hysterical Arm Paralysis	Erickson, 1954c, pp. 6–7; O'Hanlon & Hexum, 1990, pp. 52–53
1.4 Nauseated by the In-Laws	Haley, 1973, p. 153, 1985a, pp. 45–46; O'Hanlon & Hexum, 1990, pp. 226-227
1.5 Watching Fish	Haley, 1985b, pp. 55–57; O'Hanlon & Hexum, 1990, pp. 209–210
2.1 Breaking the World Record	O'Hanlon & Hexum, 1990, pp. 321–322; Rosen, 1982, pp. 103–105
2.2 There Can Be Only One Jesus Christ	Haley, 1985a, pp. 229–230; O'Hanlon & Hexum, 1990, pp. 287–288; Rosen, 1982, p. 201
2.3 What Are You Going to Do about It	Gordon & Meyers-Anderson, 1981, p. 31; O'Hanlon & Hexum, 1990, pp. 329–330
2.4 Doing Things Slowly	Erickson, 1980; O'Hanlon & Hexum, 1990, pp. 230–231

(Continued)

Case Descriptor	*Source Material*
2.5 Voyeurism	Haley, 1985a, p. 105; O'Hanlon & Hexum, 1990, p. 146
3.1 Three-Day Headache	Haley, 1985a, pp. 63–64; O'Hanlon & Hexum, 1990, pp. 89–90
3.2 The Childless Couple	Erickson & Rossi, 1985, pp. 197–198; O'Hanlon & Hexum, 1990, pp. 239–240
3.3 Becoming Christ-Like	Gordon & Meyers-Anderson, 1981, p. 43; Haley, 1973, p. 28; O'Hanlon & Hexum, 1990, pp. 291–292
3.4 Wasting Time in Therapy	Erickson, 1959a; O'Hanlon & Hexum, 1990, pp. 325–326
3.5 Wasting Time Somewhere Else	Haley, 1985a, pp. 286–287; O'Hanlon & Hexum, 1990, pp. 325–326
4.1 Bedwetting and Handwriting	Haley, 1973, pp. 206–208, 1985c, pp. 94–98; O'Hanlon & Hexum, 1990, pp. 105–106; Zeig, 1980, pp. 106–109
4.2 Bilateral Arm Paralysis	O'Hanlon & Hexum, 1990, pp. 120–121; Rosen, 1982, pp. 133–134
4.3 Getting Ready for a Wedding	Erickson, 1954a, pp. 224–226; O'Hanlon & Hexum, 1990, pp. 233–234
4.4 Zero Sperm	Erickson, 1950, pp. 179–182; O'Hanlon & Hexum, 1990, pp. 147–148
5.1 What Kind of an Ass Are You Going to Make of Yourself	Erickson, 1964, pp. 73–75; O'Hanlon & Hexum, 1990, pp. 278–279
5.2 That Will Pay You for Your Time	Erickson, 1954b, pp. 253–254; Erickson & Rossi, 1981, pp. 15–16; O'Hanlon & Hexum, 1990, pp. 189–190
5.3 Cinnamon Face	Gordon & Meyers-Anderson, 1981, pp. 79–80; O'Hanlon & Hexum, 1990, p. 314; Rosen, 1982, pp. 152–154
5.4 The Heckler	Erickson, 1959b, pp. 271–306
6.1 Scratching an Itch	Haley, 1985a, pp. 28–30; O'Hanlon & Hexum, 1990, p. 145
6.2 Taking Charge of the Restaurant	Haley, 1973, p. 224, 1985b, pp. 46–48; O'Hanlon & Hexum, 1990, pp. 246–247
6.3 A Cradle for Children	Gordon & Meyers-Anderson, 1981, pp. 67–69; O'Hanlon & Hexum, 1990, pp. 122–123; Zeig, 1980, pp. 164–165

(Continued)

Case Descriptor	*Source Material*
6.4 Harvey	Erickson, 1938, pp. 143–150; Erickson & Rossi, 1977, pp. 92–97, 1981, pp. 9–12; O'Hanlon & Hexum, 1990, pp. 295–296
6.5 The African Violet Queen	Gordon & Meyers-Anderson, 1981, pp. 18–19; O'Hanlon & Hexum, 1990, pp. 164–165; Zeig, 1980, pp. 285–286
7.1 The Dominant Husband	Haley, 1973, pp. 229–230; O'Hanlon & Hexum, 1990, p. 259
7.2 Dancing Nude before Bed	Haley, 1973, pp. 249–258, 1985a, pp. 123–149; O'Hanlon & Hexum, 1990, pp. 139–141
7.3 The Pianist with Stage Fright	Erickson, 1961, pp. 68–69; Gordon & Meyers-Anderson, 1981, pp. 139–140; Haley, 1985a, pp. 277–279; O'Hanlon & Hexum, 1990, pp. 191–192
7.4 The Less Intelligent Fiancé	Erickson & Hill, 1944, pp. 203–205; O'Hanlon & Hexum, 1990, pp. 223–224
7.5 Thirteen Marriages	Haley, 1973, p. 234, 1985b, pp. 168–169; O'Hanlon & Hexum, 1990, p. 252
8.1 Nude Dancing Men	Erickson, 1966, pp. 80–84; Erickson & Rossi, 1983, p. 116; Haley, 1985a, pp. 232–235; O'Hanlon & Hexum, 1990, pp. 281–283
8.2 Imposing Academic Perfection	Erickson & Rossi, 1985, pp. 122–123; O'Hanlon & Hexum, 1990, pp. 216–217
8.3 The Pimple on the Forehead	Haley, 1973, pp. 209–212, 1985c, pp. 100–106; O'Hanlon & Hexum, 1990, pp. 40–41; Zeig, 1980, pp. 109–110
8.4 Listening for Danger	O'Hanlon & Hexum, 1990, pp. 182–183
8.5 The Facial Scar	Erickson, 1927, pp. 117–120; O'Hanlon & Hexum, 1990, pp. 299–301; Rosen, 1982, pp. 64–66

Index

Note: **Bold** page numbers refer to tables; *italic* page numbers refer to figures.

For Product Safety Concerns and Information please contact our EU
representative GPSR@taylorandfrancis.com
Taylor & Francis Verlag GmbH, Kaufingerstraße 24, 80331 München, Germany

www.ingramcontent.com/pod-product-compliance
Ingram Content Group UK Ltd.
Pitfield, Milton Keynes, MK11 3LW, UK
UKHW022019211026
476876UK00010B/433

* 9 7 8 1 0 4 1 3 5 1 7 8 8 *